PROTECTING TRADE SECRETS

BEFORE, DURING, AND AFTER LITIGATION

PROTECTING TRADE SECRETS

BEFORE, DURING, AND AFTER LITIGATION

AN INSIDER'S GUIDE TO IDENTIFYING AND PROTECTING TRADE SECRETS FOR TRIAL LAWYERS AND IN-HOUSE COUNSEL

CHRIS SCOTT GRAHAM

Cover design by Tamara Kowalski/ABA Publishing.
Cover Illustration: © Bill Frymire/Masterfile.

16 15 14 13 12 5 4 3 2 1

Library of Congress Cataloging-in-Publication Data
Protecting Trade Secrets Before, During, and After Litigation / by Chris Scott Graham.
p. cm.
Includes index.
1. Trade secrets—Law and legislation—United States. 2. Actions and defenses—United States. 3. Civil procedure—United States. I. Title.
KF3197.G73 2012
346.7304'8—dc23 2012028163

ISBN : 978-1-61438-735-0

Discounts are available for books ordered in bulk. Special consideration is given to state bars, CLE programs, and other bar-related organizations. Inquire at Book Publishing, ABA Publishing, American Bar Association, 321 North Clark Street, Chicago, Illinois 60654.

www.ShopABA.org

Contents

Dedication ix

About the Author xi

Introduction xiii

Chapter 1
Identifying the Proper Plaintiff—Standing, Ownership, and Stakeholders 1
1. Ownership and Standing 2
2. Ownership and Development 5
3. Identifying the Proper Stakeholders within a Plaintiff Group 9
4. Taking the Litigation History 11
5. The Preliminary Technical Check 16
6. The Business of Trade Secret Litigation: Identifying the Client's Goals 19

Chapter 2
Legal and Business Considerations in Identifying the "Proper" Defendant(s) 25
1. Identifying the "Legally Correct" Defendants 26
2. Creating the "Legally Correct" Defendant and the Use of Pre-suit Demand Letters 30
3. Procedural Issues Impacting How One Handles the "Correct" Defendants 38
4. Considering the Business Impact When Naming Otherwise Legally Correct Defendants 43
5. Dealing with the "Foreign Defendant" and the "Aider and Abettor" 52

Chapter 3
Identifying the Trade Secrets, Internally and During the Action 57
1. Preparing an Identification of Trade Secrets for Internal Planning 57
2. Designation of the Trade Secrets During the Discovery Phase 64

3. Amending the Trade Secret List Before Trial 77
4. Preparing the Identification of Trade Secrets for Trial 80

Chapter 4
Identifying the Nature and Type of Trade Secret Misappropriation, Addressing the Statute of Limitations, and Action Items for the Pre-litigation Checklist 85
1. Identifying the Particular Form of Actual Misappropriation 86
2. The Inevitable Disclosure Doctrine 92
3. Addressing Threatened Misappropriation 96
4. Observations on the Statute of Limitations 98
5. Action Items for the Pre-litigation Checklist 102
   a. Witness Investigation 102
   b. Information Management and Document Retention/ Collection 105
   c. Internal "PR" 109
   d. External Public Relations 109

Chapter 5
Identifying Additional Claims to Pursue and Preemption, Pretrial Resolution Scenarios and Mediation, Anticipating Fee Awards and Statutory Bad Faith 113
1. Identifying Additional Claims to Pursue and Preemption 113
2. Pretrial Resolution Scenarios and Mediation 117
3. Anticipating Fee Awards and Statutory Bad Faith 119

Chapter 6
Choosing between Jurisdictions and Alternative Venues: Federal versus State Courts, Jury versus Bench Trials, Arbitrations, and Proceedings before the ITC 125
1. Selecting Federal or State Court, and between Alternative Venues 126
   a. Personal Jurisdiction 126
   b. Subject Matter Jurisdiction 128
   c. Illustrative Factors When Evaluating Multiple Potential Venues 130
2. Jury and Bench Trials 135
3. Whether to Proceed by Way of Arbitration 141
4. Pursuing Misappropriation Claims Before the ITC 145

Chapter 7
Protective Orders and Document Preservation Orders 149
1. Protective Orders 150
2. Preservation Orders 167

Chapter 8
TROs, Preliminary Injunctive Relief, and Expedited Discovery 173
1. The TRO 174
2. The Preliminary Injunction 177
3. Expedited Discovery 182

Chapter 9
Special Masters, Court-Appointed Neutral Experts, and Technical Advisors 189
1. The Use of Special Masters 190
2. Handling the Process of Court-Appointed Neutral Experts and Technical Advisors 200

Chapter 10
Addressing the Elements of Reasonable Efforts to Protect Secrecy and Independent Economic Value 205
1. Addressing the Requirement of "Reasonable Efforts" as a Means of Implementing Public Policy 206
2. The Evidentiary Significance of the Requirement of Reasonable Efforts 209
3. The Relationship between Reasonable Efforts, Independent Economic Value, and Available Remedies 214

Chapter 11
Headstart Injunctions and Other Forms of Post-judgment Equitable Relief 219
1. "Preliminary" and "Permanent" Injunctions in Trade Secret Litigation 220
2. Availability of Headstart Injunctive Relief to Address Acts of Misappropriation 221
3. The Impact of Reverse Engineering and Preliminary Injunctive Relief on the Duration of a Headstart Injunction 224
4. Setting the Breadth of a Headstart Injunction 225

5. The Impact of Headstart and Future Damages on the Scope of Injunctive Relief and Conditional Use Injunctions 226
6. Addressing Divergent Private and Public Interests When Considering the Potential for a Headstart Injunction 228

Chapter 12
The Impact of Contractual Boilerplate Provisions on Trade Secret Litigation 231
1. The Arbitration Clause 232
2. The Choice of Law Clause 239
3. Venue/Jurisdiction Clauses 241
4. Fee Clauses 245
5. Integration Clauses 247
6. Indemnification Clauses 249
7. Release Clauses 252
8. Marking Clauses 255

Chapter 13
The Trade Secret Fitness Audit 259
1. Key Objectives of the Fitness Audit 260
2. Identifying the Trade Secrets Existing within the Universe of Business Information 261
3. Identifying/Addressing Risk Factors to the Protection of Trade Secrets 264
   a. Employer/Employee Relationships 264
   b. Special Consultants and Contractors 268
   c. Multicompany Collaborative Relationships and Joint Ventures 269
   d. Customer Relationships 270
4. After the Audit 271

Appendix: Stipulated Protective Order for Litigation Involving Patents, Highly Sensitive Confidential Information and/or Trade Secrets 273

Index 293

Dedication

With grateful thanks to my colleagues at Dechert LLP, for their encouragement, and to my wife, Susan, and brother, Lyle, for their keen eyes and helpful edits.

About the Author

Chris Scott Graham is a partner in Dechert's intellectual property group, chairing the trade secret practice, and between 2005 and 2010 was the managing partner of Dechert's Silicon Valley office. He addresses all aspects of intellectual property rights, handles a wide variety of complex civil disputes, conducts public and private investigations, and is often selected to act as an ADR neutral with special expertise in acting as the arbitrator and mediator. He has extensive experience in all manner of civil disputes, including securities fraud and shareholder class actions, and has particular experience in trying cases involving trade secret misappropriation, patent and copyright infringement, privacy issues, unfair business competition, and false advertising.

Introduction

Trade secrets are an essential component of a well-rounded intellectual property portfolio, particularly in areas of commerce where other means of protection, such as patents and copyrights, provide inadequate or uneven protection. Whether considered under the Uniform Trade Secrets Act (UTSA) or viewed in light of the common law approach, the breadth of available protection can be extensive. Regardless of the precise delineation of elements in any particular jurisdiction, the concept of trade secrets has been applied broadly to cover both technical information (including methods, programs, and designs) and nontechnical information (from client lists and accounting records, to a recipe for fajitas), as long as the content gives the trade secret owner a competitive advantage by reason of the secrecy of that information. But the breadth of potential coverage creates difficulties even as it adds scope.

As a general commercial/technology litigator practicing in Silicon Valley for well over 25 years, I have handled several dozen trade secret cases. Each case has been different because of the variety of relationships in which misappropriation occurs, as well as the tremendous focus on the specifics of the information in question when trade secrets have been compromised. The majority of cases involved very dense technology, from microprocessor designs to recipes using polymethyl methacrylates. The subjects of other cases were less "technical," ranging from financial data to customer lists, including one case that involved the theft of a physical Rolodex (the old-fashioned kind) that contained contact information developed over several years. Many cases I tried to judgment, either in a courtroom or through arbitration, with a few handled all the way through exhaustion of all appeals. An even larger number settled before trial, both with and without the use of formal mediation.

Of course, all of these cases had issues and procedural considerations that trial lawyers must address in any civil matter. But the unique nature of trade secrets as a means of securing intellectual property rights, and the importance of these matters to my business clients, have made these cases the most interesting and created some of the greatest challenges.

Although many companies have sophisticated processes in place to capture the inventions and expressions of ideas that may be subject to patent or copyright protection, few companies give significant thought to the practicalities involved in the protection of their trade secrets until a question of misappropriation arises. Because the guidelines for classifying information as a trade secret per se are more ephemeral than traditional means of protecting intellectual property, experienced trade secret owners understand the importance of establishing comprehensive protocols to ensure they have identified their secrets, and retaining the ability to compel others to treat their proprietary information as a trade secret. Unfortunately, however, for many companies the first step to creating protections for this type of information—recognition of the value of trade secrets to the overall IP portfolio and to the operations of the enterprise—does not occur until after an overt act of misappropriation. When those events arise, company executives have a tendency to demand rapid action from their general litigation counsel, who in turn may not have experience with the practical issues that exist when handling trade secret litigation.

To address this need, this book explores the questions of trade secret identification, protection, and economic value from the standpoint of what executives, the board of directors, and the general counsel must consider when faced with the prospect of trade secret litigation. While the main focus is on the trade secret owner, due consideration is given throughout the text to corresponding issues facing an alleged misappropriator.

When assisting in a situation involving trade secret misappropriation, one of the more important functions of the practitioner is the ongoing process of educating the client on practical as well as legal issues that exist in this discrete area of intellectual property rights. Few clients are interested in a bare recitation of the legal elements of the claim. Of course, knowledge of legal specifics is essential in order to provide appropriate advice. But clients rarely applaud the practitioner who avoids taking a firm position on the probable outcome of a case through the "on the one hand . . ." game. Instead, clients want assistance evaluating risk so that they can determine cost and value, calculate the potential return on the investment necessary to take action, and, finally, assess the business downside from inaction.

The practitioner must help the client define and identify the types of information they should seek to protect as a trade secret. The practitioner must also educate the trade secret holder (and its employees) on which steps must be implemented to adequately protect those secrets. To provide the highest level of assistance, the practitioner must also be familiar with practical issues that arise during trade secret litigation, first by confirming the extent to which the client has the "right" to proceed and against whom, and then by providing advice on the best course for enforcing that right. Finally, before filing suit, the practitioner must advise the client on the benefits obtainable through judicial action, as well as the limits on what can be achieved, to ensure that the risks and expense of proceeding are justified.

This book is not a traditional "practice guide," with references to specific elements of a claim or defense, and does not provide string citations to leading appellate decisions to see how the requirements inherent in any particular aspect of the proceedings should be addressed. Rather, the approach taken here is akin to what a practitioner experiences at a whiteboard session with his or her litigation team, with everyone brainstorming to identify potential pivot points on the issues at hand. These points, sometimes legal and other times "practical," are those occasions where a decision can dramatically impact the nature or course of the proceedings. Once those points are identified, the team can discuss the best approach in light of particular rules in a given jurisdiction that influence, or even constrain, how an issue can or must be addressed. This approach reflects the fact that case law governing intellectual property rights in trade secrets is not fully uniform, but rather is subject to the legislatures and judicial decisions of the various states. This non-uniformity exists notwithstanding the adoption of the Uniform Trade Secrets Act in the majority of the states. The approach taken here also reflects the fact that selection among several alternative pivot points often revolves more on the strategic value of the decision to the client's business, instead of a rote application of identifiable legal principles. Thus, instead of a casebook approach or an analysis of specific appellate decisions, this book focuses on the practical side to protecting trade secrets through identifying and discussing realistic issues the practitioner may face in this area.

CHAPTER ONE

Identifying the Proper Plaintiff—Standing, Ownership, and Stakeholders

The call comes in from a prospective client, asking the lawyer to handle a trade secret misappropriation matter. The issue is urgent, explains the client, as the information taken is critical to the success of the client's business and the misappropriator is in the process of taking steps to compete using this information. "What," asks the client, "should we do, and how quickly can we do it?"

The intitial response of most lawyers is to focus on their own experience, background, and abilities to handle the matter. After all, trade secret litigation is a specialized area with many intricacies in the applicable legal principles and, when the trade secrets involve highly sophisticated processes or designs, technical experience in the subject matter is a welcome, if not necessary, plus. Only after the lawyer is successful with the ability to "sell" his or her expertise, and is handed the assignment, does the discussion then turn to elucidating the options for addressing the conduct of the defendant. But the careful trade secret practitioner understands that an immediate flurry of activity directed outward toward the defendant, while perhaps satisfying the agitated client in the near term, results in a missed opportunity to gather information that can shape the nature and course of the assignment, and may mask issues that have legal and practical consequences that will be increasingly difficult to address with time.

Thus, at the beginning of the relationship with the client, one of the first areas of inquiry the careful practitioner must consider involves the process of identifying whether the client is the "proper" person or entity to be named as the plaintiff. And, at the initial engagement meeting, the practitioner should be prepared to discuss a host of issues that touch both on business realities and legal requirements, provoking consideration of "ownership," "standing," and a great deal more.

1. Ownership and Standing

In the majority of trade secret cases, there is no dispute regarding plaintiff's ownership of the information that constitutes the trade secrets in question. The plaintiff can demonstrate the "how, when, where, why, and who," as well as chain of title with respect to the creation, compilation, or development of the information, so that no issue will arise with respect to whether the client is the proper plaintiff. But, as the answer to the question of ownership depends in part on the conceptual nature of the interest in the trade secrets as applied by the jurisdiction in which the suit is filed, as well as, in part, on the difference between "ownership" and "standing," one should not merely assume that the client is the correct party to be listed on the plaintiff side of the caption.

Preliminarily, when considering issues of ownership and standing, a trade secret litigator should review recent appellate decisions in the jurisdiction in which the suit will be filed to determine the philosophical approach to trade secrets as followed and applied in that jurisdiction. One school of thought is that a trade secret is in the nature of property, such that the nature of the dispute will involve variations on well-accepted property rights that may exist in an object or thing, which are being damaged or destroyed by the adverse use. An alternative school of thought does not treat trade secret disputes just as involving property, but instead focuses on protecting the *relationship* between the parties at the time the secret is disclosed. The protected relationship, contractual or confidential, is one to which, as Justice Holmes observed, "some rudimentary requirements of good faith" are attached. "Whether the plaintiffs have any valuable secret or not, the defendant knows the facts, whatever they are, through a special confidence that he accepted. The property may be denied, but the confidence cannot be. Therefore the starting point for the present matter is not property . . . , but that the defendant stood in confidential relations with the plaintiffs . . . ." *E.I. du Pont de Nemours Powder Co. v. Masland* (1917), 244 U.S. 100, 102, 37 S. Ct. 575, 61 L. Ed. 1016.

The distinction between trade secrets as a property right and a relationship tort becomes readily apparent when viewed in the context of the statute of limitations, as the relationship nature of trade secrets will result in a single cause of action for misappropriation, accruing upon the conduct that causes a rupture in the relationship. However, the property-based nature of trade secrets will still result in continuing damages, arising from the defendant's ongoing use of the misappropriated information. Initiation of otherwise stale (and thus time-barred) claims can be avoided by exploring how this distinction is handled in the jurisdiction where the suit is contemplated, well before any complaint is filed.

"Standing" is not coextensive with "ownership." As a litigation concept, when a party is in federal court, standing looks at the ability of the plaintiff to establish a right to judicial action separate and apart from the substantive merits of the underlying claim. In many state courts, standing is simply a requirement that the action be maintained in the name of the person who has the right to sue under the applicable substantive law.

Standing issues often result in confusion over differences between the right to sue, and the applicable remedy to which the plaintiff may be entitled. A former owner of a trade secret may have "standing" to sue (e.g., for damages that arose during the period of its ownership) even though it may not have the right to injunctive relief, as it is not the "current" owner of the trade secrets. When considering the question of standing, the discussion is more appropriately focused on whether the plaintiff can establish the element of a misappropriation cause of action that considers whether there has been a breach of a duty owed to the plaintiff, rather than a question that depends on the relief that may be available.

By misappropriating a trade secret, a defendant does not generally breach a duty to a plaintiff who lacks an attribute of ownership at the time of accrual of the misappropriation cause of action. However, having some aspect of ownership at the time of accrual is completely separate from what must be in existence at the time of suit or during the proceedings. Just as the "destruction" of a trade secret (by, for example, posting the information on the Internet, and thereby destroying its secret nature) does not divest a court from its authority to adjudicate the nature and extent of potential relief, divestment of ownership of the trade secrets prior to the initiation of suit does not cause a plaintiff to lose the right to sue for damages suffered prior to divestiture. The corollary is also true—that an acquirer of a trade secret does not, simply by acquisition of the trade secrets, have the right to sue for improper use that preceded the acquisition.

Similar to the rule against splitting a chose in action, only one party has the right to sue for improper use: the party that owned the rights to the trade secret at the time of improper use. This is simply an application of the general rule that a right of action for damage to property is distinct from the title to the property, such that a transfer of the latter will not abrogate the right to sue on the former (although a trade secret holder is well advised to consider expressly reserving the rights of action for infringement that may have occurred during the period of its ownership, to avoid the possibility that a court will find those rights assigned along with the legal title to the trade secrets being transferred).

A defendant faced with a suit by a former owner, suing on claims that postdate that party's ownership, can count on procedural safeguards. If there are multiple suits filed by the prior and current owners, the defendant can consider seeking consolidation, interpleader of the current owner if there are potentially conflicting demands by various claimants, or initiation of a cross-action against the non-appearing claimants that seeks a declaration of the rights and interests of all who claim an interest in the trade secrets in question.

When the trade secret lawyer is representing the rights of a subsequent owner, there are a number of protections that need be considered with respect to any pending or threatened litigation by the prior owner against a third party. Upon acquisition the subsequent owner can obtain a representation and warranty from the prior owner that there are no known acts of infringement by third parties, and/or an express right to sue over any such acts.

To the extent litigation is pending at the time of sale, the trade secret lawyer should take careful steps as part of the due diligence process to examine the pleadings and related litigation documents, so as to either adjust the price to reflect the risk of litigation, or to seek adequate assurances or warranties from the seller. The subsequent owner can also seek, if the purchase proceeds, to join the litigation by a petition to intervene or similar procedural mechanisms allowable in the jurisdiction in which the action is pending. Of course, the subsequent owner can also determine that, as it is not a party to the present suit, it will not be bound by a judgment adverse to its interests (such as a judgment that finds the information does not constitute a trade secret), and that anyone who fails to respect the status of the information as a trade secret does so at the risk of a separate lawsuit notwithstanding the prior judgment. This last possibility does not leave the defendant unfairly subject to multiple suits, as it can seek joinder of the subsequent purchaser into the pending action, or consolidation of any action that the subsequent purchaser may have commenced, as long as the prior action is still pending at the time of the filing of the new action by the subsequent purchaser.

2. *Ownership and Development*

The foregoing issues of ownership all deal with temporal aspects, which in turn impact the nature of relief. But there are other aspects of ownership related to development that the trade secret lawyer should investigate prior to filing suit.

"Ownership" is sometimes used as short hand for challenging the ability of the plaintiff to establish that it, or its predecessors or assignors, actually created the trade secrets. If the plaintiff cannot establish the record necessary to respond to this challenge, the defendant may be able to argue successfully that the plaintiff either does not have the right to sue (because of defective title, in that the "true" creator of the trade secret never relinquished title to the plaintiff), or that the information simply does not qualify as a trade secret, as the plaintiff cannot establish that the secret nature of the information was maintained continuously (not being the creator, the plaintiff cannot establish that the information was always within its control, or that of its predecessors or assignors).

Like development of a chain of evidence necessary for authentication and admission, or a chain of title necessary to establish proprietary rights, the practitioner must determine whether breaks in the chain will cause problems establishing sufficient continuity of development or exclusive control over the creation and maintenance of information to satisfy this definitional aspect of a trade secret (in that it was not "known" to the public, or to others who can obtain economic value from its disclosure or use).

When representing an individual or well-defined group of individuals who contend that their trade secrets have been misappropriated, the trade secret lawyer has a discrete universe of people to work with to compile the history of the development of the trade secrets and the subsequent maintenance of the secrecy of the information. A software programmer, for example, should be able to demonstrate documentation efforts sufficient to confirm the development history of the source code. This can be in the form of notebooks documenting algorithm development or some form of version-control system software used to track all of the development work and changes in the file sets. Version-control software is particularly helpful where there are multiple contributors to development, as it also allows several developers (potentially widely separated in space and/or time) to collaborate and document their development efforts. In low-tech industries, the documentation may be as simple as looking for original hard-copy Rolodexes (in the case of a customer list) or the individual's work files.

Once a record of development or acquisition is compiled, the practitioner should look for indicia of reasonable steps under the circumstances to maintain the secrecy of the information in the form of nondisclosure agreements (NDAs), password protection systems, and access restrictions. Through these sources, among others, the practitioner can determine whether there are glaring problems that will preclude creating a record during trial, affirmatively in their case in the chief or later in response to an affirmative defense, that his or her clients created or developed the trade secrets and thereafter engaged in reasonable steps to maintain the secrecy of the information. In contrast to requirements for establishing conception in a patent case, contemporaneous memorialization or independent corroboration may not be required as a matter of law, but is always more powerful than any oral testimony provided well after the dispute has arisen.

When representing a corporate entity, the task for the practitioner can be more challenging, as the records of creation or development may be disbursed over poorly defined groups or in different geographic locations. Records may also have temporal gaps, especially where the development occurred over lengthy periods of time and/or during the course of multiple acquisitions, divestitures, or reorganizations of corporate entities, groups, or divisions.

The passage of time also presents the problem that employees involved in the development of the trade secrets may have left, sometimes to the competitor alleged to be using the trade secrets at issue, highlighting the need to push a preliminary investigation into this aspect of ownership well prior to filing the action. In this situation, the focus turns on identifying an individual who can set forth the history of development of the secrets on behalf of the company. By either his or her position, experience at the company, familiarity with the books and records of the entity, or a combination of these factors, that individual must be able to establish that he or she is qualified to speak on behalf of the company, even on matters that may not have been known at the time that they occurred. Further, even if internal politics at the corporate entity create obstacles to complete collaboration, that individual must be willing to work closely with the practitioner—as the "champion" of the issues—to create the necessary foundation for admissibility of his or her testimony. As few employees view assisting in a trade secret case as a helpful way to increase their chances at promotion, here it may be necessary to obtain confirmation from that individual's direct supervisor that cooperation and collaboration are now viewed as an important aspect of their job.

When the trade secrets in question were acquired from another person or entity, the task of establishing this aspect of "ownership" is more complicated than simply authenticating the transactional documents evidencing the transfer of the right and title to the trade secrets. The fact that the title documentation, provided by the seller, may have a warranty that the information constitutes a bona fide trade secret will not suffice, as it only creates a right of action against the seller if the opposite is established. Additional steps, along the lines set forth above, must be taken to ensure that the party from whom the trade secrets were acquired (or, conceivably, their predecessor in interest) indeed developed or created the trade secrets and maintained the secrecy of the information through the acquisition (and afterwards). In this sense, the practitioner handling the transaction hopefully included a provision in the transfer documentation that requires ongoing cooperation from the seller.

Trade secrets acquired from an entity that is in the middle of, or has passed through, a bankruptcy proceeding have additional and unique challenges. These include the lack of warranties, the difficulty in obtaining crisp descriptions of what was transferred, the potential paucity of efforts undertaken at the bankrupt entity to maintain secrecy during the period of its ownership, the ability of the debtor estate to reject executory contracts and, finally, the specific rights of licensees with respect to intellectual property rights notwithstanding rejection.

Trade secrets created through joint development efforts with another company or individual (such as an individual contributor, or consultant retained for a particular project) pose other problems. These include difficulties in obtaining records of ownership and development, determining who owns which trade secret and the potential for resolving disputes over ownership before initiation of suit against the current misappropriator, and ascertaining what rights, if any, have been granted to others by pre-existing contracts or which arise by operation of law—especially where the entities or individuals are located in a foreign jurisdiction that may allocate intellectual property (IP) rights in a manner inconsistent with the law in the United States. Joint development efforts involving universities and governmental agencies pose unique issues that must be explored. These issues relate to ownership, the right to limit exploitation, and the ability to pursue claims on behalf of all owners.

Joint development of a trade secret also means that the practitioner must establish who has the right to publish and control publication (as well as determining whether publication has occurred), who has the right to patent inventions based thereon, whether applications for patents have been filed in the U.S. or any foreign jurisdiction, and finally the ability of the joint venturer to unilaterally license the misappropriator to the use of the trade secrets, and whether it has done so.

3. Identifying the Proper Stakeholders within a Plaintiff Group

A plaintiff "group" can exist anytime the client is not an individual. Groups exist where there are multiple named party plaintiffs or when there are joint owners. Groups can also exist when there is only one plaintiff but there are factions within an entity plaintiff. Groups within a business entity may consist of a single person. When that person, either by nature of his position or her relationship to the factual matter that gave rise to the dispute, has some aspect of authority or influence over the matter, that person's buy-in is important for the ability of the practitioner to proceed. As the practitioner usually lacks complete insight into the group's internal dynamics, the best course is to ask the immediate client representative to assist in identifying all individuals associated with the client who may have any type of interest in the matter—these are the stakeholders—and to describe the nature of their interest. Dealing with an individual party plaintiff may pose certain challenges, but in that situation at least there is only a single decision maker involved in the process.

In the situation involving a plaintiff group, the practitioner must evaluate the formal and informal hierarchical structure of the group in order to achieve efficient and collaborative results. The formal structure is generally apparent in a corporate setting and typically follows a standard organizational flow chart. In this regard, the practitioner must make clear how that organizational flow will impact his or her interactions with the client as well as the decision-making process. For example:

- To whom is the practitioner to direct her reports and in what fashion (emails to one or some, copies to others, etc.?

- Who is the ultimate decision maker within the client group with respect to this matter?
- Are there different levels of authority (e.g., minor procedural decisions being made by in-house counsel and substantive decisions made by a business person)?
- To what extent does the matter require involvement from the CEO or the General Counsel, or are ultimate decisions left to the judgment of the department/division manager?
- If settlement discussions occur, who has the authority to settle on behalf of the company? While some decisions can be made at lower levels of management, "materials" settlement terms may even require Board of Director approval.

Addressing these questions at the start helps a practitioner to both learn more about the client and its needs and to integrate into the formal operations of the plaintiff group.

The informal structure within the plaintiff's group, and the stakeholders associated with that group, can be harder to discern even for a practitioner who has represented the same client in other matters. In particular, informal structure includes those who may have the ability to influence decisions, even when their own position in the organization suggests that the matter will not affect their role. For example:

- Are there individuals who may be impacted by the expense of litigation because it impacts their budget directly (as where the expense of litigation is charged against the P&L of their division, rather than an expense allocated against the legal department or bundled into G&A)?
- Will the process of litigation require use of headcount in a division, otherwise allocated in an annual plan to projects the division has been tasked to complete within a certain time frame and within a certain budget?

- Are there individuals who may be impacted substantively by the litigation, such as where the trade secrets are essential to the success of the division, or where the non-monetary aspects of a settlement (through a cross-license or business arrangement) impact how their business operations are viewed or valued by the company?
- Did anyone in the entity have responsibility for drafting any documents, including contracts or correspondence/emails, which may be central to the dispute in a positive or negative fashion? Will they create problems if their work product is internally criticized?
- Will the likely percipient witnesses be interested in assisting, or instead have personal reasons to avoid having any part in the proceedings, such as may occur when the alleged misappropriators are their former colleagues or current friends?

Learning as much information as possible in these areas can allow the practitioner to evaluate and minimize practical problems in acquiring proof for trial, substantive problems in developing litigation goals, and interpersonal problems in maintaining an effective working relationship with the client.

4. Taking the Litigation History

In medicine, a doctor regularly commences each visit with a review of the patient's medical history, including prior experiences with other health-care professionals and the current treatment regime, before turning to the complaint that occasioned the visit. This process serves the dual function of identifying the nature of the current problem, as well as furthering the professional-client relationship. Lawyers, even when beginning a new relationship, tend to miss this important step.

A party's litigation history can provide a wealth of information and insight into how they might be affected by the pendency of litigation.

- Has the client previously been sued, or is it currently being sued?
- If so, what types of claims were involved in the cases, and where were their venues?
- How much was at issue, and what was the client's experience with the expense of the process?
- What were the result(s)?

Answers to these questions suggest the way in which the party will approach or resolve the current dispute, indicate areas where there may be opportunities and potential problems as the matter proceeds, and guide a level of discourse appropriate to the client's sophistication.

If the client has never been involved in litigation, it is highly likely that they have no idea regarding the hidden costs of a lawsuit calculated in terms of executive involvement, or the range of absolute dollars in fees and costs typically spent in the course of trade secret litigation. The time it takes for a lawsuit to progress from initial filing to judgment, and then through appeal, can be extensive. A neophyte party must be conditioned to the prospect that, once begun, the end date for litigation (absent a business solution mid-course) no longer is within its control. Even if they have some experience in commercial litigation, they may be unaware of the significant expense of trade secret litigation. Recent studies, aggregating numbers from trade secret litigation filed throughout the United States when the amount in controversy was under $25 million, show an average cost to each side on the order of $1.6 million. For larger amounts in controversy, the average cost to each side for trade secret litigation jumps to $3.2 million.

Making explicit the potential and anticipated expense of litigation in advance of filing serves several functions. First, it forces the client to look carefully at the value of what it is seeking to protect. Indeed, have they even taken any steps to quantify that value? Are they willing to spend in excess of $1 million to sue for an injunction to stop the use of trade secrets that bring less than that sum to the bottom line? Are they willing to dedicate the internal personnel to support the litigation, whether by members of the internal legal team and/or by the individual contributors who will act as percipient witnesses? Second, elaborating the anticipated budget early in the process avoids, if not eliminates, disagreements later over the expense of the process and reduces fee disputes. Clients are rarely pleased with significant litigation expense, but an outlay discussed in advance is always preferable to an invoice for services rendered that exceeds the amount contemplated.

When discussing litigation history, the type of prior litigation experienced is equally important as the amount of litigation experience. A party with a great deal of general commercial litigation is, in some ways, more problematic than a neophyte, as their experienced-honed expectations are more difficult to modify. With these experiences under their belt, they may be less inclined to effectively listen to advice because they have "been there, done that." Even experience in other forms of IP litigation can have this effect. In particular, patent litigation, even when involving the same technology, is far different from trade secret litigation in terms of the strategies, substantive considerations, and procedural issues to be addressed. "Pure" patent lawyers in particular tend to see trade secret litigation as a less sophisticated and simpler means of IP protection and can be unpleasantly surprised by the reality they face in both the courtroom and the press.

Armed with the litigation history, the practitioner can better understand the client's litigation philosophy, as that will drive how they respond during litigation, their goals for the litigation, and the manner in which business solutions should be considered, approached, and handled. Is the client litigation-averse? If so, does that philosophy derive from a prior litigation experience? Here the practitioner can discuss these experiences to assist the client in understanding how the present case is different (or not) and how to avoid the same concerns arising again. Does the client's philosophy derive from the potential economic downside of the present action, real or imagined, from customers who are also doing business with the other side, or as a result of a negative outcome in the case? If so, those risks can be addressed to ensure that they are appropriately quantified and, if possible, minimized (and, if merely imagined, harmonized with more likely scenarios). Does their philosophy stem from how the relevant business community or marketplace may view the litigation, as is the case where a large, established player sues an upstart and seeks to put that party out of business? A response that considers market spin and an aggressive press/investor relations strategy may address these concerns.

If the client is litigation-oriented, a separate but related set of issues arise. A client who is comfortable with litigation (not to mention those who actually enjoy it) may believe the civil system of jurisprudence can be a tool of business competitiveness, manipulated to its advantage in the market. This sort of litigation-oriented client can be dangerous to the system and the practitioner. Success often breeds contempt, and a practitioner representing a party who already has a number of victories under its belt must remind the client that its ongoing obligations during litigation are no different (perhaps even greater) than those of the party who has never before seen the inside of a courtroom. Further, the practitioner must be mindful of the overly elevated expectations that a litigation-oriented client may have, as the practitioner will be the likely scapegoat should those expectations not be realized.

In addition to furthering the "know thy client" philosophy behind taking a litigation history, the practitioner should be aware of facts existing by reason of any prior litigation that may impact the potential for litigation success, such as by triggering the running of the statute of limitations. In trade secret litigation the action must be brought within three years after the misappropriation is either discovered or, by the exercise of reasonable diligence, should have been discovered. Information developed in a prior action may present facts that place the client on notice that other misappropriators exist.

While under the Uniform Trade Secrets Act a continuing misappropriation constitutes a single claim against a given defendant, multiple defendants may give rise to multiple claims for misappropriation, each with its own statute of limitations, and even if there is continuing use of the information by any one defendant. For purposes of the running of the statute of limitations, the proper focus in this situation with respect to a potential defendant is not upon that defendant's actual state of mind, but rather upon the plaintiff's suspicions. Prior litigation involving the same trade secrets, or even the same technology, should thus be considered to determine the date upon which the client first had any reason to suspect that the currently targeted defendant obtained or used the information with the knowledge, or with reason to know, that the information included the client's trade secrets. That date should be used to calculate whether the action may be time-barred.

Prior litigation involving claims other than trade secrets can nevertheless impact the trade secret claims, regardless of the identity of the prior opposing parties. In particular, any litigation involving the same technology (or products in which the technology plays a part) can create issues in favor of the defense. In prior patent litigation, the client, as either plaintiff or defendant, may have taken positions with respect to patent documents or prior art that will support the argument that the evidence in the prior action disclosed the relevant information currently in issue, thus eliminating the secrecy needed to sustain a trade secret claim. This defense has a sound legal basis, for information disclosed in a published patent application (or in other public prior art) is not secret and is not subject to trade secret protections. Damages models used in prior patent litigation may also impact the value of future trade secret litigation if a model covers the current claims such that a court would decide that the possibility exists of a double recovery.

Releases executed in connection with the resolution of prior litigation can also provide the current defendant with a defense. This arises when the scope of the release is overly broad with respect to the claims released (when the potential defendant was a signatory to the release) or when the scope of released parties now extends to the prospective defendant, because that defendant has acquired the previously settling party, or simply where the definition of "Released Parties" covers these defendants. In the latter case, this can occur when the release specifies not only named defendants but also includes a boilerplate list, such as "each of their respective past and present predecessors, successors, heirs, assigns, parent companies, subsidiaries, divisions, equity holders, owners, members, managers, partners, directors, officers, employees, contractors, agents, representatives, consultants, accountants, counsel, insurers, associates,

Affiliates, and all Persons acting by, through, under or in concert with them, or any of them." Asking the client to provide copies of settlement agreements to review prior to filing suit can avoid unpleasant surprises that are sure to arise shortly after service of the complaint.

5. *The Preliminary Technical Check*

The definition of a trade secret varies slightly by jurisdiction, as do the particular types of information that fall within the scope of trade secret protection. However, there is a common theme with respect to concept of civil trade secret protection: For information to qualify as a trade secret, it must not be generally known to the public or, more specifically (in the absence of wrongdoing) to the client's competitors; it must confer some sort of economic benefit or advantage to the owner from not being generally known; and it must be the subject of reasonable efforts to maintain its secrecy.

The essence of a trade secret, therefore, is the client's possession of information that can either be made known to, or withheld from, others *at the option of the client.* This is the fundamental difference between a trade secret, a patent, and a copyright. A patent protects a novel idea, in particular an invention, against use or appropriation by others. A copyright protects the particular expression of an idea, even though the idea itself may remain unprotected. By contrast, trade secret law is not so limited and does not just protect "ideas" as such.

A trade secret may consist of something not ordinarily considered to constitute an idea (such as a concept or even a conceptual expression), but rather a fact or collection of facts, such as lists of tolerances or customer addresses. Further, trade secret protection does not exist as much with respect to the particular idea or the fact itself, but rather to the information that may disclose the idea or fact to a third party. Consistent with the relationship nature of trade secret protection, the rights that exist with respect to a trade secret center on the right to control the dissemination of this information.

Thus the ability of the client to clearly identify the information claimed to have been misappropriated is critical to any trade secret claim, as well as to the ability to muster an effective defense. Accordingly, trade secrets plaintiffs who pursue their claims in a California Superior Court must, prior to commencing discovery, be able to "identify the trade secret with reasonable particularity." California Code of Civil Procedure, § 2019.210. Other courts, while not making identification of trade secrets a prerequisite to conducting discovery, have warned plaintiffs of the risks they run on the merits by failing to identify specific trade secrets and instead producing long lists of general areas of information that contain unidentified trade secrets.

While the initial meeting with a client is not the best time to attempt to extract a detailed identification of the trade secrets in issue, this is an opportunity to begin the process of educating the client about the need for such identification and the difficulties that may arise in that process. The question to the client can be as simple as asking if they can readily define their trade secrets and, if the answer is yes, whether they have done so. Within the scope of information they seek to classify as a trade secret, unsophisticated clients routinely include that which is readily available to others, or which does not, in and of itself, provide any competitive value from the fact that it is not generally known. Asking if they are able, at the initial meeting, to specify the information in question provides an opportunity to discuss the requirements for classifying information as a trade secret in order to assist in the further process of refining the list to a more readily defendable group. Where the information is of a technical nature, any discussion on trade secret identification without the presence of technical contributors will likely miss on how to distinguish the information from that which is known to others in the scientific or technical community. This may entail having the client focus on the individuals within the client organization who have the appropriate knowledge and expertise, or it may involve a discussion of available experts who can assist in the process, or a combination of both.

When the information is of a non-technical nature, such as a customer list or preferences, the discussion must include the assignment of responsibility for compiling and presenting information in a manner that allows ready categorization, as well as for confirming that these categories of information are, in fact, not readily available to others. In this regard, while a conclusion that the information is readily available with some minimal expenditure of effort will not, by itself, preclude the ability to claim trade secret status, this will have a significant impact on the damages that might be awarded and the prospect of obtaining injunctive relief. A court will be reluctant to permanently enjoin a party from using information that could be readily compiled from various sources, even if it concludes that the defendant misappropriated the information in order to accelerate its ability to compete. A headstart injunction may issue, but its duration might be so limited that obtaining that relief will hardly justify the expense of the action.

The preliminary technical check should include inquiring whether the client has a history of disclosing its trade secrets to actual or potential customers, vendors, or other third parties. If so, the client should be asked to compile a detailed list of all third parties indicating when and under what circumstances the disclosures occurred, and the steps taken (e.g., in the form of NDAs or similar contractual arrangements) to ensure that the party to whom the information was disclosed continued to have an obligation to maintain the secrecy of the information. A client who may have provided documents that reflect some (or even all) of the trade secrets in issue to its vendors—that is, disclosed its trade secrets to "a limited number of outsiders for a particular purpose"—does not automatically forfeit the right to seek trade secret protection. In the course of common business practice, such disclosure is often necessary for the use and exploitation of a trade secret.

Furthermore, while it is part of best practices to have explicit documentation of the obligation to maintain confidentiality, the attributes of particular relationships can impose an implied duty of confidentiality on the part of the person to whom the disclosure is made. For example, this implied duty has been found by at least one court to arise as a matter of law in the context of the negotiations for the sale of a business. It has also been found to arise in the context of a vendor-vendee relationship, even in one situation where several hundred employees of the vendee had access to the documentation that contained the trade secrets, and copy controls did not exist.

As the obligation to maintain the secrecy of information is one measured under the standard of "reasonableness," maintaining absolute secrecy is not necessarily required, and the question often is submitted to the jury for determination. Thus, with respect to such disclosures, the client should be queried as to its awareness of any instances where the obligation to maintain confidentiality was not honored and, if so, the steps taken to address the breach. These are all facts that are likely to come out during discovery. Being aware of these situations before filing provides an opportunity to ameliorate the impact of early disclosures by modifying the description of trade secrets to eliminate those where secrecy may have been compromised by an unrelated third party. Waiting until the facts come out during litigation creates the risk that the defendant can divert attention to the prior disclosures as a means to deflect attention from its own conduct, even when the prior disclosure impacts only a subset of the information claimed to have been misappropriated.

Even where the client confirms that it has never previously disclosed the trade secrets to any third parties, the practitioner should engage in an initial survey of the steps to maintain secrecy of the information with respect to the misappropriator in question. Is there documentation specific to the misappropriator, such as an employment agreement or proprietary inventions agreement for employees, or NDAs or provisions in joint development agreements for consultants or business partners? What security safeguards are in place for computer systems, both electronic (inter- and intra-office network firewalls and passwords) and physical (access to office suites, networks, USB ports, printers, or copy machines)? The level of security should be commensurate with the type of information, in that the obligation to maintain secrecy must be "reasonable under the circumstances."

6. *The Business of Trade Secret Litigation: Identifying the Client's Goals*

Litigation is not the main business of the client. It is a distraction; it is a money pit; it does not advance the goals of the operation. Most clients dislike being in or near litigation. But when litigation must be contemplated seriously, the practitioner serves the client best by avoiding rhetoric that will merely serve to inflame passions or prick executive egos. Litigation over principle is rarely satisfying to the client over the long term. Regardless of the need to create the appearance to the outside world of an aggrieved or injured party, internally the prospect of litigation should be considered dispassionately in the same way as any other investment: is there a sufficient return on the investment to justify making the investment in light of the potential risk?

The CFO of the corporate client will be able to quickly explain that return on investment (ROI) is a performance measure used to evaluate the efficiency of an investment. To calculate ROI, the benefit (return) of an investment is divided by the cost of the investment; the result is expressed as a percentage or a ratio. The ROI formula is sometimes expressed as follows:

$$\text{ROI} = \frac{\text{Gain from Investment} - \text{Cost of Investment}}{\text{Cost of Investment}}$$

This formula uses the term "gains from investment" to refer to the proceeds realized. In a simplistic sense, if the proposed investment does not have a positive ROI, or if alternative opportunities have a higher ROI, then the investment should be not be undertaken.

In applying the formula to trade secret litigation, the cost of investment alludes to more than the hard-dollar cost, expressed in terms of attorney fees and costs (filing fees, court reporter fees, expert witness fees, and so on). The hard-dollar part of the cost of investment is relatively easy to quantify through the preparation of litigation budgets. More difficult are the intangible, or "soft," costs of investment. These soft costs are typically expressed in terms of management time, lost opportunities, market perceptions/reactions, and so forth. While the practitioner is not usually in the best position to quantify these soft costs, he or she is in a very good position to underline the existence of these costs with the client to ensure that there is an express appreciation of their existence before suit is commenced.

In order to assist the client in applying the formula, however, the practitioner must first fully understand (and assist the client in articulating) the goals that the client seeks to achieve through the contemplated litigation.

A court can offer only limited relief in connection with civil trade secret litigation. It can only enter a judgment that awards monetary and/or some form of equitable/injunctive relief. The court cannot order a defendant to apologize, or issue a mea culpa. But, in addition to a monetary award or injunctive relief, the fact of litigation may also be considered by the client to have an independent benefit, with the disruption to the defendant and market impact on third parties (including customers of both the client and the defendant) being part—or even all—of the client's overall goals.

Monetary goals are the simplest to use in calculating the potential ROI. If the best possible result is an award of $1 million (calculated, for example, by a determination of lost profits caused by the misappropriation), and the hard-dollar cost of investment is also $1 million, in the absence of some other nonmonetary benefit, it does not take a financial genius to see that the potential economic return does not justify the investment. More difficult are the intangibles that arise on both sides of the equation.

On the "return" side, one needs to consider whether there is a "message" the client wants to send to the market, or to its other employees, regarding its willingness to protect its trade secrets regardless of expense. Does it see the defendant as a market risk in that, left unchecked, it will take market share even apart from the use of the trade secrets? Does the client thus want to create "FUD" (fear, uncertainty, and doubt) in the marketplace such that, by reason of the pendency of the litigation, customers may not be willing to engage with the defendant? In some markets the mere pendency of trade secret litigation will cause customers to delay their purchasing decisions until the litigation has been resolved. This can create a period of time that will allow the client to stabilize key relationships or starve out a fledgling competitor.

In connection with these types of "market goals" the practitioner must consider, and be prepared to advise the client concerning, the risk that the client's conduct (and, in particular, conduct outside of the courtroom in publishing the pendency of the litigation) will create or give rise to cross-claims (such as trade libel, interference with business relations, unfair business practices, and violations of the Lanham Act). While various iterations of the litigation privilege (statutory in California and developed by the case law in other jurisdictions and in federal court) may provide a defense to such cross-claims, in cases where business disruption appears to be a primary goal of the client, the practitioner should redouble efforts to ensure that his or her own obligations (that exist under Federal Rule of Civil Procedure 11 and similar state laws) have been satisfied by the time the claims are filed.

The "cost of investment" side of the analysis also includes consideration of the soft costs previously mentioned. These costs are far more intangible, and thus difficult to monetize, but are real nonetheless. Where the client group has several stakeholders, there will be different views on the value of entering into litigation—hawks and doves. The hawks will downplay the soft costs related to business distraction, and the doves will underscore these distractions and the potential for unfavorable market reaction as the "true cost" that must be evaluated. In mediation, we often focus defendants on the positive intangible value of settlement, which will exist by reason of having the psychological burden of the Damocles sword of litigation no longer hanging over their heads. There are psychological burdens of a similar nature on plaintiffs, less recognized, that exist by reason of the presence of litigation and the distractions it can cause for an organization, especially if well publicized. Here the practitioner serves the client best by facilitating an open and honest discussion of these issues.

The risk calculation in determining ROI involves both what may emanate from the judgment and from events outside of the courtroom. There is first the risk of harm that that flows immediately from an adverse judgment. As the prevailing party, the defendant will be entitled to an award of its costs, and the client will not be able to recover any of the fees and costs it incurred. There is also the potential that the client will be responsible to reimburse the defendant for its attorney's fees, which can be assessed against the plaintiff when a fee clause exists in the contract asserted as giving rise to the duty of confidentiality, or if the court concludes that the claim of misappropriation was made in bad faith. There is the potential that the defendant will turn plaintiff and file a new action to assert a claim of malicious prosecution, trade libel, or interference.

The adverse judgment can also create the risk of a finding that the information did not constitute a trade secret so as to be unprotectable vis-á-vis a third party. If the court concludes that the information does not constitute a trade secret because the information was in the public domain, that ruling could have an adverse impact on any pending applications or issued patents related to that technology. A publicly traded company that touted its trade secret technology as basis for the valuation given in its IPO could face a significant drop in share value and market capitalization, followed by the inevitable shareholder suits. If the court concludes that there is a defect in the plaintiff's title such that it cannot assert ownership of the trade secrets, the plaintiff thereafter cannot rely on those trade secrets as a basis to preclude use thereof by any third party.

CHAPTER TWO

Legal and Business Considerations in Identifying the "Proper" Defendant(s)

When an individual walks out the door with trade secrets in hand, who to name as a party defendant seems fairly obvious. But when the original misappropriator takes these trade secrets to a new employer or joins with others to start a competing business, the choice is not so simple. Should the complaint name only the original misappropriator? Is there value in sending a demand letter to the new employer or business? Is there a notice requirement before the new employer or business can be included in the suit? Are there potential problems if the suit does not immediately name everyone who may have interactions with the original misappropriator? What are the risks if several suits are filed seriatim, e.g., first against the original misappropriator, and later against his or her new employer or business venture?

Identifying these legal issues is a critical service the practitioner must be able to perform for the client. These considerations start with the applicable requirements for identifying the proper party/parties and quickly involve tactical decisions that bear on the manner in which the case is handled and the ability to bring subsequent suits if necessary. But these decisions are not made in a vacuum. The client must also consider the impact these decisions may have on its business in the larger sense.

1. *Identifying the "Legally Correct" Defendants*

Some forms of protecting intellectual property rights, such as patent infringement suits, apply a strict liability standard as the prerequisite for judicial relief. "Reasons" for use of the IP are irrelevant to a prima facie determination of patent infringement, regardless of the defendant. By contrast, other forms are more defendant-specific. For example, a claim for trade secret misappropriation is a form of intentional tort and involves an analysis of the putative defendant's state of mind. For liability to attach, the evidence must establish that the defendant knew—or had reason to know—that the act of acquisition was wrongful. But, just as liability is not limited to those persons involved in the original act of acquisition, steps can be taken by the practitioner to "create" the necessary state of mind in third parties in order to satisfy the requirements for obtaining judicial relief.

In addition to wrongful acquisition, "misappropriation" under the Uniform Trade Secrets Act is defined to include the unauthorized disclosure or use of a trade secret by a person who knew (or should have known) that his knowledge of the trade secret exists as a result of a duty to maintain confidentiality, or through the wrongful act of another. Through this broad definition, all persons who are shown to have participated in an intentional tort can be liable for damages suffered by the plaintiff. The fact that a given individual or entity was not part of the initial acts of acquisition of the trade secret is not a shield to liability.

The different forms through which misappropriation can occur (acquisition, use, or disclosure) create the possibility of multiple-party defendants who may or may not have engaged in different forms of wrongful conduct, or who were involved at different points in time. Thus, while for any given defendant there can be only a single claim for misappropriation in most jurisdictions, arising upon the particular initial action that constitutes an act of misappropriation, there can be multiple independent acts of misappropriation by various parties, which gives rise to separate claims against each of these potential defendants.

In deciding whether there are sufficient facts to argue an extension of liability beyond the initial acquirer to another individual or entity, such that they can also be named as a party defendant, one must consider that the definition of "use" under the Uniform Trade Secret Act is very broad. Use has been found to exist where the confidential information was employed in manufacturing, production, research and development, marketing goods that embody the trade secrets, and soliciting customers through knowledge gained from the trade secret information. Use can also exist where the information serves as a basis for future development efforts. But use of information constituting a trade secret does not subject that person to liability when the action was without knowledge that the trade secrets are owned by another, or were acquired through improper means. Therefore, a key aspect in determining whether to name any particular individual or entity as a party defendant centers on (1) the extent to which, at the time the complaint is filed, they know (or received facts that place them on notice) that the use of the information is wrongful, and (2) the nature and scope of the relief being sought.

A frequent scenario involves a former employee who has taken trade secret information to his or her new employer. Should the complaint also name the new employer? The facts available may not indicate whether the new employer instigated or had knowledge of the theft, or even has any indication that its new employee may have done anything improper. However, the nature of the job to be performed by the former employee often suggests an increase in the risk of use and disclosure of the trade secret information. Alternatively, there may be a pending transaction through which the trade secret information may be publicly disclosed or transferred to others absent prompt action. In either case, holding off until the time is "right" to file a subsequent suit naming the new employer or transferee may be too late to unring the bell.

A trade secret owner faced with this situation may not have the luxury of time in which to first send a warning letter to the new employer before initiating judicial action. Regardless of the good faith of the new employer or transferee, when the risk of disclosure is high, it is unacceptable to wait until a record of sending demand letters and addressing noncommittal responses can be created. Rather, in these circumstances the practitioner must elevate speed as a priority over preparation of a record in order to protect the client's interest in maintaining the information as a secret. For this reason it is prudent to couple a complaint that provides notice to the defendant of the existence of the trade secrets with a request for a temporary restraining order, or preliminary injunction, in order to preserve the secrecy status quo. The newly named party defendant (who may claim not to otherwise have been aware, or previously on notice, that it is in possession of and in the process of beginning to use the trade secrets) will be placed on actual notice as soon as the company is served with a complaint. In this fashion the trade secret owner "creates" a legally correct defendant. While there can be no damages awarded against the new employer for events that precede the filing and service of the complaint, as any prior possession or use by that party defendant would not be with the requisite state of mind and therefore would not be wrongful, in this situation the goal with respect to this party is injunctive relief to prevent the disclosure, dissemination, and subsequent use of the trade secret information.

When the trade secrets are already in use by the new employer or business entity, the practitioner should consider whether it can attach liability for pre-filing damages through application of the doctrines of respondeat superior and vicarious liability. Under these doctrines, the lack of a wrongful state of mind by a managing officer or director of the corporation is not an absolute bar to an award of damages. Instead, the crucial question considers the application of principles of agency and asks whether the agent was acting within the course and scope of her employment. And, in addition to liability for damages when the new employer or business is found to have acted through its authorized agents, corporations and other business entities can be directly liable for misappropriation when the wrongful acts of the initial misappropriator have been ratified.

Further, the officers or directors of a corporation, or the owner of a business entity, may face exposure for liability in their individual capacity for this intentional tort, even when they were not personally engaged in the original tortious conduct, or where the act of wrongful acquisition preceded their involvement. Direct liability can exist for these individuals without the need to establish that they personally used the trade secrets, as long as it can be shown that they knew, or should have known, of the use of the trade secrets but nevertheless failed to take steps within their power to stop the tortious conduct. In this context, their actions can constitute an independent wrongful act as well as a ratification of the original wrongful acts. Liability through ratification should also be considered where an individual takes effective control of the business entity, with notice of sufficient facts to justify a finding that they "knew or should have known" of the initial acts of wrongdoing, but still failed to take action to prevent ongoing harm to the trade secret owner.

The potential for direct personal liability does not mean that exposure exists for an officer, director, or business owner whenever they simply fail to immediately accede to demands set forth by the trade secret owner in a complaint or a pre-filing cease-and-desist letter. Public policy does not support liability on this limited basis, as it would unduly hamper competition and stifle innovation if one company could effectively squelch competition merely by the filing of a suit or the delivery of a demand letter. Whether and when the risk of liability has begun to attach to a "subsequent misappropriator" can turn on the nature of the details provided by the trade secret owner and the actions taken in response. For example, a letter that merely indicates a belief that a subordinate employee has taken some unspecified information creates less risk to the new employer than a lengthy missive that provides details of the manner of taking and the specifics of the information involved. If the officer, director, or business owner has not been provided with detailed information relating to the alleged acts of wrongdoing, or claims in response to such information the right to rely on expert advice, reports, or opinions developed in addressing the claim of misappropriation, their liability exposure is reduced as long as their conduct is reasonable in light of the circumstances.

The potential for liability—or the potential to "create" liability—thus compels the practitioner representing the trade secret owner to consider carefully whether there are steps that can increase pressure on the new employer or business entity. The practitioner must investigate whether individual officers or directors can be legally named as party defendants, given the circumstances, and the extent to which there are additional steps that could or should be taken in order to create the specter of liability for these additional defendants.

2. *Creating the "Legally Correct" Defendant and the Use of Pre-suit Demand Letters*

Not every trade secret dispute should be addressed by filing a complaint as quickly as possible, nor does every matter justify seeking a request for a temporary restraining order. In some cases pre-litigation activities designed to develop a record of efforts to gain information from the potential defendants, and which serve the purpose of placing them on notice of the incipient dispute, provide greater long-term benefits than can be gained through immediate juridical action.

In many situations, the client may be aware of facts that suggest acts of misappropriation but cannot be sure that the former employee has actually taken documents that contain its trade secrets, or the scope of that which was taken. The client may not even be sure that the former employee has gone to a new employer or a competitor. The former employee may not know that he or she has taken materials the client considers confidential, or has no intention to use the materials to compete. Indeed, mere possession by itself is not always actionable misappropriation. Alternatively, a business entity now doing business with the individual with whom the client has a concern may not be aware that it has possession of the client's trade secrets. These are cases when pre-litigation efforts to reach out to the alleged misappropriator, or the persons with whom he or she wishes to do business, may result in steps that will provide full and complete protection of the trade secrets. The new employer, not aware previously of the concerns held by the trade secret owner, might wish to avoid any dispute and therefore readily work with the trade secret owner to implement steps designed to fully address any risk of harm by reason of the improper use of the trade secrets. In these scenarios, a pre-dispute demand letter has the potential of achieving satisfactory results.

A pre-dispute demand letter should be written in a manner that brings to the attention of the recipient the client's concerns regarding the potentially improper possession, use, or disclosure of the trade secret information. Of course, it should also be written with the secondary audience—the court and the jury—in mind. A firm but respectful tone is more effective with both audiences than a letter full of hyperbole and threats. Even a letter that is brief, devoid of details regarding who did what and when, at a minimum places a stake in the ground that can be later referenced should the recipient claim that there cannot be a finding of liability due to a lack of notice.

The more detail provided in the letter, the harder it can be for the recipient to later claim a lack of awareness regarding the nature and scope of the problem. These details could include the basis for the duty to maintain secrecy (such as including references to, or copies of, agreements that contain the contractual obligations), references to the actions of the primary actor that suggest improper acquisition of the confidential information, specifics regarding the type of information at issue, the potential ways in which the information might be used, the manner by which a particular assignment of the individual at the new place of employment might create the risk of use due to overlap in positions, and the harm that could result from any use or dissemination of the information.

In addition to demanding immediate cessation of use, the letter could demand certain additional steps, including the immediate preservation of documents or records that might be sought through discovery should the matter proceed to litigation, and a request that the recipient immediately return all materials and property of the client. On this last point, the demand letter should not request "destruction" of the information as an alternative to its return. Compliance with this demand will result in significant hurdles in ascertaining the scope of what was misappropriated, and will provide the defendant with a strong response to any subsequent claim that it spoliated evidence.

A greater level of detail places the recipient in a position where a simple response (such as "don't worry, we honor the intellectual property of others") becomes facially insufficient. To avoid appearing cavalier, the recipient is placed in a position of having to conduct a reasoned investigation or to take more particularized steps to address the claimed manner of use or potential disclosure. If it does take such steps, those efforts are potentially subject to discovery. If it does not, it is exposed to a claim that its conduct post-notice was willful and supports an award of exemplary damages. But regardless of the level of detail in the letter, the recipient is placed in a position where it must decide whether and how to respond. It could answer with a categorical denial, or demand further details, or indicate that it is conducting an investigation and will respond further in due course, or provide an explanation or defense. In any case, the client can then decide what to do next depending on the response.

As a document scrutinized by the recipient for clues to the intentions of the drafter, the practitioner must think about the implicit messages conveyed by the choice of addressees and signatories. Merely contacting the former employee, with the letter signed by the manager of the former employer, may not result in any response and can leave the former employee an "out" by simply claiming that the letter was not received. Registered letters will establish receipt but are often left unclaimed at the Post Office. Including a cc to the General Counsel of the new employer is less likely to result in the letter being disregarded, but is also more likely to result in the new employer immediately seeking outside legal assistance. The probability that outside legal counsel will be quickly involved increases if the trade secret holder prominently copies its own outside counsel. If the letter is addressed to the CEO of the new employer but signed by a "low-ranking" manager in the employ of the trade secret holder, the chance of a delay increases, as that letter will likely be passed off to others for handling. A letter addressed from CEO to CEO, or from General Counsel to General Counsel, more probably will receive direct reciprocal attention.

A further consideration is whether to include someone who the trade secret owner will want to have on the deposition list as an addressee or person copied. A recipient of a demand letter may well become an important percipient witness, if merely for evidence of what was not done after receipt. The converse is also true, in that the individual signing the letter has now increased the potential for a deposition. What that person knew and when, whether he or she will otherwise be a trial witness, the impact the letter may have on his or her testimony and credibility, as well as any potential privilege issues that may arise should all be considered in deciding who is the best person on behalf of the trade secret owner to appear as the "author" of the demand letter.

If the answer to the demand letter is a complete failure to respond, or a written "blow-off," the client is then placed in a position where it must take further steps immediately or be faced later with the defenses of waiver or laches. Having made the effort to reach out to the other party, however, the client has minimized the risk that it will be sued for malicious prosecution should it later fail to establish wrongdoing on the part of the responding party. By contrast, if the response includes a reasoned analysis of the situation and concludes with the view that the recipient neither has possession of nor will use the trade secrets, rather than initiating suit against that party (in the absence of facts that suggest the imminent threat of harm by failing to seek judicial assistance), the client should then respond with a confirmation that makes clear it is relying on those representations in deciding not to take any further action at the time. But the practitioner should still calendar the expiration of the statute of limitation, based on a calculation that assumes the assurances from the recipient will not serve to later toll the statute, and the client should be cautioned to be extra-vigilant for any information that would suggest that the assurances were false or incorrect.

Consistent with the need to implement a strategy to preserve rights for potential use down the road, the client should create a repository that details the information to which the alleged misappropriator had access, and which secures copies of all documents (such as contracts, emails, or memoranda) that may be relevant in case the dispute later heats up. The risk in the interim is that dissemination may occur, which will destroy the trade secret status of the information and leave the client only with the right to seek damages for the loss but unable to obtain injunctive relief. To guard against this eventuality, the client should be counseled to explore a patent strategy to acquire IP protection via the Patent Act for what was known to be or potentially could be acquired by the misappropriator, or which will require its continued cooperation as a named inventor.

The practitioner representing the individual or business entity that has received a letter suggesting that it is in possession of trade secret information should not counsel her client to merely ignore the letter. Almost any reply is better than an unanswered demand. Absent a response, should litigation later ensue, in addition to addressing the underlying claim of misappropriation, that party will have to explain why it did not respond. The failure to respond before the action begins can negatively color the more important explanation at trial of why misappropriation did not occur.

Steps available to the practitioner in responding, in particular to develop a record that his or her client engaged in efforts reasonable under the circumstances to investigate, include asking for greater details regarding the specifics of the trade secrets and the nature of the acts that are alleged to constitute misappropriation, as well as a further explication of the actions the trade secret holder desires from the recipient of the letter. The recipient should make clear, where appropriate, that there is insufficient information to form a detailed response. If an investigation has been (or is being) undertaken, internally or through the use of experts, to support a determination that the recipient either has not done anything improper or that there is no risk of resulting harm, the recipient should consider providing these specifics. In either case, the trade secret holder is now placed in a position of having to decide whether to take judicial action or to respond further with additional information.

If the response to the initial demand letter is substantive, or suggests that a further response will be provided that reflects the results of an internal investigation, the recipient must take steps to be able to later substantiate the point made, whether of the manner in which the internal investigation is conducted or the activities involved in the retention of an outside expert. Where the recipient is not the initial alleged misappropriator, it should consider whether a preliminary report can be developed, in a form suitable for presentation to the court, which concludes that the trade secrets are not required in order to conduct its business, especially if other evidence suggests that misappropriation or other wrongful conduct occurred. As an interim step, this report will be helpful, should the trade secret owner seek broad-form preliminary injunctive relief that might effectively shut down the business operations of the respondent, by narrowing the scope of any injunctive order.

In any event, an investigation undertaken by the recipient should focus on establishing sufficient facts to reasonably support either the conclusion that there was an absence of acts that constitute misappropriation by the investigating party (because the information as described does not constitute a trade secret or because acquisition, use, or disclosure by that party simply did not occur) or that specifies steps that can be taken to suspend any activities that might involve the use of the allegedly misappropriated information. If the investigation includes the latter recommendations, the recipient of the demand letter must undertake steps well documented to implement that advice.

Any response by the recipient of a demand letter should also request the trade secret holder to confirm that it has retained any documents that may bear either on the acts of misappropriation as alleged or the claimed harm, and which relate specifically to the recipient. By concluding the response with an indication that the recipient now considers the matter closed in the absence of being provided additional facts, pressure is placed on the trade secret holder to either provide more information or take legal action. If the legal course is taken, the trade secret holder will now have to address, in the battle for the sympathies of the court or jury, why it did not simply respond further to what the recipient will attempt to characterize as a reasonable request for additional information.

The choice of addressees and signatories in the response, in the same manner as the demand letter, can send express as well as implied messages. If the person signing the response is a junior-level executive, the trade secret owner may feel that the responding party is not taking the matter seriously enough. Conversely, if the person signing is too senior, the responding party may send the unintended message that it has a significant concern over the statements being made in the demand letter, as opposed to any express statement of having evaluated the matter and decided that there is no cause to proceed further. In addition to ensuring that the right message is being sent, the choice of who should sign the response should be evaluated from the standpoint of whether that person will otherwise be a witness, and whether they will now become a witness by reason of having signed the letter (as they will be asked about any affirmative statements or factual representations in the letter). Having outside counsel sign the response may lend gravitas to the situation but will also elevate it to a different level by the trade secret owner.

In deciding how to proceed, the party responding should not necessarily feel compelled to address the response to the signatory on the demand letter. Is there is a person more senior or with whom the responding party already has some form of helpful relationship (whether through prior interactions that give rise to an aura of credibility or even as simple as having been previously introduced at industry events)? The responding party should consider including that person as an addressee, or even as a party merely being copied, if it will facilitate the dialogue.

Care should be taken in drafting and circulating pre-litigation demand letters. Statements that allege a person has misappropriated trade secrets can be defamatory per se, as they suggest a crime or are injurious to another in their trade, business, or profession. Trade secret owners, and particularly their employees involved in sales, should be cautioned that the use of these letters for marketing purposes will—at a minimum—distract the court from addressing the central issue of misappropriation, and can create an impression that the claim is being asserted for ulterior purposes. Worse, the improper publication of demand letters can provide the defendant an effective cross-claim. However, when made in anticipation of litigation and circulated only to those persons and entities who have a direct interest in the matter, these demand letters are subject to a litigation privilege in most jurisdictions, even when they are sent to persons other than the individual directly being accused of misappropriation.

The boundaries of the litigation privilege may vary from jurisdiction to jurisdiction, but as a general rule protect the author even if the alleged wrongdoer is eventually cleared of any wrongdoing, as long as the letter served a legitimate purpose tied to the subject matter of actually contemplated litigation and was not used in bad faith for anti-competitive purposes. For this reason, the practitioner should carefully review any demand letters to be sent by the client, as well as any letters to third parties, which provide notice of the incipient dispute or pending litigation, to ensure that such communications fall within the applicable privilege as articulated in the relevant jurisdiction. Otherwise, in addition to constituting the factual basis for a defamation counterclaim that exposes the client to damages, the wrongdoer now has an alternative explanation to provide the jury for the trade secret owner's pursuit of the action in the first place (i.e., the desire to use the claim of misappropriation in order to gain market share, or otherwise disrupt the business efforts of the alleged wrongdoer).

Sending a pre-suit demand letter also creates the small risk that the recipient will take advantage of the warning that a suit is likely and file a preemptive suit for declaratory relief. The accused misappropriator could seek an adjudication that the information does not constitute a trade secret, that the alleged trade secret owner is not the true owner, that the statute of limitations has expired, or any other of the numerous defenses that may exist under the particular facts. Where the trade secret owner is located in a jurisdiction that recognizes the inevitable disclosure doctrine (e.g., Illinois), the alleged misappropriator may seek to file in a jurisdiction, such as California, that expressly refuses to recognize that theory of relief. Trade secret cases involving contractual non-competes have a higher likelihood of being subjected to a declaratory relief action, as the mere threat of suit by the party seeking to enforce the non-compete can freeze the business opportunity being sought by the other contracting party.

In general, there is little likelihood that the accused misappropriator will (or should) seek declaratory relief, except when there is a jurisdictional choice that could result in a difference in the applicable legal standards. Otherwise, by seeking declaratory relief, the accused misappropriator has now initiated a process that may not have been the first choice of the trade secret owner, who may have preferred to pursue a non-judicial business solution or who was merely attempting to extract concessions through empty threats. But, once legal action has been initiated by the accrued misappropriator, most trade secret owners will feel compelled to protect their position and will file a responsive affirmative claim.

3. *Procedural Issues Impacting How One Handles the "Correct" Defendants*

There are a number of procedural variables with respect to when and where to file the initial complaint. As the identities of all potential defendants are not always known at the time an action is initiated, the plaintiff must decide whether to proceed against those currently known or instead wait until further information is available. Even when all of the possible defendants are fully identified, a single action may not be possible if they are not located handily in a single jurisdiction. There may be choices among different forums that benefit the plaintiff, as well as jurisdictional restrictions that limit the potential for filing in federal versus state court. When the complaint is first filed, the plaintiff must decide if all of the substantively correct potential defendants could or should be named in a single action or separated procedurally by filing several actions, and whether it has retained sufficient ability to maneuver procedurally in order to address situational difficulties as they arise.

The prospect that several defendants may have some involvement in the matters giving rise to the claim is an issue that involves the statute of limitations, as the failure to timely name a given party who is in possession of the trade secrets can destroy the ability to protect these secrets in the future. Under the delayed-discovery rule, applicable in most jurisdictions, the cause of action for misappropriation begins to run with respect to all potential defendants as soon as there is notice to the trade secret owner of the existence of the injury. In some state courts a plaintiff can avoid expiration of the statute of limitations with respect to unknown defendants (defendants whose identity has not been yet ascertained), even where they may have participated in the original wrongful conduct, by naming fictitious "doe defendants." The plaintiff must still be diligent in conducting discovery addressed at ascertaining the identity and involvement of additional defendants, and then must make a motion to amend through which it can substitute the "real" defendants in place of the doe defendants. When this process is followed, the amendment is said to "relate back" to the date of the initial filing of the complaint for purposes of determining whether the action was timely filed in light of the statute of limitations.

While ignorance of the existence of an injury or cause of action may delay the running of the statute of limitations until the date of its discovery, the general rule is that the plaintiff's ignorance of the identity of the defendant will not toll the statute as to that defendant. By comparison, in jurisdictions that do not allow naming "doe defendants" (such as the federal courts), the plaintiff must be diligent to either name all of the wrongdoers when the original complaint is filed, or thereafter take steps through discovery to learn their identify and seek leave to amend the complaint (or to file a new and separate action) to add the new defendants before expiration of the statute of limitations.

Whether to name multiple defendants when filing the initial action in order to avoid expiration of the statute of limitations is a decision complicated by the fact that there is the potential for different periods of limitation when there are multiple defendants. The actions of each defendant are considered separately, and a plaintiff may have more than one claim for misappropriation, each with its own statute of limitations. This is different from saying that an act of misappropriation can give rise to multiple claims, as there is a distinction between a claim for misappropriation and the individual act (or acts) of misappropriation. In most jurisdictions, an act of misappropriation gives rise to a claim by a given plaintiff against a given defendant only once, at the time of the initial misappropriation, subject to the discovery rule applicable in that jurisdiction. Each new misuse or wrongful disclosure by that defendant is viewed as augmenting the single claim of misappropriation (and the misappropriation is seen as continuing) rather than as giving rise to separate claims. This reasoning does not preclude the plaintiff from having separate claims against each one of multiple defendants, based on their own involvement in the continuing misappropriation. When the original misappropriation is continuing, therefore, while only one claim may arise against the original defendant, there may be one or more additional claims with respect to any other defendants who may be later involved.

In order to deal with the statute of limitations issue, the choice facing the attorney representing the trade secret owner ranges from naming all of the known individuals in the suit at the time it is filed, adding them to the same suit over time as discovery develops support for the claims, or filing separate suits, with each directed at different party defendants. With respect to additional potential defendants, the practitioner should be sure to track the last date on which these parties should be named in any pending or newly filed action in order to avoid the statute of limitations. Even though these additional defendants may not actually know that they are improperly using the trade secrets, a court may conclude that the statute of limitations began to run when the plaintiff had any reason to suspect that the defendants knew, or should have known, that they had acquired or improperly used the trade secrets.

Separate from consideration of the statute of limitations, when there are multiple potential defendants, jurisdictional issues impact whether some or all are legally correct for the desired venue. A civil claim for trade secret misappropriation is a state law claim, and access to federal court (in the absence of adding a claim, based on the same basic set of operative facts, that poses a separate federal question) depends on the existence of diversity jurisdiction. Adding one or more from a pool of several potential defendants may destroy diversity. As subject matter jurisdiction can neither be created by consent nor waived by the parties, this is a procedural matter that cannot be resolved by a stipulation. Thus, if a federal court venue is desired, the plaintiff may have to forgo naming one or more of the diversity-destroying defendants. If the plaintiff finds it tactically beneficial to name all defendants in a single suit, it instead must file in state court. The opposite analysis is also true, in that a plaintiff may decide that it is best served by being in state court. By adding an individual defendant to the action for purposes of destroying diversity, the plaintiff can avoid the potential that the primary defendant will remove the action from state to federal court.

In contrast to subject matter jurisdiction, an objection to the lack of personal jurisdiction can be waived by the parties. But, in the absence of a pre- or post-filing waiver, a plaintiff will still be limited in its ability to pursue several defendants in the same suit if it is unable to convince a given court that there are sufficient contacts such that the court may exercise personal jurisdiction over all defendants. However, a successful motion to dismiss by one of the other defendants, on the grounds that the court lacked personal jurisdiction, will not impair the ability to proceed against the remaining defendant(s).

In addition to the traps that arise by reason of the statute of limitations, and the jurisdictional questions that exist as gatekeepers for suits involving multiple defendants, the client must be made aware of the various ways in which claims against subsequent parties may be lost or hampered if it decides to pursue several defendants individually or seriatim. The first of the two choices to be made strategically, when the client does not desire to pursue all defendants in a single action, is whether to contemporaneously file multiple actions against the several defendants, with each defendant named in a separate action. The second choice reflects a process of filing consecutive actions to gain procedural separation of the cases to impede efforts by the defendants to consolidate the actions.

Both procedural options may be a good choice when there are different issues involving proof of liability, or with respect to the presentation of damages, such that there is a risk that the trier of fact will be confused if multiple defendants are named in a single action. For example, on the question of proof of liability, if widely divergent steps have been taken by the post-original misappropriation defendants to investigate after delivery of a cease-and-desist letter, the trier of fact may be confused over the question of the extent to which it should find remedial efforts—reasonable with respect to one party—inure to the unearned benefit of another. On the question of damages, there may be different markets impacted by the operations of the various defendants, which will result in confusion over a lost-profits analysis. Likewise, there may be different benefits to each of the defendants from their improper use of the trade secrets that may confuse the way in which an unjust enrichment award is crafted.

When multiple actions are considered, the plaintiff needs to be aware that an unfavorable result in one action on liability may preclude it from pursuing any of the other actions because of "one way" res judicata, or collateral estoppel. For example, the court in the initial action may conclude that the information in question does not constitute a trade secret. This type of threshold finding applies to any other defendant, and a defendant in the separate or subsequent action may thus be able to avoid liability without having to undertake any effort to establish a defense. By contrast, the plaintiff cannot take advantage of either principle against a defendant in one of the subsequent actions should it prevail in the original action, as that defendant did not participate in the prior action and therefore is not bound by any of the prior findings. This does not mean that a court in the subsequent proceeding will not be influenced, even if only informally, by the judgment in the plaintiff's favor from the prior action, especially if the judge presiding is the same. But that potential, standing alone, is a meager benefit when weighed against the potential downside risks.

Where the plaintiff decides to file multiple actions, it can anticipate that the defendants in the subsequent actions will scour the record of the earlier actions to identify findings or admissions that can be used to their benefit. Aware of the potential for being sued in a subsequent action (or named in a separate but unconsolidated action), potential defendants may encourage or support efforts by the named defendant in the initial action, including providing assistance in the preparation of discovery that may assist their own efforts in a later action. The plaintiff, responding to this discovery, will not have the right to serve reciprocal discovery upon the subsequent or potential defendants, and must be mindful that its verified responses may be used against it in the subsequent actions. Ameliorating this risk is the fact that the plaintiff can use the discovery devices available in the initial action, including the use of third-party subpoenas, to build a record against the subsequent defendants before they have been sued and have standing to object.

The practitioner representing a defendant named in a subsequent or separate action has to consider whether the benefit of being named separately outweighs the benefit of being one of many defendants in the initial action. Even though it may not be bound under principles of res judicata or collateral estoppel to the terms of a judgment previously entered, a point that weighs in favor of separation, there are many ways in which the plaintiff can introduce a prior favorable judgment in a subsequent proceeding to influence the trier of fact. For example, it may have included a copy of the judgment in a cease-and-desist letter that it sent to the subsequent defendant. The cease-and-desist letter, along with the prior judgment attached as an exhibit, is then offered into evidence to show that the subsequent defendant was on notice of facts that gave rise to its obligation to have investigated fully. The jury, even if instructed that this defendant is not bound by the findings in the original judgment, is sure to be swayed by the existence of a judgment already entered, and will be more likely to make findings in accord with those in the prior judgment.

Options available to a defendant in this situation include seeking consolidation of the actions in full or, for purposes of the liability phase only, with separate juries for purposes of determining the amount of damages, if any. It can also seek coordination of the proceedings to minimize conflicts in legal or factual positions among the various defendants. One or more of the defendants in the various actions can move for the appointment of a special master, particularly for supervising discovery, as that will result in a de facto consolidation of discovery to the benefit of the defendants (who can take advantage of the admissions contained in any of the sworn discovery responses from the plaintiff and can choose to either participate in depositions taken in a given action or merely attend as a spectator rather than as a participant, and thereby reserve the ability to later depose the same individual in the subsequent proceedings).

4. *Considering the Business Impact When Naming Otherwise Legally Correct Defendants*

The ability to identify the legal prerequisites to naming an individual or entity as a party defendant is a critical skill. There must always be a legally justifiable basis for naming any defendant, supported by a reasoned investigation. If there is not, the practitioner should decline to proceed.

But the client must consider more than the judicially imposed requirements before proceeding with the case. A host of business issues play into the decision whether to include a particular party, and a sophisticated client rarely sees litigation as an isolated aspect of its business.

An important aspect of the decision of who to include as a party defendant involves how the litigation will be viewed by the various constituents that impact the client's business. Messages, express and implied, intended or not, are sent and received by a variety of third parties when a company turns to litigation. The cost of litigation also is affected by the decision of whom to include. These business issues and financial considerations, impacting all of the parties to the suit, are tied both to the nature of the suit and to the decision of whom to name as a party defendant.

Assisting the client to make reasoned choices in developing its business case for naming any otherwise legally correct defendants requires a healthy understanding of the goals the client wishes to achieve through litigation.

- Is this a "one and done" action, where there is no reasonable chance the client's path will ever again cross that of the potential defendants?
- Is this litigation for "competitive" purposes, such that the client desires it to have an impact that extends beyond the action and further in scope than the parties named therein?
- Do the parties have a preexisting relationship that provides ongoing benefits or obligations that could be affected by the action and the parties that could be named therein?
- Are there other real or potential future interactions between the client and third parties, including one or more of the potential defendants, that must be considered?

Sometimes the client has not fully considered what it wishes ultimately to achieve, or the impact that litigation will have on its broader business interests. Before litigation is commenced, the practitioner must help the client fully identify that which it wishes to achieve, and to counsel the client regarding the legal ability to reach those goals and the practical likelihood of success given the information available. If the goal includes broader market impact, the practitioner should suggest the client consider soliciting the advice of marketing professionals. These individuals can provide insight on the impact the suit may have on the marketplace, as well as assist in messaging throughout the course of the action. When and if the goals of a client change over the course of a lengthy action, the practitioner has an ongoing obligation to push the client to continue to consider and articulate its newly identified goals, to ensure that everyone is focused on the same end-game, and to assist in a reevaluation of the litigation investment in light of any changes in desired results.

Where the client has multiple employees and the potential defendants include one or more former employees, the practitioner should discuss with the client how those who remain may view the litigation. These individuals could be important witnesses for the client or potentially adverse and called by the defendants on a number of topics. In deciding how best to proceed, consider the following:

- Will the current employees be cooperative with respect to the internal investigation?
- How forthright will they be with counsel in preparing for their testimony?
- Is there a risk that they will try to shape their testimony one way or the other in order to assist one side over the other?
- Will they become a conduit for information to their former colleagues regarding decisions concerning the litigation, placing friendship over loyalty to their employer?
- Is there a risk that they may be evaluating their own future with the company, or opportunities that may exist elsewhere, when considering what they have learned about the suit?
- Will the action be seen as an anti-competitive attempt by the client to ward off attempts by the new employer to recruit from the client's remaining employees?

The existing employees will certainly take into account the differences between how the client deals with those who left on "bad" terms when compared to those who left on "good" terms. For any of these reasons, the client needs to be actively aware that these remaining employees will evaluate who is being sued, apart from whether there are legally clear grounds for the suit, and may potentially feel even more sympathetic to the former employees if a "fair" basis does not readily appear.

Where multiple former employees may have to be named, the client can also consider whether it is possible to ameliorate the negative visual impact of suing a number of former employees by staggering joinder of the various defendants, depending on what discovery may develop, with the most culpable-appearing defendant being the first to be named. Less culpable individuals can then be approached with an offer to resolve the matter short of litigation, as long as they provide full cooperation. Since cooperation from the remaining employees can provide a significant advantage to the client throughout the course of an action, internal "marketing" efforts should be implemented to educate the remaining workforce regarding the basis for and importance of the litigation. This process should start early and continue throughout the pendency of the action. Status reports can be provided to selected groups of employees so the client can educate these groups regarding the stages of the action, what each side is doing, and the meaning these actions may have to the outcome. In a smaller entity in particular, these educational efforts can reduce the number of inaccurate rumors, avoid distraction, and help to explain the impact the litigation may be having on the business, particularly where the expense of the action has an economic toll on the company. This process of internal marketing can further serve a prophylactic purpose by educating the remaining employees on the importance of the trade secrets and the willingness of the company to take affirmative steps to protect its investment in those assets.

Similar to the fact that the suit will send messages to the remaining employees, a client's competitors will draw inferences and base conclusions on the manner in which the client approaches the action. In this regard, the question is centered not just on who is named, or even if the potential exists that the competitor may be added, but also on the nature of the competitors to whom the message is being sent (intentionally or inadvertently).

- Will one party take the lead and act as the decision maker for the defense group, such as where a group of former employees goes to work for the competitor, who then responds on behalf of everyone named as a defendant?
- Will some of the defendants hang back, riding on the coattails of more aggressive defendants?
- Are there potential indemnity obligations, contractual or equitable, such as between joint venturers?
- Are the decision makers at the competitor litigation-averse, such that they will draw from prior negative experiences in reaching the conclusion that the trade secret owner is not someone against whom they want to litigate?
- Does the client want to develop or capitalize on a reputation for using litigation as a business tool to dissuade its competitors from challenging its market position?
- Will neutral customers view the litigation favorably to the client, or believe that the client now puts supply chains at risk?
- Is it likely that the competitor will fund the defense, such as where individual defendants are being accused of using the information to further the business of that competitor?
- Are the individual defendants able, under the Labor Code (or similar statutes, contracts, or agreements), to tender the defense to the competitor, who will then fund the defense in its role as their new employer or business partner?

The ability to afford protracted litigation, which every party assesses in light of its own unique situation, is based as much on the temperament of the person ultimately in charge of running the business as it is on an objective analysis of the strength of the balance sheet. As such, when a direct competitor is a potential defendant to the action being contemplated, motivating issues and pressure points that exist independent of the litigation should be considered in the assessment of the impact this defendant will have on the cost and success of the action. If the competitor sees the action as a catalyst for engaging in a larger battle over market share, the client must be ready to allocate resources disproportionate to the matters directly in issue. Alternatively, the competitor may be interested in seeking a rapid solution when the mere existence of the action will have an impact on an upcoming event involving the competitor, such as an IPO that may have to be delayed. The client may find value in the fact that the competitor is seeking business with a common customer, who will insist that the action be resolved before approving a design win for a device that may be embroiled in the dispute. If the competitor is litigation-savvy, its litigation experiences may suggest that it will be "comfortable" dealing with the cost and distraction of litigation. If so, pursuing them as a party defendant in a borderline case may not be a good business decision. Does this competitor have the ability to assert counterclaims, such that the suit will expand dramatically beyond the issue that justified initiation? Are they currently involved in one or more actions, or have prior actions been recently resolved? These areas can be fertile ground for information on their approach to litigation and their ability to address or withstand additional litigation, and may assist in identifying common friends and enemies who can be a source of assistance or trouble as matters progress.

The reactions of independent third parties must factor into the decision-making process. Customers who are concerned with pending litigation because of the impact it may have on their supply chain, or on the ability of the client to provide contracted-for services, will find ways of placing pressure on the client. They will want to know whether their information has been compromised, or if team members assigned to their projects are being affected. Purchase orders can be delayed, requests for proposals may seek additional information, and representations and warranties concerning ability to perform may be requested. These concerns are not directed solely at the plaintiff or defendant, and a proactive approach by both sides to educating their key customers can minimize misunderstandings and temper perceptions inculcated by the opponent that (with respect to the plaintiff) the litigation was filed merely for anticompetitive purposes, or (with respect to the defendant) the theft was by an entity that is no longer innovative, transformative, or able to perform.

Companies that have no direct involvement in the events giving rise to the action but may have been approached to provide economic support to the defendant group, or that are contemplating an acquisition of a defendant business entity, will look carefully at any pending litigation in evaluating the strength of an investment or the risk of repayment. This could mean a failure of funding sources for a start-up or the derailing of a potential exit strategy, which in turn can increase the client's leverage to drive a business solution. Alternatively, involvement by an extraneous and otherwise "neutral" company may result in a different avenue through which to pursue a business solution with the defense group.

How the jury may view who is named as a party defendant is a separate governor to be considered by the client when the strategy involves naming everyone possible. There may be some individuals for whom liability is "iffy." If they do eventually participate at trial as a named defendant, the risk exists that their lack of culpability will permeate how the jury views the case against the primary defendants. Even if dismissed prior to trial, the jury is likely to hear that they were named as a defendant and wonder why they no longer are participating in that capacity. Alternatively, if a marginal party has even a tangential role in the events leading to suit, the risk exists that the participating defendants will use the "empty chair" defense, pointing to the unnamed party as the "true" wrongdoer. As the jury is likely to wonder why that individual was not included as a party defendant, the remaining defendants can try to deflect responsibility by suggesting that the role of the non-party had some impact that should lessen their liability. The trial judge may also take into account the parties named—or who could have been named. The failure to have all parties before the court may impact the decision whether to order injunctive relief, or the scope of relief. If the court concludes that some of the defendants should not have been named, this may affect the amount awarded when confronted with a request for an award of fees to the prevailing party, as additional parties tend to increase expense.

The existence of a funding source for the defense is a consideration that should be evaluated in deciding who to name and in what capacity. An individual who was a former employee but is now working for a competitor will want to argue that the activities alleged are broad enough to cover his or her efforts on behalf of the new employer, within the course and scope of their employment, such that the new employer should provide a defense either in the form of retaining counsel for the employee or providing funding for the employee's counsel. In several jurisdictions, the Labor Code or similar statutes require the employer to reimburse an employee for the costs of defense necessarily incurred when the employee discharges his or her obligations, as long as the employee is sued for conduct that allegedly occurred in the course and scope of employment.

Likewise, in many jurisdictions the Corporations Code addresses the corporate employer's duty to indemnify an individual sued in his or her capacity as an officer, director, or other agent of the company. The duty of the new employer is one of reimbursement when the employee is successful on the merits (with the company having the right, but not the duty, to reimburse when the employee is not successful, as long as he or she acted in good faith and reasonably believed the actions were in the best interests of the company). Whether defense costs should be advanced as they are incurred, rather than being reimbursed after the matter has ended, and whether the defense should be provided by the same lawyer representing the employer, are difficult decisions that can be affected by the nature of the allegations in the complaint. The initial reaction of many clients is to shape the allegations in a way that will limit the chances that the new employer will provide defense funds during the pendency of the action. However, the entity providing the funding may ultimately play a positive role in reaching a business solution, especially when it is responsible for paying the monthly invoices for defense services rendered.

If it appears likely to the new employer that it will also be added as a named defendant, it will have to consider whether to absorb the expense of retaining separate counsel—one for itself and another for the individual defendants—or have one firm represent the defense group as a whole. If it chooses to save the expense of separate counsel, the opportunity may arise where the client can take advantage of the potential conflict of interests that can flow from joint representation. Sometimes the conflict is not apparent when the representation begins, and becomes obvious only after the lawyer has acted on behalf of all of the party defendants.

While potential conflicts can be addressed through execution of waivers, joint representation may not be possible if there is an actual conflict, such as where the party defendants have adverse interests in some aspect of the case. If continued representation of all members of the defense group is not possible, the defense counsel must determine whether it can continue to represent at least one of the clients (typically the new employer is preferred for financial reasons), as the other defendants are now "former clients." While informed consent by all parties can address this issue, the defense group may have difficulty where counsel obtained information confidential to one party that it wants to use over the wishes of the other defendants. At a minimum, the situation has the potential for sowing confusion and distrust among the defense group, with the potential that inconsistencies will appear in their presentations, as they no longer can closely coordinate their efforts.

An alternative source of defense funds for one or more of a defense group may also exist in the form of insurance. Claims for unfair competition, theft of trade secrets, or misappropriation are not typically covered by the standard comprehensive general liability policy (or are subject to an IP exclusion). The willingness of the carrier to provide a defense, even if subject to a reservation of rights, most often results from language in the complaint that is sufficient to trigger the duty to defend on the basis that it alleges a form of advertising injury. For example, there is a distinction between copying a style of doing business, such as a plan for interacting with consumers and getting their business, and copying a particular product line that might be attractive to consumers. The former involves the "outward appearance or signature of a business," which may fall within an advertising injury provision in a policy of insurance, whereas a traditionally non-covered claim for misappropriation of trade secrets involves the theft of the information relating to the inner working of a plaintiff's products or business.

Whether in the form of a CGL, E&O, or D&O policy, insurance coverage has the positive aspect of being a potential source of contribution to a settlement pool for achieving a business solution. It can be a negative when it becomes a source of funding for defense costs, which results in defendants being able to litigate without attention to the economic worth of the matters in issue. When choices exist in how one may plead a case, such that allegations can be included to either increase or decrease the potential for coverage, the client should be advised of the ramifications that coverage may have on the way in which the case plays out.

5. *Dealing with the "Foreign Defendant" and the "Aider and Abettor"*

Eager to put pressure on the primary defendants, the client may ask whether it is possible to add individuals or business entities located outside of the United States. The client may wish to name entities or individuals who it perceives as having provided assistance or support to the more culpable defendants, even though these parties were not directly or actively involved in the acts of misappropriation. Even with the assumption that one can satisfy the obligations existing by reason of Federal Rule of Civil Procedure 11 or its state court counterparts, the expense and distraction caused by the addition of remote or tangential defendants can outweigh any perceived benefit. Once these difficulties are considered, the client will be in a better position to decide whether the potential defendant is worth the additional problems that arise as a result of adding it to the lawsuit.

Where one or more of the potential defendants is not a United States resident and is neither incorporated nor doing business in the United States, a number of procedural hurdles exist that impact the decision whether to add them as a defendant. Can they be served and, as a practical matter, what will be the difficulty, cost, or potential for extensive delay in that process? Will service be recognized legally in their "home" jurisdiction, such that their attendance will be required? If they do not have a presence in the United States or an agent for service of process, service hurdles can cause a number of problems that will prevent the efficient handling of the action. While service often can be accomplished on most foreign defendants under the terms of the Hague Convention, there are a number of countries (such as Taiwan) that are not signatories. There may be no ability to formally effect service of a summons issued by a U.S. court to defendants who are resident in these countries. If the trade secret owner proceeds with the case on the basis that it served the summons in compliance with the laws of the United States, the resulting judgment may not be honored in the foreign jurisdiction. Likewise, however, even where the Hague Convention applies generally, each signatory nation has its own procedural hurdles that must be satisfied to accomplish service in a manner that will satisfy both the United States court and the requirements of the signatory nation.

Even if service can be effected in a manner that will satisfy the due process concerns of a U.S. court, will the client be able to effectively enforce a resulting judgment in the foreign jurisdiction? The lack of assets located in the United States subject to attachment, or minimal future business activities in the United States that might serve as an incentive for the foreign defendant to comply, can make pyrrhic the initial success in acquiring a judgment. The foreign jurisdiction may not be willing to domesticate or honor the United States judgment, and an award of injunctive relief will thus lack any extra-jurisdictional effect. These are some of the concerns that should be considered as part of the value proposition whenever the client wishes to add additional foreign-based defendants.

When the potential defendant was not an active participant in the acts and has not directly acquired, used, or disclosed the trade secrets, alternative theories of liability exist as a basis for joinder, including "aiding and abetting" and "conspiracy." However, these theories add elements to the misappropriation cause of action that must be established at trial. For example, to satisfy the elements of aiding and abetting, the client will have the burden of proving that the "aider and abettor" rendered substantial assistance to the primary wrongdoer, and did so with the requisite scienter, in addition to establishing the existence of an independent wrong committed by the primary offender.

Conspiracy allegations can be helpful to reach otherwise unrelated third parties. While such allegations do not frame a separate cause of action in many jurisdictions, the allegation of a conspiracy provides a basis for imposing a type of vicarious responsibility for the acts of one party upon several defendants. But, like aiding and abetting, establishing the proof of a conspiracy adds a number of elements to the underlying misappropriation claim. Under most articulations of civil conspiracy, the plaintiff must also establish that the object or course of conduct to be accomplished was a result of a meeting of the minds between two or more persons. Further, as the purpose of the conspiracy must itself be unlawful (or lawful but accomplished by unlawful means), the court may not merely infer from the underlying wrongful conduct the agreement necessary to form a conspiracy.

Defendants listed as co-conspirators will generally attack the claim by arguing that the factual allegations are insufficient to state a claim. This mode of response occurs especially when the averments merely state that each of the secondary defendants agreed with the primary defendant(s) to do "something" that eventually facilitated the use of the trade secrets. Faced with allegations suggesting a conspiracy to misappropriate trade secrets, these defendants will contend that the plaintiff must present factual support for the claim that each defendant specifically agreed to help the primary actor while *knowing* that plaintiff's trade secrets would be used. In this regard, a mere agreement to do something that also happens to aid in the commission of a tort, without more, is rarely sufficient to constitute a civil conspiracy. Neither is it sufficient for the plaintiff to point to the fact the former employee took the trade secrets to his or her new employer or business partner, as there generally can be no civil conspiracy between a corporation and its agents.

The trade secret owner should be counseled that, while adding defendants can place pressure on a defendant or defense group to reach a business solution, the client cannot succeed on a claim for civil conspiracy without establishing that each of the alleged co-conspirators agreed to do something in furtherance of the conspiracy while knowing of its improper purpose. When the client wants to add parties as co-conspirators, it must be mindful of the complexities necessary to establish all of these additional elements, as well as the expense and distraction that can result, which could potentially deflect focus on wrongdoing by the primary actor.

CHAPTER THREE

Identifying the Trade Secrets, Internally and During the Action

Identification of the trade secrets sets the tone for the case, initially guiding the court and the parties in discovery and ultimately shaping the arguments to be presented at trial. The trade secret owner is expected to know what has been misappropriated and will be asked to specify those trade secrets with particularity. But identification of the trade secrets in a complex case is not a static event. The process begins with the earliest client meeting and continues throughout the proceedings. As information develops and evidence is uncovered, details emerge that shape the specifics of the claims. Challenges to the adequacy of the identification of the trade secrets are expected, as the defendant will seek narrowing clarifications. While additions to the list of trade secrets during the course of the action is possible, amendments are neither automatic nor without potential consequences to the broader case.

1. Preparing an Identification of Trade Secrets for Internal Planning

A trade secret owner typically wants to file a complaint as quickly as possible after learning of facts that suggest misappropriation. At the earliest stages there is often a lack of complete knowledge regarding the full extent of what has been taken. But even when the trade secret owner has a good understanding of what has been misappropriated, different people associated with the owner may have inconsistent views regarding whether that information constitutes a trade secret of the business. What should be claimed as having been misappropriated—at its heart a legal issue—

becomes an internal business/political debate. Sometimes philosophical differences arise from technical viewpoints that diverge, with internal "experts" disagreeing about the criticality of some aspect or another. On other occasions the differences may be grounded in business considerations unrelated to the ability to qualify the specific information as deriving value from being secret. Internal politics can also play a role in the process of selecting the person within the company primarily responsible for management of the case, which in turn will affect the process of deciding what will be included on the list of asserted trade secrets.

It is imperative that the practitioner, from first involvement in the matter and well prior to the filing of a complaint, manage the process of convincing the trade secret owner that its best interests lie in dedicating the time and resources necessary to conduct a comprehensive internal analysis of the universe of information that may have been misappropriated. This process must begin before launching an external campaign against the misappropriator. From that larger body of information, the practitioner can then shape the list of trade secrets that will be used in prosecuting the case. Waiting until after the complaint is filed can result in the trade secret owner taking positions in its role as the plaintiff, either in the allegations of the complaint or in connection with an early request in discovery, that can be troublesome should the investigation uncover new or different facts that require changes in strategy.

Identifying an internal client "champion" is an important step in the process. This person needs to have, by reason of his or her existing role in the organization or as a result of specialized knowledge of the information in question, the ability to drive internal consensus regarding the universe of applicable trade secrets. While this person is not necessarily a member of the client's internal legal department, it must be someone who has the authority to work with the practitioner and his counterpart in the legal department. The champion acts as a primary conduit for gaining internal information, allowing the practitioner to have a single point of contact on technical issues. By serving as an internal buffer, this individual will minimize conflicting and confusing directives on non-legal issues.

While the employees of an operating entity always claim to know the most about the contents, existence, and nature of the trade secrets to be asserted, invariably the information provided will include aspects that are not entitled to protection. This overinclusion must be addressed early in the process, no matter how "special" the information is to the client. The practitioner, even when reasonably skilled in the art, can best avoid unpleasant confrontations with the client over what should be included by the simple expediency of retaining an independent "early expert" to help prepare the list. This person should be well versed in the technology and the markets in which it is being used. As these early experts are not viewing the defendant's information, at this point the candidates do not have to qualify under a stipulated protective order. Depending on their availability or inclination, these individuals may act as testifying experts. But even if their role is limited to consulting, they can play an important role assisting the client in the internal investigation and analysis. Because this person is from outside the organization, he or she will be more comfortable in pointing out problems with any aspect of the list of proposed trade secrets, whether because there is an indication that the information already is publicly available, or due to some aspect that does not provide any independent economic value by not being known to the general public or others who could make use of the information. As a "neutral" person, the early expert can also help ensure the information containing the trade secrets is described with reasonable particularity, and in a manner that will distinguish the items from matters generally known to persons skilled in the particular industry.

In working with the client to compile the list of trade secrets, it can be helpful for the practitioner to first make sure the client has a working understanding of the differences between the three main methods of protecting intellectual property rights in information. Even sophisticated clients confuse the fundamental difference between a patent, a trade secret, and a copyright. A patent protects a novel *idea,* in the form of an invention, against use by others. Patents do not provide protection for facts standing alone, and, although willful infringement can result in enhanced damages, the defendant's mental state is not an issue when infringement is considered.

Copyright law does not protect ideas per se, but rather addresses copying of the particular *expression* of those ideas. A trade secret can include nonpublic expressions of an idea, as well as something not ordinarily considered to constitute an *idea* (a conceptual datum), but which instead consists of a *fact* (an empirical datum), such as a list of customer preferences or ingredients in a recipe. But, similar to the limits on copyright protection, a trade secret is not exactly the idea or even the fact itself. Rather, trade secret law protects nonpublic information through which that idea or fact can be communicated or disclosed to another.

In light of the differences between trade secrets, patents, and copyrights, it is critical to any trade secret claim—and to any defense—that there is a clear identification of the information alleged to have been misappropriated. Here is where the distinction between information and facts/ideas can become tricky. A description of various features, functions, or characteristics of the design and operation of a software product does not, by itself, designate protectable information as such. While the unique designs that comprise software may constitute the basis for a trade secret, such that information concerning it (the source code) could be misappropriated, it is the information and not the design itself that must form the basis for the claim.

The client may want to assert as having been misappropriated a lengthy list of items that it considers to constitute its trade secrets. There is a cost-benefit analysis that should be considered when deciding whether to claim many, versus a few, trade secrets. First, the longer the list ultimately provided to the other side, the greater the volume of discovery that the owner will receive in response. This exchange of discovery will include detailed inquiries into creation/development of each aspect of every trade secret, the manner in which every item is different from that which is in the public domain, and whether there are damages flowing specifically from the acquisition, use, or disclosure of each particular trade secret different from those that result from the existence of any of the other trade secrets allegedly misappropriated. This is a balance factor that will impact both sides, as the trade secret owner can propound more complex discovery where the trade secret list is lengthy and itemized in excruciating detail.

Second, as more detail is provided, the potential increases for arguments over aspects that are not expressly within a category, and the concept of a negative pregnant applies. This is an issue for the plaintiff, although one can attempt to ameliorate the problem by including catchall categories in the description. Third, there is risk of confusing the judge prior to trial, and the jury during trial, when a lengthy list includes tertiary items. The strength of opinions from plaintiff's testifying expert will dissipate when the opinions have to cover all of the different aspects. If one or more of these items is dubious, the defendant will undoubtedly focus the jury on these matters as a way of casting doubt on the entire list.

If possible, the trade secrets should be grouped together in an organized fashion, with more generalized items followed by their natural subparts. If that is not feasible due to the nature of the trade secrets, the client should be asked to focus on the items that are truly significant, such that an injunction against use of these alone will stymie any business plans by the defendant that involve use of any of the secret information. If this route is considered, the practitioner must also carefully consider the timing relative to the statute of limitations, as the statute will run in most jurisdictions as to all of the trade secrets misappropriated, even though fewer are being asserted at any given time.

Difficulties can arise when "ownership" of the trade secrets is not clear, such as when they flow from the results of a joint development agreement. Analyzing the issue as a chain-of-custody question will help identify ownership gaps. This is an area where careful vetting of the list prior to commencement of the action is critical. This process should include a review of any joint venture or development agreements to ensure that there are no hidden ownership questions that will arise at an inopportune time. While there is no obligation on the part of the plaintiff to join all actual or potential co-owners of the trade secrets in order to create standing, as is required when suing for patent infringement, the defendant can assert a number of affirmative defenses when there are third parties who may claim a right to ownership or a license to use. The licensure defense can involve the defendant claiming immunity under a blanket license from the third party that could be read as covering the trade secrets. The defendant alternatively may immediately seek to acquire such a license from the third party as soon as it learns of the ownership issue. At a minimum, a gap in ownership can be used to establish a lack of wrongful intent (if the defendant can claim that it understood the trade secrets to belong to someone other than the plaintiff, and was acting with the understanding that its use of the trade secrets was permitted).

When the trade secrets relate to high technology, in the form of a method or process for developing a product or its design or attributes, the practitioner must determine whether any aspect of the proposed trade secrets have been disclosed in the process of acquiring a United States or foreign patent. In acquiring a patent, the applicant must disclose the invention in a document that will become publicly available, and must be prepared to distinguish the formula, manufacturing process, or device from matters within the general knowledge of persons reasonably skilled in the art. During the process of obtaining a patent, the U.S. Patent and Trademark Office (USPTO) will often provide one or more rejections to the application (an "office action") on the basis that the invention as described in light of the prior art would have been "obvious" to persons of reasonable (or "ordinary") skill in the particular industry. The applicant will then have an opportunity to respond to these office actions, either by explaining to the patent examiner why the prior art does not render the invention obvious or by amending the claims as proposed in the patent application, which describes the invention. All of these exchanges become part of the public "file wrapper" at the USPTO and are therefore subject to discovery in trade secret litigation. Once the patent application is published, and certainly once the patent has issued, any trade secret information that may have been contained in these exchanges is now public and no longer is entitled to trade secret protection. A defendant will therefore seize upon the disclosures in these exchanges to argue that the information is not entitled to trade secret protection, either because it is now disclosed in an issued patent or because (as found by the USPTO) the information already was obvious to the public.

When an issued patent correlates to the same areas as identified by the client in its proposed list of trade secrets, the client should be asked to describe, in light of the exchanges with the USPTO, what it is about the formula, manufacturing process, or device that distinguishes it from the patent or matters of general knowledge within the industry and thus makes it a trade secret. Further, if the information is part of an existing application, such that the claims of the patent will cover the use of the information, the client should be advised to consider whether it would be better to wait until the patent issues and then sue for patent infringement rather than for misappropriation, or potentially for both. The trade secret claim, in that situation, could address back damages and the patent claim future use. Deciding whether to assert a trade secret claim or to wait until the patent issues and then sue for infringement must also take into account whether the defendant will be able to take advantage of the delay in order to assert patent law defenses of estoppel (which can preclude a plaintiff from pursuing an action for infringement) or laches (which can limit the amount of damages that may have occurred prior to commencement of the action).

Part of the process of preparing the identification of trade secrets for internal planning purposes thus involves whether the following questions can (or likely will) be answered:

- Can the plaintiff, as to each item, meet its obligation to establish the existence of a trade secret?
- Does evidence exist, separately for each item, that suggests the information was improperly acquired by the defendant? This issue focuses priarily on information that the client believes to be among the larger body of misappropriated information, but which has not been used (or for which there is no ability, absent discovery, to ascertain whether it is being used. This is a problem that exists, for example, where the trade secrets consist of information incorporated into portions of source code that cannot be detected in the normal operation of the executable version).
- What likelihood exists that the defendant will be able to demonstrate independent development for each item?

2. *Designation of the Trade Secrets During the Discovery Phase*

A plaintiff must, at some point in the action prior to submission of the matter to the jury, commit to a final list of the trade secrets on which the claim of misappropriation is based. Having invested the time and effort prior to filing the complaint in preparing the wider list of trade secrets that could be asserted, the practitioner is now ready to respond to the obligation during the action to identify the specific trade secrets at issue. However, the timing and contents of the designation of trade secrets allegedly misappropriated varies from jurisdiction to jurisdiction.

The complaint in a trade secret action rarely provides more than a generalized description of the trade secrets. By contrast to an action for statutory copyright infringement, which precludes commencement of the action prior to registration of the copyright, there is no requirement to register or identify the trade secrets before the plaintiff may file suit. The lack of pleading detail is partly due to the fact that a particularized description in a publicly filed complaint would negate the right to claim trade secret protection for the information as disclosed therein. In addition, a plaintiff is appropriately reluctant to provide a list in the complaint lest the defendants later argue that such enumeration—absent amendment of the pleadings—comprises the outside parameters of the items in issue. Where federal-type notice pleading is permitted, the description can be even sparser, with the charging allegations seldom providing more than a bare recitation of the elements of the claim. The Uniform Trade Secrets Act itself provides no guidance on the issue. Where enacted, it codifies a body of substantive rights without containing an express procedural obligation to identify the trade secrets in the course of litigation.

A minority of jurisdictions direct the plaintiff to provide a comprehensive identification, through a designation served early in the action, as a means of case management. Some states, like California, address the case management issue by statutorily providing that the plaintiff cannot commence discovery relating to the trade secrets until they are described with "reasonable particularity." Here the focus primarily is on whether the standard of "reasonable particularity," in the particular jurisdiction, requires only an identification of the materials that contain the trade secrets (such as a reference to a "marketing plan," or even the specification of a manufacturing manual that contains a list of tolerances used in production of an item), or an itemized specification of the trade secrets themselves (which would involve a recitation of the specific aspects of the plan, or the aspects of those tolerances, that are the actual trade secrets).

California's requirement of providing a designation that identifies the trade secrets before commencement of discovery is not included as a part of the Civil Code, nor is it part of the Uniform Trade Secret Act as adopted in California. Rather, the statutory requirement (commonly referred to as Section 2019.210) is located in the Code of Civil Procedure as part of the Civil Discovery Act. While Section 2019.210 is a procedural statute and not binding on a federal district court sitting in diversity, many federal judges and other state jurisdictions are receptive to the parties using the requirements of Section 2019.210 as a guideline in drafting the initial discovery plan.

Section 2019.210 provides:

> In any action alleging the misappropriation of a trade secret under the Uniform Trade Secrets Act . . . , before commencing discovery relating to the trade secret, the party alleging the misappropriation shall identify the trade secret with reasonable particularity subject to any orders that may be appropriate [to preserve the secrecy of the trade secrets in judicial proceedings].

Section 2019.210 does not expressly require that a trade secret claimant explain how the alleged trade secret differs from the general knowledge of skilled persons in the field to which the secret relates. Rather, such an explanation is required only when, given the nature of the alleged secret or the technological field in which it arises, the details provided by the plaintiff are inadequate to permit the defendant to learn the boundaries of the secrets, to investigate defenses, or to permit the court to understand the designation.

A plaintiff attempting to comply with Section 2019.210, or its equivalent in other jurisdictions, may wish to provide a designation (a Trade Secret List) that identifies the trade secrets in as generalized a fashion as possible. In this way the plaintiff retains room to maneuver as discovery proceeds in order to avoid missing aspects of the trade secrets that might come to light, or being limited in the scope of discovery to propound to the defendant. The defendant will typically respond to a generalized list by objecting that it provides an insufficient description. In particular, where the descriptions are in the form of a citation to voluminous documents, or even portions of source code, the concern is that the information obscures rather than refines the description. In addition, a defendant may point out that the trade secrets are not described with reasonable specificity, especially where the Trade Secret List does not expressly distinguish the information from matters generally known to persons reasonably skilled in the particular industry.

Although a trade secret claimant is not required in every case to particularize how the alleged trade secret differs from what is known generally in an industry, whether a designation adequately distinguishes the allegedly protected information from general knowledge is a function of the particularity of the designation in light of that which is being claimed. This distinction hinges on the extent to which the description is sufficient, given the nature of the alleged secret and the level of sophistication of the technology, to permit the defendant to ascertain whether and in what way the information is distinguishable from matters already known, and to permit the court to fashion appropriate discovery.

A trade secret that comprises information on a customer list for an existing business will not require as much detail as a disclosure that purports to claim incremental variations or advances in the state of the art for a highly specialized technical field. Absent a showing by a defendant that the details alone, without further explanation, are inadequate to permit it to discern the boundaries of the trade secrets, to prepare available defenses, or to permit the court to address disputes over the scope of appropriate discovery, the plaintiff is not required to particularize how the alleged secret differs from matters already known in the field. In applying this balance of interests, the practitioner can take some comfort in the idea that the identification in a trade secret designation—at this early point in the proceedings—is to be liberally construed, such that any reasonable doubts regarding its adequacy are to be resolved in favor of finding it sufficient to allow the plaintiff to proceed with its discovery to the defendant.

In preparing the designation of trade secrets, the focus should not be limited to whether the categories of information qualify as a trade secret. In addition, the practitioner should conduct a careful review of the pre-filing analysis, in light of whatever additional information has been obtained, to determine whether there is (or is likely to be) evidence of misappropriation of each identified secret by the named defendant. It is a mistake to include trade secrets for which the client lacks any evidence of actual acts of misappropriation among those where there is an evidentiary basis to show means, motive, and action (such as unusual manipulation of files, evidence of transference of files to external storage devices, and heavy use of external printers as reflected by the printer "spool" files). Defense counsel will focus their presentation on those trade secrets where there is a lack of evidence of misappropriation.

When there is continued uncertainty regarding the full extent of misappropriation, or a lack of evidence as to some categories of trade secrets, there is a tendency to include in the early designation indefinite words, such as "includes" (as in "the list of trade secrets set forth below includes . . .") or "comprising." The intent in using these words is to avoid providing the defendant an exhaustive list, as "including" or "comprising" means to contain as part of something, and thus indicates a partial list. Similar problems exist when the plaintiff appends language at the end of the list that consists of a catchall phrase (such as "and all related research, developments, and improvements related thereto"), or indicates the possibility for an endless list of potential combinations (such as "each of the foregoing trade secrets, in combination with one or more of the others"). For each of these examples, a partial identification becomes tantamount to no identification at all, as the plaintiff has not been pinned down on the parameters of the case being alleged. A defendant, upon receipt of a trade secret identification that has this type of language in its preamble or conclusion, should object and insist on a closed-ended list.

The primary goal in objecting is to force the plaintiff to narrow the list as a natural course of having to provide greater specificity. A narrower list is more precise, which ensures that everyone involved has reasonable notice of the issues that the defendant is being expected to face, and will assist in the efforts to properly limit the scope of discovery to those aspects of the defendant's business that relate directly to the alleged trade secrets. This avoids a situation where the plaintiff can rummage unfettered through all of the defendant's business operations under the guise of searching for its trade secrets. Apart from the expense entailed when a plaintiff can engage in such unrestricted trade secret discovery, there is a substantive danger to the defendant. Whatever information the plaintiff uncovers in the possession of the defendant, if it comes anywhere close to what was or could be described by the plaintiff in the Trade Secret List, will be claimed as plaintiff's trade secret property, either directly or by constituting a derivative work developed through the defendant's knowledge of the trade secrets.

A defendant's secondary but less laudable goal in asserting this form of objection is to delay the plaintiff's efforts regardless of the true sufficiency of the list. As the defendant has no procedural impediment equivalent to that which the plaintiff must satisfy before it can propound defensive discovery, seriatim objections to the sufficiency of the list by the procedurally savvy defendant can gain an extended discovery headstart. The fact that this discovery may result in responses that provide the same information as is required for the Trade Secret List does not obviate the plaintiff's obligation to provide the information in response to both.

Objections to the sufficiency of the disclosure can be in the form of a direct objection to the Trade Secret List, before the defendant responds to any discovery served by the plaintiff. Alternatively, the defendant can wait until it is the time to serve a formal response to the discovery and include the objection as part of its responses. In either case, the plaintiff then has to decide whether to provide more detail in an amended list, to which the defendant is likely to again object, or to seek more immediate assistance from the court in the form of a motion to compel discovery responses. Either method will result in some delay of the plaintiff's right to obtain substantive discovery responses. However, if the plaintiff declines to voluntarily revise the Trade Secret List to provide more specificity, and instead brings a motion to compel substantive responses to the discovery, the delay will be substantial, as many months may pass before the court is able to make a determination of the sufficiency of the Trade Secret List.

Rather than applying the passive approach of setting forth objections in discovery responses and waiting for the plaintiff's reaction, the defendant can actively seek judicial assistance through a motion for protective order. The benefit to the defendant flowing from this option lies in the court then being required to consider the sufficiency of the Trade Secret List without the potential distraction of the relevancy of the particular discovery requests and the sufficiency of the responses. As with all discovery motions, of course, the defendant will first have to meet and confer with the plaintiff and seek a voluntary amendment of the Trade Secret List to meet its concerns. In addition, should the meet-and-confer prove ineffective, the defendant will have to provide evidentiary support for the motion, typically in the form of an expert witness declaration to the effect that the trade secrets are too vaguely described to distinguish the information being claimed from the larger body that is already known in the particular industry. If the parties cannot resolve their differences, the court will have a narrow question to consider, and its order will either direct the plaintiff to provide an amended Trade Secret List or overrule the objection and permit the plaintiff to commence with its substantive discovery.

The plaintiff, in addressing a contention that its designation does not reasonably distinguish the information, will typically use a supporting declaration from an independent expert. A statement (affidavit or declaration) from its own employees on this issue is evidentially acceptable, but has marginal probative value by comparison. The declaration should do more than merely recite the items on the Trade Secret List, and then opine that these descriptions are "reasonably particular" and constitute protectable trade secrets. Instead, the expert should provide some analysis why the items provide value from the fact of being secret, the factors considered, and the reasoning employed. While the plaintiff can use the same expert that assisted in the earlier internal process of culling the trade secrets from the client's broader universe of information, the defendant potentially can also request a deposition of that expert on the subject of his or her declaration before the court rules on the motion in which the sufficiency of the trade secret identification is in issue. If deposed, that expert will be asked to produce his or her entire file, and there will be issues of privilege to consider regarding the choices made in accepting and rejecting aspects of the plaintiff's internally suggested trade secrets.

Budgetary constraints permitting, an effective course is to retain a separate testifying expert who has never previously worked with the client on this particular matter, and thus had no involvement in the creation of the list of alleged trade secrets. This testifying expert can opine on the sufficiency of the Trade Secret List without having to defend his or her role in its creation, and explain why that information, as described, can be distinguished from the information that is already publicly known. Lacking any prior involvement, this form of declaration has significantly higher probative value, especially as the court is not making a conclusive determination as to whether the information in fact constitutes a protectable trade secret.

A defendant challenging the sufficiency of the trade secret statement can booster the presentation through its own expert declarations. These are intended to demonstrate similarity between the language used in the statement and that in publicly available journals or articles, in order to illustrate the failure of the Trade Secret List to distinguish the matters claimed from those known to the public. However, as a challenge to an identification of trade secrets should not be treated as a mini-trial on the merits, the question for the court is not whether the alleged trade secrets are, in fact, in the public domain. Evidence submitted by the defendant's expert to that effect is appropriately disregarded. The defendant should be directed to instead make that type of showing on a motion for summary judgment.

There is a substantive risk to the plaintiff with any form of motion relating to the sufficiency of its trade secret designation, whether the motion is one that seeks to compel discovery responses or the defendant's motion for protective order. The ability to challenge the adequacy of a Trade Secret List is not meant as a means for the defendant to eliminate claims on the merits. The plaintiff should not be required at the discovery stage of the proceedings to provide the same level of exacting detail that may be required to prevail at trial. However, the process of addressing the adequacy of the disclosure can easily become a de facto mini-trial over the merits of the misappropriation claim, albeit without all of the procedural rights and protections that exist at the time of trial. This can occur when dueling experts are involved, if the court inadvertently issues an order that "finds" in favor of the defendant's experts. If left unchallenged by the plaintiff, there is a probability that the order will be used thereafter by the defendant in support of a request for a summary adjudication of the dispute on the merits.

The risk of this outcome can be minimized when the plaintiff has created a record of trying to address the defendant's discovery concerns by meeting and conferring, and also by providing an iteration of the Trade Secret List that attempts to address the substance of the objection. These attempts can also reduce the risk that the court will order a further disclosure, problematic both for the substantive harm that the order can have on the scope of the secrets asserted and for the fact that the plaintiff cannot proceed with discovery until it has served the amended list. Of course, the defendant is likely to renew its objections, having secured a favorable ruling for the court on the initial motion. During this period of judicial involvement, although the plaintiff is precluded from being able to gather evidence from the defendant, the defendant is not precluded from proceeding immediately with discovery, or even pursuing a motion for summary judgment.

In those jurisdictions that do not have an express procedure that sets forth the timing or necessary contents of an early designation or Trade Secret List, and in particular where the plaintiff is not required by rule or statute to identify its trade secrets with reasonable particularity before commencing discovery, the defendant has a two-pronged attack it may mount. First, it must address the issue immediately through discovery aimed at the substantive allegations. In federal court the defendant must rely on the normal discovery procedures under the Federal Rules of Civil Procedure, including the mandatory disclosures under Rule 26 and the discovery tools provided in Rules 30 through 36, to force the plaintiff to provide a specification of the trade secrets. Here the recommended choice consists of propounding a focused initial set of interrogatories and taking a deposition of the entity's designated representative.

Serving requests for admission under Rule 36 will not elicit a list of the trade secrets, as it is the function of requests for admission to narrow the scope of a case by removing issues, rather than providing for the acquisition of substantive information. While they can also be used to determine the plaintiff's contentions, narrative responses to the requests for admission are not required, and other discovery devices are far more effective for this task. Requests for production of documents under Rule 34, seeking the production of all materials that contain, disclose, or embody the trade secrets, will generate a large pile of materials (and a larger set of objections), but will lack any particularized identification of what specifically in the pile constitutes the trade secrets.

An illustrative set of initial trade secret interrogatories under Rule 33 is as follows:

> **Interrogatory No. 1:** Please identify, with specificity and in a manner that explains how the alleged trade secrets differs from the general knowledge of skilled persons in the field to which the secret relates, all of the alleged trade secrets that you allege or contend Defendant misappropriated or misused, including but not limited to as alleged in the complaint.
>
> **Interrogatory No. 2:** For each alleged trade secret identified in response to Interrogatory No. 1, please identify: (a) all persons who have or have had rights to the alleged trade secret, other than your existing employees; (b) the nature and source of the rights; and (c) all efforts by any person to maintain the secrecy or confidentiality of the alleged trade secrets.
>
> **Interrogatory No. 3:** For each alleged trade secret identified in response to Interrogatory No. 1, please identify all persons (other than your existing employees) to whom the alleged trade secret is known or has been disclosed and describe, in detail, the circumstances under which it became known or was disclosed,

including but not limited to: (a) the date on which the alleged trade secret was disclosed or became known to such persons; (b) the specific terms on which the information was disclosed or became known, such as pursuant to a confidentiality agreement; (c) all documents or agreements relating to the disclosure; and (d) all places or locations where the alleged trade secret may be found or accessed.

Interrogatory No. 4: For each alleged trade secret identified in response to Interrogatory No. 1, please describe, in detail, each instance in which you allege or contend that the Defendant misappropriated or misused the alleged trade secret, including but not limited to: (1) the date of the alleged misuse or misappropriation; (b) all persons involved in any way in the alleged misuse or misappropriation; (c) the specific manner in which the Defendant is alleged to have engaged in misuse or misappropriation; and (d) with respect to any method you allege or contend that the Defendant misappropriated or misused, the location of each portion of such method in any source code, product, or in the public domain.

Interrogatory No. 5: For each alleged trade secret identified in response to Interrogatory No. 1, please identify: (a) all agreements relating to the alleged trade secret including but not limited to the parties and the terms of the agreements; and (b) all copyrights and patents relating to the alleged trade secret including but not limited to the owners, licensors, licensees, assignors, or assignees of those copyrights or patents.

Interrogatory No. 6: For each formula, pattern, compilation, program, device, method, technique, or process identified in response to Interrogatory No. 1, please identify the origin of the formula, pattern, compilation, program, device, method, technique, or process, including when, where, and by whom formula, pattern, compilation, program, device, method, technique, or process was created.

While these interrogatories are targeted to an identification of the items being alleged as the misappropriated trade secrets, their use as a parameter-setting device is limited. As a practical matter, responses to interrogatories are written by counsel, filtering the information provided by the client, and are thus both replete with objections that marginalize use and details that are sanitized to reduce preclusive value. They also are readily supplemented, without significant restrictions as long as sufficient time remains before the discovery cutoff to propound further discovery.

In jurisdictions that do not have (or apply) a rule similar to California's Section 2019.210, trying to obtain the information through interrogatories is helpful, but, without motion practice to force supplemental responses and to address the inevitable objections, these will rarely provide information that is sufficiently clear or that will limit the trade secret owner as the matter goes forward. By contrast, when the plaintiff is a business entity, the defendant can significantly bolster the value of these interrogatories by serving a deposition notice under Rule 30 (or its state court counterpart) that directs the entity to designate one or more of its officers, directors, or managing agents, or some other person to testify on its behalf.

An entity notice under Rule 30 must include a list of matters for examination, and in response the entity must sufficiently educate the designated witness to be able to testify knowledgeably on those matters. That testimony is then binding on the entity. To avoid arguments over the extent of the witness's preparation, or objections to the categories on the basis that they are ambiguous or overly broad, precision is more important than breadth. For example, the notice could constitute just three categories on which the entity must provide a designated witness:

(1) A SPECIFICATION of each of [Trade Secret Owner's] TRADE SECRETS including, but not limited to, as alleged in the Complaint filed in this action, which Defendant allegedly misappropriated. The term "SPECIFICATION" as used herein with respect to information claimed to constitute the TRADE SECRETS shall be construed to require an identification of each of the TRADE SECRETS with reasonable particularity, and to provide the factual basis for the claim that such information

(a) derives independent economic value, actual or potential, from not being generally known to the public or to other persons who can obtain economic value from its disclosure or use, and (b) was and continues to be the subject of efforts that are reasonable under the circumstances to maintain its secrecy.

(2) The date(s) and manner in which each of the TRADE SECRETS was allegedly misappropriated.

(3) For each of the TRADE SECRETS as alleged in the Complaint filed in this action, a description of all information detailing the expenditure of "time, money and resources" in developing the alleged trade secrets including, but not limited to, how much time was spent and by whom; how much money was spent and in what manner; and what type of resources were expended and in what manner.

The defendant should focus this deposition on eliciting as much specificity as possible in order to limit the plaintiff's ability to change at trial what it claims to constitute the trade secrets. The interrogatory responses can be shown to the witness, who will then be asked to expand upon that which the response identifies. The testimony of a witness who was unable to provide a reasonable level of specificity, or who attempts to provide open-ended responses, should not be permitted to stand unaddressed. As long as a decent record is obtained, these situations provide a good vehicle for bringing the lack of specificity to the attention of the court. The request for judicial assistance can now be buttressed by an enumeration of the problems that arise when the defendant has not provided a fair indication of the trade secrets in dispute. Should the court agree, and direct the plaintiff to provide a witness who can testify to a reasonable level of detail, the defendant will have narrowed the claimed trade secrets and gained an order that can be later used as a basis for a motion in limine to exclude any information not provided by the corporate designee.

The deposition notice for the representative of the business entity can also be accompanied by a request, under Rule 34, to produce documents and tangible things at the deposition. A simple and concise request could be phrased as follows: "All documents and things alleged by [Trade Secret Owner] that set forth a written description of each of the TRADE SECRETS." To avoid a situation where the deponent brings a large stack of materials to the deposition that has not been previously produced, and therefore not reviewed by counsel for the noticing party, the same categories should be included in a separate Rule 34 Request for Production that specifies a date of production that is at least a few days prior to the deposition.

Next, and in addition to seeking an identification of the trade secrets through discovery, the defendant should seek a protective order from the court asking that it direct the disclosure of the trade secrets alleged to be in issue before the plaintiff can engage in any form of discovery. For example, Texas courts have stayed discovery until such time that a trade secret plaintiff has specifically identified the allegedly misappropriated trade secrets. The same rationale that underpins the provision for early identification in the California Civil Procedure Code is applicable—a plaintiff claiming trade secrets misappropriation should not be able to use discovery as a fishing expedition to justify or further bolster its claim. When the case is in federal district court, the process is the same. There is little burden in demanding an early specification, as Federal Rule of Civil Procedure 11 requires an attorney to certify that the representations made to the court in pleadings and other filings were "formed after an inquiry reasonable under the circumstances." Presumably counsel for the trade secret owner satisfied Rule 11 and has "some" understanding of the scope of the trade secrets allegedly misappropriated.

The motion for protective order should request both an identification, in order to allow the court and the parties to determine the scope of relevant discovery for this case, and a stay on discovery by the plaintiff until such time as an acceptable identification has been provided. Courts applying the Federal Rules have routinely compelled plaintiffs to identify the alleged trade secrets before obtaining discovery from defendants, to assist the court and the parties in structuring discovery and determining relevancy. All of the policy issues that exist with respect to an early Trade

Secret List apply with equal force regardless of the jurisdiction, and the guidelines in California regarding the adequacy of a list submitted under Section 2019.210 will inform the court in a different jurisdiction of the considerations that could guide its deliberations. When making this motion, the defendant must, of course, first engage in a comprehensive meet-and-confer process. Similar to the discussions that are described above, when an early Trade Secret List is being challenged, during this exchange of views the defendant must articulate the reasons why it needs to have a further identification and the difficulties and burdens that will occur if the identification is not forthcoming before discovery commences.

3. *Amending the Trade Secret List Before Trial*

A plaintiff may seek to amend or supplement its Trade Secret List as the case proceeds and discovery responses are reviewed. Evidence may be uncovered that establishes acts of misappropriation with respect to "non-designated" trade secrets, identified by the client during the pre-filing investigation but not included in the early designation because of a lack of evidence at that time. However, amending the list of trade secrets as the case progresses is not automatic, and unilateral attempts will be met with an objection, as an attempt to broaden the designation is a significant issue of concern for all defendants. In particular, they will be concerned that an amendment will be written to simply describe the "old" (previously designated) trade secrets in a manner that includes what was uncovered during discovery, without having to provide supplementary discovery responses. This concern is not without merit, which is why jurisdictions that require an early identification stress the importance of providing the defendant with reasonable notice of the issues that must be met at the time of trial, in addition to reasonable guidance in ascertaining the scope of appropriate discovery under these circumstances. With reasonable notice, the defendant is better protected from first learning on the eve of trial the full extent of trade secrets allegedly misappropriated, and thus they are in a better position to form complete and well-reasoned defenses.

The submittal of a list of trade secrets is a representation by the plaintiff to the court that the disclosure is a complete statement of the secrets in issue based on information known to date. In the absence of a request for leave to amend being made and granted, especially in those jurisdictions that require an early Trade Secret List as a case management tool, the court may restrict a plaintiff to the original disclosure. Should there be an attempt to stretch the bounds of the disclosure late in the proceedings, to meet a motion for summary judgment, or to counter an opinion expressed by the defendant's expert, the court may exclude evidence relating to the "new" secret as being an impermissible attempt to "broaden" the original list. For example, the plaintiff may argue that, while an aspect of functionality listed in the statement is not itself the secret, the existing categories are sufficient to include the secret "how to" of that aspect related to its method of operation. The defendant will argue, in turn, that this distinction is inappropriate. And, as the plaintiff has not made a formal request to amend its trade secret designation, the court should hold that the "how to" details are inadmissible. The focus of the court in this situation will be:

- Should this information have been included earlier, and if so, what is the reason for the delay in it being provided?
- Could the plaintiff have easily written its Trade Secret List to reflect this difference?
- Did the plaintiff provide some manner of additional information, thus placing the defendant on notice, but without revealing all of the technical details that compose the trade secrets?
- Did the defendant previously have fair notice of the distinction between the original designation and the proposed additional information?
- Was there adequate notice to the defendant of the need to conduct further inquiry in light of other aspects of the proceedings, such that the defendant is not being ambushed?
- If adequate notice was not previously provided, is there a way to allow the plaintiff to proceed on the merits that will not unduly prejudice the rights of the defendant?

- Is the distinction between the information in the designation and what is now being provided one that should have been raised by the plaintiff through a formal request to amend the Trade Secret List?

When the plaintiff has taken the initiative, and a motion to amend is seasonably made, the concern that it is trying to stretch the boundaries of its initial Trade Secret List, standing alone, is not a basis to deny a request for an amendment. Plaintiffs often want to amend the disclosure of the trade secrets as a case proceeds and discovery is obtained, as the full extent of theft is rarely understood when a case is filed. The proposed amendments can range from iterations on existing trade secrets to additions of completely new categories or items.

To the extent the jurisdiction requires an early identification, in opposing a request for leave to amend, the defendant should consider whether the court will apply the same requirements that must be satisfied for a plaintiff to amend the complaint, with the degree of difficulty increasing as the case moves closer to the trial date and the prejudice to the defendant increases (in terms of having the time or ability to conduct, or the need to repeat, discovery). To overcome an objection to the proposed amendment in these jurisdictions, the plaintiff should be prepared to document how it determined through discovery that the defendant misappropriated additional or new trade secrets, and the promptness of its actions upon that discovery, in order to establish good cause in the same manner that is required to amend a pleading.

In those jurisdictions that do not have an express requirement of an early disclosure, the question for the defendant in evaluating how to respond will focus more on whether the plaintiff seasonably amended its prior disclosure or supplemented its discovery in light of what has already transpired in the case, and whether allowing inclusion of the additional descriptions will prejudice the ability of the defendant to respond to the merits of the claim.

Regardless of the timing or method of disclosure, and whether it occurs as a result of rule or as a response to a request through discovery, when an itemized specification is being provided that sets forth details of the actual trade secrets in issue (rather than points to where they can be located elsewhere in the records being produced), the plaintiff should ensure that the information is protected against the further wrongful dissemination, use, or access to the trade secret information by the defendants. These protections can exist by reason of local rule that requires confidential treatment or, in the absence of a local rule, can be obtained through entry of a formal protective order. Issues to consider in connection with entry of a stipulated protective order are discussed in Chapter 7.

4. Preparing the Identification of Trade Secrets for Trial

Regardless of the timing of disclosures through discovery or the level of specificity provided during the pretrial phase of an action, at trial the plaintiff must describe the subject matter of the trade secrets with sufficient particularity to separate this information from matters of general knowledge in the public, or the special knowledge of those persons skilled in the trade. As a legal matter, how this requirement is satisfied varies from jurisdiction to jurisdiction. As a practical matter, satisfaction of this requirement will also vary depending on whether the case is tried to the bench or a jury, as the court is far more likely to impose a stricter requirement of specificity on the plaintiff when the presentation is to a jury.

The lack of a uniform standard exists with respect to different types of trade secrets, and this aspect can provide an unwelcome trap for the unsuspecting plaintiff. Non-technical trade secrets, like customer lists and marketing methods, will not require the same degree of detail as enhancements on existing technological methods of operation. In some circumstances, a reference to imprecise terms such as "dimensions and tolerances" contained in engineering drawings and blueprints can be sufficient to identify and claim the trade secrets set forth in these materials, but only because the documents as a whole constitute the trade secrets. In other cases, the plaintiff may provide a description too vague and inclusive to satisfy the requirement of separating where the real secrets lie from the balance of the information. The plaintiff may find that it failed to describe the trade secrets with sufficient particularity when the reference is merely to the source code as a whole, or the specifications and requirements of a process or system, with the court holding that there was a failure to identify where the trade secrets may be located, or to separate those aspects from that which is already known to those in the trade.

An argument often supplied by the plaintiff, who lacks the ability to provide fine details, starts with the premise that the secret is actually an amalgamation of previously known individual elements. Thus, for example, a client may wish to protect information put together over time regarding its customers, including detailed information about their needs, preferences, purchasing history, and pricing information. While it is correct that a compilation can constitute a trade secret, such that the entirety of the item as a whole constitutes the trade secret, by taking this position and declining to provide greater specificity concerning the portions of the customer list that are truly unique, the plaintiff creates for itself several risks. The court could conclude, from the evidence presented, that there are aspects relating to the customers, such as their addresses and contact persons, that are already well known to the trade. In a software case, a similar result can flow from a finding that the code in issue is derived from open source code. If the plaintiff has not done any more than identify the customer list or the technology as a whole, and left as a mystery exactly what aspects are the "true" secrets, the court may conclude that the plaintiff has not met its initial burden to prove either the existence of the secrets or that it is the creator/developer of the aspects that constitute the protectable information.

Alternatively, the court could find that the entirety of the identified information is not a secret as it does not (in haec verba) satisfy the element of providing independent economic value by being maintained as secret because of other sources of similar information or products based on the same open source code that are publicly available. Even if the court agrees that the information as a unitary whole constitutes a trade secret, due to a lack of understanding how the business operates, it may conclude that mere possession and use of the list of customers, or an executable version of the software, does not satisfy the requirement of knowledge of the trade secret.

While the process of providing exacting details regarding the trade secrets can be an operational headache in the middle of trial, shortcuts in this evidentiary presentation should be avoided. If the defendant requests a special verdict, the plaintiff must be prepared to support evidentially each trade secret independently. The record for the trial court and on appeal must be sufficient to support a finding that the information as presented satisfied the plaintiff's evidentiary burden. A foundation must be established to admit into evidence the same information that is necessary to satisfy the discovery-based obligation to identify the trade secrets with reasonable particularity, and they must be distinguished from that which is generally known to the public. Particular care must be paid to the aspect of *why* the trade secrets provide independent economic value, as that information is the foundation to finding that the information constitutes a trade secret, as well as for an award of damages that resulted from the misappropriation.

When there is a lack of specificity in the description of the trade secrets, a separate issue will exist in structuring and thereafter enforcing post-trial equitable relief. A post-trial permanent injunction can be prohibitory (enjoining use, possession, and/or dissemination of the trade secrets) or mandatory (directing the defendant to turn over the items in its possession that constitute or embody the trade secrets). In either case, the enforcement mechanism is contempt proceedings. As contempt proceedings for the violation of a civil injunction are quasi-criminal, the order setting forth the injunction must meet certain levels of specificity to satisfy due process concerns over adequate notice of the conduct being prohibited.

In determining whether an injunction is enforceable through contempt proceedings, the inquiry by the court focuses on whether the person subject to the injunction was reasonably able to determine from its express terms what he or she may or may not do. Depending on the jurisdiction, this may be both an objective and a subjective test, in that the court will consider both what a "reasonable man" would have understood and what the defendant did in fact understand. In assessing whether the order is too ambiguous, the court will not enforce an injunction that forbids an act in terms so vague that persons of common intelligence would necessarily guess at its meaning, and differ as to its application, with the language of the injunction interpreted in light of the record that discloses the kind of conduct that is sought to be enjoined.

A defendant can easily defend against a broadly worded injunction that merely provides "do not misappropriate (unspecified) trade secrets," or that fails to provide a description of what was encompassed by the "trade secret business" or the "technical information." Likewise, many courts are uncomfortable enforcing an injunction that contains nonstandard verbs such as "concepting," or sets forth descriptions that lack clarity regarding their outer boundaries, such as the phrase "including any information that is substantially similar to the foregoing." The injunctive portion of the judgment should identify only the specific trade secrets, and not information "substantially similar to" the trade secrets.

One way to address potential concerns over the lack of specificity is to incorporate the Trade Secret List by reference into the judgment. This can be accomplished by physically attaching a copy of the list as an exhibit to the judgment, and filing both under seal to maintain the confidentiality of the information. A public version of the judgment, without the attachment, is then filed in the regular court records. Alternatively, the plaintiff can incorporate a readily identifiable document without including a physical attachment, as long as it is one that was produced during the course of the action and that provides the necessary degree of specificity. Either way, in order to enforce the injunction through contempt proceedings, the record from the underlying action must provide the defendant with a clear disclosure of the kind of conduct that is enjoined—possession, use, and/or disclosure of readily identifiable trade secrets—in addition to a sufficient identification and definition of the trade secrets. In this way the plaintiff and the court can satisfy any due process concerns the defendant may raise subsequently.

CHAPTER FOUR

Identifying the Nature and Type of Trade Secret Misappropriation, Addressing the Statute of Limitations, and Action Items for the Pre-litigation Checklist

A claim for trade secret misappropriation involves a highly factual inquiry, given the amorphous nature of information that can constitute a trade secret, the different types of conduct that can constitute an act of misappropriation, and the need to delve into the intent or knowledge of the parties. While the focus most frequently is on conduct alleged to constitute "actual" misappropriation, liability is sometimes predicated on inevitable disclosure or as a result of threatened misappropriation. As neither the Uniform Trade Secrets Act nor the Restatement of Torts defines these terms, or delineates as mutually exclusive the categories of conduct that constitute misappropriation, a course of actionable conduct may have attributes that relate to each.

From the first filed pleading and continuing throughout presentation of the case, the practitioner must consider the nature of the conduct by the defendant that he or she wishes put before the jury and the manner in which that conduct is described, as the form of misappropriation will bear upon the case to be prepared and the issues to be tried. Underlying this analysis is the question of when the claim arose, as statute of limitations issues are not always based on clearly defined triggers.

During the process of conducting a pre-filing analysis, there are action items involving identification of potential witnesses, locating and compiling relevant documents, and the process of management of internal and external public relations. These are action items where the client's input and assistance are invaluable. A short pre-filing checklist will streamline the process once the action is under way.

1. Identifying the Particular Form of Actual Misappropriation

Under the Uniform Trade Secrets Act, actual misappropriation can be based on several forms of conduct, falling within three major categories: (a) acquisition of the trade secrets by improper means, (b) use without consent, or (c) disclosure without consent. These categories allow extension of liability past the initial acquirer, based on the reasoning that a person who knowingly exploits the illegal acquisition of property owned by another should not find himself in a better position than the original misappropriator. A typical charging allegation will touch upon all three categories in order to avoid missing any possible basis for misappropriation ("By the conduct as alleged herein, Defendants have improperly acquired, used, and/or disclosed the trade secrets. . ."). Most jurisdictions do not require, at the pleading stage, specific allegations that set forth how the trade secrets were acquired by or transferred to the defendant, or the manner in which the trade secrets were actually used in the defendant's new business.

The first step in investigating a claim of misappropriation is to focus on the target defendants, typically the original misappropriator, to consider his or her role and the best applicable category. For example, the former employee who downloaded confidential files and is now using this information in his new job has wrongfully acquired and is now wrongfully using the trade secrets. But did the new employer wrongfully acquire the trade secrets, or is their use the only improper act? From these facts, standing alone, the answer is not clear. Has either the former employee or the new employer improperly disclosed the trade secrets, and is the manner of use by the former employee at the new business a disclosure of one to another? If the former employee is merely using information to the extent it is contained in his or her memory, was the initial acquisition wrongful or merely "any subsequent use"? Is there a difference in the potential relief, and is assertion of a wide variety of different allegations necessary, or will they merely confuse the jury?

Wrongful acquisition may be actionable in itself without the need to establish subsequent use or disclosure. For the jury to conclude that the acquisition was "wrongful," the plaintiff must show more than just passive receipt of the secrets by the defendant. Since possession does not require reduction of the information to a corporeal form, a defendant may "take" trade secrets upon termination of employment by reason of the information in her memory. Mere possession of the information by a departing employee in this situation is insufficient to establish misappropriation. A subsequent employer can thus come into "possession," unknowingly and not wrongfully, of the trade secrets in the sense that their owner's former employee brings them into the business of the subsequent employer. However, when the new employer acts in a manner that suggests the intent to secure control of these trade secrets in derogation of the rights of another, either with knowledge of an adverse claim of ownership or by being placed on notice of facts that indicate the information was acquired by improper means, the purpose behind the act is implicated. The court may now step in and grant appropriate relief to the trade secret owner. The fact that there has not yet been any "use" or disclosure may curtail the ability to obtain an award of damages, but will not prevent a trade secret owner from obtaining injunctive relief.

There is a significant impact on monetary forms of relief where the plaintiff can only establish wrongful acquisition. Under the Uniform Trade Secrets Act, a trade secret owner can recover damages for the actual loss caused by misappropriation, as well as an additional award based on the unjust enrichment to the defendant as a result of the misappropriation, that is not taken into account in computing damages for actual loss. But, while injunctive relief is available to prohibit use or disclosure and to direct the return of any trade secret materials, in the absence of being able to establish actual use or disclosure, the plaintiff will not be able to show either that it suffered a loss of profits or that the defendant was unjustly enriched by the mere fact of the initial wrongful acquisition. In these situations, other than the potential for injunctive relief and an award of attorney's fees for willful and malicious misappropriation, the plaintiff will be limited to seeking an order directing payment of a reasonable royalty for no longer a period of time than the use could have been prohibited. On this point caution is advised, as the meaning of the term "reasonable royalty" is not the same as that applied in most commercial contexts.

Rather than a percentage of actual profits, a royalty-based award in a trade secret case is really an estimate of the value to the defendant of that which was misappropriated. Occasionally this means the difference in the cost to the defendant to develop the trade secrets on its own, using the actual development costs of the plaintiff as a baseline. Alternatively, the proper measure for the royalty can take the form of a calculation that the parties would have agreed to as a fair price for licensing the right to use the trade secrets for the purpose intended by the defendant at the time of the original misappropriation. In calculating what a fair licensing price would have been had the parties engaged in a negotiation over this value, the practitioner should consider such factors as:

- The foreseeable changes in the parties' competitive posture;
- The prices other licensees may have paid for access to this or similar information;
- The total value of the secret to the trade secret owner, including its development costs and the importance of the secret to its business;
- The nature and extent of the use the defendant intended for the secret; and finally,
- Whatever other unique factors in the particular case might have been affected by the parties' agreement, such as the ready availability of alternative sources of similar information.

The term "use"—whether in the context of affirmative or negative know-how (discussed below) —is commonly applied in its ordinary sense, such as when one directly exploits the secrets for his own advantage. This concept is simple enough to understand when a process or method is incorporated into a manufacturing facility, or a design is incorporated into the development of a product or device. There is an action and consequence, either in increased efficiency or output. The term "use" is not, however, so expansive as to include making further use of something that results from use of the secret. A party that was using a product manufactured by another through the use of a secret process does not "use" that process. Nor does "use" include, in the ordinary sense, merely possessing the information of another. And in jurisdictions that have adopted the Uniform Trade Secrets Act, use of the trade secrets of another is wrongful and constitutes misappropriation only if, and when, the acts of the user are accompanied by the requisite mental state.

Of the five varieties of actionable "use" listed under the Uniform Trade Secrets Act, four require the defendant to have "knowledge of the trade secret." The fifth variety contemplates the defendant's actual or constructive awareness that "knowledge of [the trade secret] *had been acquired* by accident or mistake." This wording creates the possibility that a defendant might be liable, though himself lacking knowledge of the trade secret, if he "used" it with knowledge that another, on whom his use somehow depends, had acquired knowledge of it as a result of accident or mistake. As a consequence of this expansive interpretation of "use," an officer or director of a corporation can be personally liable for "using" the trade secrets through their corporation if they are found to have known (or had reason to know) that the knowledge of the trade secrets was derived from or through a person who had improperly acquired them, or who had a duty to maintain secrecy. In this context, "use" includes any act by the corporate entity that constitutes employing the confidential information, whether through manufacturing, production, research, or development. However, for an individual to be liable for use in this context, there still has to be a showing that he was aware that the information was acquired by improper means, accident, or mistake, or received notice that the use of the information is wrongful.

While "knowledge" is another term not defined in the provisions of the Uniform Trade Secrets Act, it has been construed to mean more than a simple awareness that a body of information exists that belongs to another. Consistent with this construction, even the knowledge that another unrelated defendant is wrongfully using the trade secrets will not, by itself, give rise to liability. The practitioner should look for evidence of possession of the trade secret information by the target defendant, or someone acting on its behalf or at its direction, in a manner such that the information can be studied, disclosed, or exploited, coupled with facts that demonstrate that this defendant was on notice that such possession might be wrongful.

Notice in this context is broadly construed in the majority of jurisdictions, including, in one instance, the ability of someone who was not the original misappropriator to invest at a bargain price in a business using a sophisticated process that was based upon the misappropriated information. In these circumstances, a finding of liability should withstand a challenge on appeal as long there is a sufficient evidentiary basis for the jury to conclude that a reasonable person would have inquired further, and thus could have learned if there was a question as to whether the entity's possession of the information was wrongful.

Ownership of a trade secret allows one party to control use, and to prevent use by others. However, the essence of a trade secret is violated by its disclosure, not its use. The two words are not synonymous. One may use information without disclosing it, and the mere private use of a trade secret—even where that use is improper—does not alter its fundamental characteristic as a secret. Disclosure is an act of publication, which impedes the ability to characterize the information as a trade secret. Here the analysis is similar to the determination of whether a list of trade secrets specifies the information with reasonable particularity. Disclosing information consisting of a user-oriented description of the advantages of a product does not disclose the trade secrets that constitute the technical details of the product's architecture that create those advantages. But publishing the technical details in a trade journal is a disclosure that obviates the information's trade secret status.

Once the information is public, a prohibitory injunction that restricts further publication will not be appropriate and may run into First Amendment challenges. Rather, damages are the primary recourse for the trade secret owner, with the measure of relief calculated by using a hypothetical sale of the trade secret to the defendant. The "sale price" can be based on a number of factors, including the total value of the secret to the owner, the development costs for the secrets, and the importance of the secrets to the business.

Whether the act of misappropriation consists merely of wrongful acquisition or also involves actual use or disclosure, further caution is advised where the trade secrets consist of "negative know-how." With respect to this type of trade secret, while the right to monetary recovery can be quantified through standard economic modeling, the likelihood of securing injunctive relief is especially difficult.

While all types of trade secrets can be acquired, or even disclosed, there are significant differences with respect to affirmative use between "regular" trade secrets and those that consist of "negative know-how." Negative know-how consists of information that instructs what not to do in a given situation to maximize the potential for a positive result. As a body of knowledge developed through trial and effort, testing and analysis, or experimentation over time, it can be wrongfully acquired, used, or disclosed. As a result of having acquired negative know-how, the defendant will have an understanding of what efforts will not be successful, or which of several avenues is best to pursue over others.

Sometimes the description of a trade secret as constituting negative know-how is merely semantics. The realization of what is best, or what not to do, in a given setting exists in almost every human endeavor that involves the ability to select among one of several alternatives. The act of selection necessarily involves the rejection of every other option considered. The knowledge to use multiple iterations at prescribed temperatures might stem from the conclusion that a single application at a single temperature does not provide as good a result. The characterization of information as containing negative know-how, however, can almost always include information developed in the process of invention, or the modification of a procedure or technique. Knowing what not to do, and the mistakes to avoid, often leads eventually to knowing what to do and gains to be made. Possession of this knowledge can be very valuable, and has independent economic value from not being known to others, in terms of reduced research expense, better use of development budgets, and shortened time to market.

However, while econometric experts can quantify the value gained from the use of negative know-how, in order to opine on the amount of monetary recovery that should attach to a finding of misappropriation, courts will struggle with this concept when being asked to draft the parameters of effective and enforceable injunctive relief. Also, little value inures to the trade secret owner from an injunction that prohibits a misappropriator from using negative know-how, as enforcement of an injunction in contempt proceedings requires proof that the defendant used the knowledge of what not to do. Proving use of negative know-how in practice to establish that the wrongdoer violated an injunction prohibiting use of information that directs what not to do is nearly impossible, especially with the heightened burden of proof in the quasi-criminal context of contempt proceedings. For purposes of assisting the court in drafting language that will prohibit further use, the practitioner should consider how best to articulate negative know-how trade secrets in the alternative affirmative form of information.

2. *The Inevitable Disclosure Doctrine*

Clients are often very concerned about the security of their confidential information when a high-level employee leaves to take a similar position at a direct competitor, even when there is no overt threat of willful misappropriation. The issue that creates this cause for concern is not that the former employee may use the general knowledge, skill, or experience that was acquired during the course of the previous employment, but whether the former employee will use the more specialized knowledge, skill, or experience that incorporates the client's confidential information.

The client is not just concerned that a former employee may knowingly and intentionally use the trade secret information. Rather, even when the former employee has the highest levels of integrity, these employers are concerned that the former employee will not be able to compartmentalize the information he has in his head, and thus may be likely to inadvertently use the information. These concerns have grown dramatically as employees increasingly move laterally between companies, putting in sharp focus the balance between the rights of individuals to freely pursue their careers against the rights of employers to protect information that has been developed at great cost, or that provides value from its characteristic as a trade secret.

Where active wrongdoing exists, application of traditional forms of trade secret misappropriation does not need to balance the rights of individuals to pursue their desired calling. By contrast, most courts are reluctant to provide the same form of injunctive relief where the client can only articulate a concern that the former employee, by reason of her responsibilities at the new place of employment, could use the information that is in her mental possession. The "inevitable disclosure doctrine" addresses this situation. Where recognized, the doctrine provides a means to prevent a former employee from working for a competitor, notwithstanding the inability to prove that the former employee is wrongfully in possession of, or is overtly threatening to use, the trade secrets.

Under this doctrine, the former employee may be enjoined once the former employer demonstrates that the new job duties will "inevitably" cause the former employee to rely on his knowledge of the former employer's secrets. Without the obligation to establish the existence of injury compensable in monetary damages, an action may be filed to address the conflict between the continuing obligations of the individual to his former employer and those arising from the duties inherent in the current position. The former employer will seek an injunction ranging from one that restricts the handling of substantially similar duties (to alleviate the potential for placing the trade secrets at risk) to one that prevents the former employee from assuming any position with the competitor for a period commensurate with the "shelf life" of the secrets. In this context, "shelf life" refers to the period during which the information has value derived from its characteristic of secrecy.

Like many aspects of trade secret law, the doctrine of inevitable disclosure is not recognized in all states, or consistently applied in those states where the doctrine has found support. In some states, like California, the doctrine has been expressly rejected as being a violation of public policy as articulated in California Business and Professions

Code Section 16600. In these jurisdictions, the mere fact that a former employee possesses trade secret information as a result of prior employment is insufficient to sustain a claim, even where the individual intends to compete with the former employer in circumstances where such information would prove useful.

Where the doctrine has been applied, some of the criteria consistently used to determine whether disclosure would be "inevitable" include:

- Whether the new employer is a direct competitor of the prior employer or is providing the same or similar products or services;
- The scope of the defendant's new job, when compared to his or her prior position, and in particular whether the new position is nearly identical to the old one, such that the individual could not reasonably be expected to fulfill the new job responsibilities without utilizing the trade secrets of the former employer;
- Whether the employee has been forthright regarding his or her new position and employer;
- The extent to which the plaintiff has clearly identified the trade secrets that will be at risk as a result of the responsibilities of the new position, and whether the trade secrets at issue are highly valuable to both employers;
- Whether actual trade secret misappropriation has already occurred;
- Whether there is a non-disclosure and/or non-competition agreement between the prior employer and the individual;
- Whether the new employer has an express policy against use of others' trade secrets or has taken steps to minimize the risk; and
- Whether it is possible to place the employee in a position with the new employer where the trade secrets of the prior employer will not be at risk.

When the court concludes that some or all of these factors weigh against the former employee, the focus turns to fashioning the appropriate equitable relief. Specifically, the court will try to form an order that prohibits the continued employment of the individual, but only to the extent necessary to protect the interests of the prior employer. In some situations this will result in a complete bar. In other circumstances the order may only prohibit the individual from acting in a specified role, or for a limited duration consistent with the time-sensitive nature of the data.

The process of forming an appropriate order considers first the nature of the trade secrets and their "shelf life." Marketing and sales information tends to have a shorter shelf life than technological advancements. Few trade secrets are so pervasive in nature, and important to a company, that the individual should be precluded for all time from having any form of continued employment for the competitor. If the individual's expertise is truly specialized, this form of bar could result in the individual being forever excluded from obtaining gainful employment in the area of her training and experience. As there is no justification under trade secret law to maintain a prohibition on employment longer than the period of effective use of the information, at a minimum the court can look at the speed of developments in the area in question and craft an appropriate end date to an absolute prohibition. When the trade secrets appear to provide continued value over an extended period of time, an alternative to a lengthy absolute prohibition might consist of an order allowing placement of the individual in an unrelated area of employment with the competitor, so that she would not have any need to use the trade secrets in the normal course of her employment.

As a practical matter, those jurisdictions that apply the doctrine of inevitable disclosure are far more likely to find in favor of the former employer when there is some showing of "bad facts," on the part of either the former employee or the new employer. The concept of "bad facts" refers to conduct that can be described as constituting bad faith, "duplicity," or underhanded conduct on the part of the former employee or the new employer. Sometimes this is shown by a lack of forthrightness on the part of the employee during the course of leaving the prior employer. Other times it may be necessary to show a disregard by the former employee of his obligations, evidenced by conduct during an exit interview that suggests an unwillingness to preserve confidentiality, a refusal to confirm return of all company materials, or a refusal to acknowledge ongoing obligations to maintain confidentiality. This showing may be satisfied by the manner in which the new employer has responded to inquiries from the prior employer, or requests for assurances that its trade secrets will be protected against improper acquisition, use, or disclosure.

In those jurisdictions reluctant to apply the doctrine, the trade secret owner must address the concern that it tends to create an after-the-fact covenant not to compete and restricts employee mobility. In those jurisdictions, the prior employer must instead show some evidence of actually threatened misappropriation in order to overcome the employee's fundamental right to choose his or her employer. Other jurisdictions apply the general bar against issuance of injunctive relief in this setting, overcome only by a showing of actual misappropriation and irreparable injury for which there would be no adequate remedy at law.

The doctrine of inevitable disclosure is an example of how selection of the jurisdiction, when more than one venue is available, can impact the substantive rights being asserted. A trade secret owner who can file in both California and Illinois may choose the latter when the only claim is based on the doctrine of inevitable disclosure. But while some courts will readily enjoin a former employee based solely on the overlap in positions, most courts tread carefully when striking the balance between protection of intellectual property rights and employee mobility. Reasonable non-competition agreements can be an effective substitute for the inevitable disclosure doctrine, at least in those jurisdictions where such agreements are judicially enforceable as a post-employment restraint on competition. But to be effective as a practical matter, these agreements have to be in place before the employee has terminated his employment.

3. *Addressing Threatened Misappropriation*

The Uniform Trade Secrets Act specifically provides that an injunction may issue to enjoin threatened as well as actual misappropriation. In jurisdictions where the inevitable disclosure doctrine has been applied, that theory of liability is often described as an example of a threatened disclosure, applicable in cases where evidence of the existence of a substantial threat of impending injury is unavailable. Other courts have described the inevitable disclosure doctrine as an alternative to proof of threatened misappropriation; but in jurisdictions that have unequivocally rejected the inevitable disclosure doctrine, a sharper distinction is drawn.

To reconcile the interests of a business in protecting its trade secrets versus the right of an employee to be free to compete in the broader workforce, courts in jurisdictions otherwise hostile to the inevitable disclosure doctrine have pointed to the disjunctive in the Uniform Trade Secrets Act ("actual *or* threatened misappropriation") as a basis to grant relief even when there have not yet been any acts that constitute actual misappropriation. In these jurisdictions, for an injunction to issue, the plaintiff must at a minimum show that the defendant currently is in possession of the trade secrets *and* (1) has, in the past, actually misused or disclosed the plaintiff's trade secrets; (2) has evidenced the present intent to improperly use or disclose the trade secrets; or (3) wrongfully refuses to return the trade secrets after a demand for their return has been made.

Under all of the foregoing scenarios, the focus is on the remoteness of the threat. The fact that the initial acquisition was by proper means does not preclude injunctive relief. However, there must be more than a mere suspicion or apprehension of injury. The threat must be substantial. For example, if there is no evidence that the defendant intends to commit a future breach of an obligation to maintain confidentiality with respect to information he carries inside his head, convincing a court to issue an injunction based on the fact that there was a past breach is difficult at best.

The use of threatened misappropriation as the basis for relief arises most frequently in cases involving the need for a temporary restraining order. By definition, the defendant's actions have not matured into actual use or disclosure, and monetary relief would be difficult to obtain, as any injury compensable in damages has not yet occurred. Because of the close relationship between this basis for seeking relief and the doctrine of inevitable disclosure, in jurisdictions that prohibit the latter, the practitioner must counsel the client to proceed only where there are strong grounds to convince the court that there is a good-faith basis to seek the injunction. This is a situation where, in the absence of a reasonable indication based on admissible evidence that the threat of use or disclosure exists—other than by the mere fact of new employment—the defendant may have the ability to convince the court that the relief is sought for improper purposes (such as an attempt to intimidate the owner's remaining employees from moving to the new employer). If the court concludes that the trade secret owner is attempting to apply, sub silencio, the inevitable disclosure doctrine, and thus that the claim of misappropriation was made in bad faith, under the Uniform Trade Secrets Act attorneys' fees can be assessed in favor of the defendant.

4. Observations on the Statute of Limitations

The period in which a claim for trade secret misappropriation may be timely brought is a procedural issue that is dependent on the applicable state law even when the claim is filed in federal district court. There are differences in what constitutes accrual of the period of limitations, and thus the date of accrual, both between different jurisdictions and sometimes within the same jurisdiction, depending on the type of conduct alleged to constitute misappropriation. There are also differences from jurisdiction to jurisdiction in the length of time from accrual until expiration of the statute of limitations. There are differences in the application of the discovery rule, which might toll expiration of the statute of limitations, and differences depending on whether the trade secret owner is targeting the original or a subsequent misappropriator. Because of the myriad of potential differences that bear upon calculation of whether an action was timely filed, a complete analysis is well beyond the scope of this work. However, some of the key issues to consider are as follows:

In states that have adopted the definition of trade secrets set forth in the *Restatement of Torts*, such as New York, a plaintiff has three years in which to file suit. This time period may be extended where the continuing tort theory applies to such a claim (such as where the plaintiff alleges that a defendant has kept the secret confidential but continued to use it for commercial advantage). Texas, by contrast, historically applied the two-year statute of limitations for injury to, or conversion of, the property of another before more recently adding a specific section to its Civil

Practices and Remedies Code to provide a three-year statute of limitations for actions alleging trade secret misappropriation. The Uniform Trade Secrets Act suggests a three-year period, but the versions in some states range from two to five years. Further, under the Uniform Trade Secrets Act, the period begins when the misappropriation is discovered by the trade secret owner or when, in the exercise of reasonable diligence, it should have been discovered.

The date on which a misappropriation claim accrues can vary depending on what the party alleged to have committed the misappropriation did with the information. If the claim is based on improper disclosure, in some states the claim accrues on disclosure, and in others on the acquisition that preceded the disclosure. If the defendant keeps the information to himself and makes use of it to commercial advantage without any public disclosure, in some states the plaintiff may be able to fashion an argument that each successive use constitutes a new tort for purposes of the statute of limitations with respect to that defendant. By contrast, in California and other states that have adopted the Uniform Trade Secrets Act, a continuing misappropriation will constitute only a single claim. In these jurisdictions, a claim for misappropriation against a given defendant arises only once when the trade secret is initially misappropriated, with each subsequent use or disclosure of the secret augmenting the initial claim rather than giving rise to a separate claim.

Under the Uniform Trade Secrets Act, as well as in some jurisdictions that apply the common-law theory underlying the claim, the statute of limitations begins to run from the date upon which the misappropriation is discovered or, by the exercise of reasonable diligence, should have been discovered. Where the jurisdiction applies the discovery rule, a mere suspicion of wrongdoing may be sufficient to trigger the statute of limitations, as long as a reasonable investigation would produce facts sufficient to justify filing suit. The trigger applies regardless of whether the plaintiff has, in fact, conducted such an investigation. The differences in these rules have a number of related consequences. For example, the statute of limitations may run for all trade secrets that have been misappropriated by a given defendant, even though the plaintiff suspects misappropriation by that defendant of only one of several trade secrets. Further, to delay expiration of the statute of limitations, the plaintiff will bear the burden of establishing the time and manner of discovery, and the inability to have made the discovery at an earlier time through the exercise of reasonable diligence. One potential method of establishing reasonable diligence in this situation is through the use of an expert. To substantiate the position that information necessary to discover the claim was not available, the focus turns to a factual inquiry of whether the expert's efforts were appropriate and the trade secret owner's reliance thereon reasonable.

Further complicating the analysis, the rules implementing the statute of limitations are applied differently when the defendant is not the original misappropriator but is a third party uninvolved in the original misappropriation. The third party, as it does not have a direct relationship with the trade secret owner, is seen as having committed a "different" type of misappropriation. This distinction is most apparent in jurisdictions that consider trade secret misappropriation a "relationship" tort. As a result, there can be different claims for misappropriation among the various defendants and a different limitations period that must be calculated, even in those jurisdictions that hold that there is but a single claim and one limitations period as to the multiple acts of the original misappropriator.

There may also be a difference between the third party and original misappropriator as to what events will trigger commencement of the limitations period. Here the practitioner will have to discern whether the jurisdiction in which the action is pending will consider the period to begin to run for the third party when: (a) the trade secret owner reasonably should have suspected that the third party also acquired the trade secrets, regardless of the extent of the knowledge of that third party as to the "true" ownership of the information; (b) the third party knew, or was on notice, of the possibility that he or she was not in rightful possession of the information; or (c) the trade secret owner first has any reason to suspect that the third party either knew or had reason to know, when he obtained or used the trade secrets, that the information was actually owned by the trade secret owner.

When the practitioner is being asked to immediately file a complaint, on the checklist of action items to cover is whether the claims are time-barred. In making this analysis, the conclusion that the defendant may be able to mount a colorable statute of limitations defense is different from a situation where it becomes clear that the claim is time-barred on its face. This analysis is one where the practitioner can, in the absence of clear facts to the contrary, err on the side of concluding that the action can be timely filed. Rather than ruling against the client at the outset, the practitioner can deal with the factually complex issues that exist when addressing the issue as a matter of course during the pendency of the action. If the issue appears evident from the facts alleged on the face of the complaint, the practitioner will also have to add facts that "plead around" the statute in order to avoid a demurrer or motion to dismiss. In any event, the burden of asserting and establishing the defense rests on the defendant.

However, where the question of misappropriation is close, such as where an employee has gone to a competitor and the client is concerned—but not sure—that there may be use of its trade secrets, best practices in client counseling may lead to a course of action that does not involve immediately filing an action. In this situation, the best strategy may consist merely of sending a demand (or warning) letter to put the new employer on notice, and then waiting to see if there is any indication over time that suggests actual trade secrets use. At the point where the facts show evidence of use or threatened disclosure, the client will have better substantive grounds on which to file.

In implementing this strategy, the practitioner must make a careful determination of the date on which a court would likely conclude the period of limitations began to run, and the date on which the period will thus expire. These dates must be communicated clearly to the client, preferably in writing, who must be warned of the "drop-dead" date on which an action must be filed, or any rights will be irretrievably lost. To protect the client from losing rights, for internal calendaring purposes the dates should be calculated with a strong bias toward an early commencement and expiration date, as expiration of the statute of limitations is both an absolute bar to assertion of the claim as well as one of the major sources of malpractice claims.

5. *Action Items for the Pre-litigation Checklist*

Before a complaint is filed, the practitioner representing the trade secret owner has complete command of the calendar, subject only to the demands of the client and the potential for expiration of the statute of limitations. Once the action is commenced, however, the practitioner no longer has unilateral control over the time sequence of events. The schedule is now determined by the court's requirements and availability. A trial date, once set, drives all other dates, including the discovery cutoff, time periods for motion practice, and various pre-trial obligations, including identification of exhibits, preparation of motions in limine, and related tasks. The few choices that remain are heavily influenced by demands from the opposing parties. Providing the client a pre-litigation checklist of action items that address the process of compiling information needed during the course of the action will help avoid unnecessary distractions thereafter.

a. Witness Investigation

There are three "sets" of witnesses: those under the control of the client, neutral third-party witnesses, and hostile witnesses, whether or not under the control of the adverse parties. The pre-litigation checklist should direct the client to begin the process of determining and identifying those individuals who are key witnesses for either side, what they will likely say, and whether there is a need to develop additional witnesses with knowledge of certain subjects in anticipation of future issues that are likely to arise.

Witnesses under the control of the client include current employees and retained experts. This category also includes individuals who have already indicated their willingness to assist in the matter. The client should be asked to provide the most current contact information for each such identified witness, a brief description of their relevance to the dispute, and a summary of the anticipated nature of their testimony. A schedule should be set to interview, at least preliminarily, these "controlled" witnesses to confirm their willingness to assist, to evaluate the value of the testimony they may offer, and to determine their appropriateness to participate. The initial interview can be fairly short, as it is intended more as an initial point of contact than an exhaustive interrogation.

Neutral third-party witnesses may include former employees and current customers, vendors, or others who have dealt with either side to the dispute, and who are likely to have information relevant to the matter. A plan of action should be prepared for contacting these witnesses, to take into account that some may be willing to speak initially only to a client representative with whom they have previously interacted. Some of these witnesses, especially third parties who are former employees, are not "hostile" in the sense of actively seeking to support the adverse party, but they will be unwilling to participate due to a reluctance to be seen as taking sides. Some will simply refuse to discuss the matter absent a subpoena, due to their hostility to the client or the position the client is taking. Others will be willing to accept a "friendly" subpoena to avoid the appearance of cooperating. Knowing who will be friendly and who will be hostile before filing can provide valuable insights into the development of a discovery plan and deposition schedule. For these proposed third-party witnesses, the practitioner should consider:

- Does the client "know" how it will testify? If so, how?
- Have they been interviewed and, if not, who best should conduct the interview? A private investigator can be used, should there be a possibility the witness will go sidewise, and an independent witness will be needed to impeach their testimony.
- What do they add to the suit, and is their presence likely to make a difference in the outcome? A long list of potentially "helpful" witnesses, who will provide testimony on tertiary issues or who are merely cumulative, is not as important as selecting a focused list of witnesses who will address the key issues.

- Will they testify voluntarily? Will they prefer first being served with a "friendly" subpoena?
- Are they located in a jurisdiction where their testimony at trial can be compelled? If not, or if any other reason (such as health) suggests they may not be able to appear at trial, should a "trial deposition" be conducted to preserve their testimony? Trial depositions are very different from discovery depositions, primarily in that they are designed to memorialize known testimony in an admissible form. The latter, by comparison, are directed toward eliciting unknown testimony in order to gauge what can—or might be—presented during the proceedings.
- While these witnesses may appear friendly, are there risk factors that exist, such as prior employees who may harbor hidden grievances, or entities (including customers or vendors) who are doing business with both plaintiff and defendant?
- Is the defendant aware of the existence of these witnesses, and the potential that they may testify? If not, is there an obligation to disclose their existence before the discovery cutoff?

During the process of witness identification, expert consultants can be vetted and retained, both for testimonial and non-testimonial purposes, in order to gain maximum depth and breadth of expertise, and to take them out of play for the adverse party. In-house experts should also be identified, to assist as a "consulting" expert or for testimonial purposes, with the caveat to consider the potential disruption to the business as a result of the time spent using such individuals as testifying experts. For all of these proposed expert witnesses, the practitioner should consider:

- Who are the preeminent experts? The client should retain separate experts to cover the distinct areas: liability, security, and damages. Liability experts provide support for the characterization of the information as a trade secret. Are they knowledgeable in the business or the market in which the client participates? Do they understand what constitutes general knowledge in the industry? They must be able to discuss how the information was developed, its manner of use by the client, and its value to the business. Security experts involve opinions on the reasonableness of efforts to maintain the information as a secret and may provide testimony on the manner of access, especially when the evidence involves a forensic analysis of computer systems. Damages experts, whose opinions may address lost profits, unjust enrichment calculations, and reasonable royalties, are often not retained until later in the proceedings. However, they should be brought on board early in the process. Apart from ensuring their input is available to assist in shaping financial discovery that will bear on their opinions, their preliminary assessments of the value of the case can guide the client in determining how much it should invest in pursuing litigation. If the damages expert concludes that the amount of the potential recovery reflects a sum well below the cost of litigation, advising the client before litigation dollars are spent will reduce the possibility of a fee dispute when the action is over.

- Should the client "lock up" experts who are well considered in their field, even though it does not intend to use their services, to prevent the adverse party from retaining them?
- Do existing positions or consultancies affect the expert's ability to review materials that the adverse party will produce under a protective order that restricts dissemination?
- Are they available? Trial judges are notoriously inflexible in moving trial dates because an expert has a scheduling conflict. The practitioner must be sure that the expert's other commitments leave sufficient time to handle the assignment, and that key aspects of their analysis are not left to the junior members of the team, with the expert merely reading the report on the way to the deposition.

b. Information Management and Document Retention/ Collection

The process of identifying and selecting the trade secrets to assert should involve the contemporaneous identification of documentation that memorializes the trade secrets. These materials may consist of a wide variety of items, such as development team notebooks, source code data files, customer lists, or manufacturing recipes. Materials may be in hard copy, located in individual offices, in file rooms, or in offsite storage. Electronic storage means may have been used, including email servers, individual hard drives, and backup tapes. But the production of documents sufficient to identify the trade secrets is hardly all that will be requested by the adverse parties. Among other materials, they will want documents related to creation of the trade secrets, to the claims of misappropriation that reflect the "how and why" of the conduct alleged, and those materials that reflect whether the information was maintained as a secret. The requests will include copies of agreements—such as nondisclosure agreements, contracts, and proprietary inventions agreements—with employees, customers, vendors, or others who may have known, or been in contact with, the trade secrets. Documents bearing on the method and quantification of damages will be sought.

Determining what type of documents may be needed to support the client's case is the first step. The next step is to construct a document audit, laying out for the client how it can be implemented and determining the costs, risks, and benefits of searching for documents in light of the potential claims at issue. Some of these activities include the following:

- Review company document retention policies and determine whether such policies pose compliance/spoliation concerns. All policies or protocols that automatically delete or destroy hard copy or electronic materials should be suspended until a further review for relevant materials has been completed.

- Evaluate with the client the pros and cons of electronic litigation databases and other tools for document management. To facilitate this analysis, solicit bids from outside vendors that provide information on timing, cost, and scope of services. Request and check their references.

- Consider and investigate insurance coverage and notice issues in case of an assertion of cross-claims. Conduct this investigation of insurance even if the client is not currently aware of any basis for cross-claims, as the obligation of a carrier to fund a defense runs from the date of tender, not from the later date on which the carrier accepts the tender.
- Determine which employee(s) has an understanding of the different methods used by the company to organize and maintain the books and records. Conduct an interview of such employee(s) to determine the scope and location of sources for potentially relevant documents.
- Send a memorandum to employees informing them of the need to retain all relevant documents. In a large organization, the recipient list will be less than all of the employees, but business concerns over disruption in the workplace must be tempered by the litigation risk should a relevant witness inadvertently destroy important documents simply because she was unaware of the need to retain the materials. This memorandum should not simply ask employees to preserve all "relevant" documents, but rather should provide a specific description of the categories of documents (i.e., "All documents relating to ___") that must be preserved. The memorandum should also be clear that both hard-copy and electronic documents should be preserved, and provide guidance as to whom they should contact with any questions. While this memorandum arguably is privileged, as being sent by or at the request of counsel, it should be prepared with an eye to the fact that it might be provided to the court, should there later be a dispute over whether the client properly took steps to locate and preserve relevant documents.

- Identify a person within the organization to be in charge of the process of collecting relevant documents from the other employees, agree on a plan of action for document collection, and begin the process of implementing that plan.
- As part of the plan of action for document collection, the client should send a further memorandum to its employees (or, alternatively, to a select subset of employees) instructing them of the process to follow in gathering all hard-copy and electronic documents responsive to certain categories that must be produced, while cautioning them to still preserve the balance of materials in case of further requests.
- Gather the hard-copy documents collected by the individual employees. Copy these documents, returning originals to the employees for safekeeping. A document-tracking inventory chart should be prepared. This chart indicates the source of documents collected, the date of collection, and the location of the collected documents when they are held in different media. If it is insufficient to rely upon individual employees to collect all relevant electronic documents, derive another methodology consistent with the client's organization for collecting and reviewing potentially relevant documents. This process may include the imaging of drives from all or certain employees. Alternatively, instruct individual employees to place their electronic documents on a centralized file server, from which the legal team can then review and print out relevant and responsive materials.
- Conduct a search of all other potential sources for relevant hard-copy and electronic documents, including any documents for employees who have departed the company. The search typically includes document storage warehouses or centralized filing locations; filing cabinets; office closets; computer hard drives, including recycled drives; floppy disks or Zip disks; e-mail and other servers; and backup or archived tapes.

- Be prepared to conduct a search for previously deleted documents, which may involve computer forensics activity. Have an agreed approach to document the efforts at information management and document collection, including identification of an individual on behalf of the client to be in charge of the process suitable for providing a declaration, or submitting to a deposition if necessary, over the adequacy of the efforts in case of a later dispute.

c. Internal "PR"

Rumors are prevalent whenever a business files a lawsuit. Without any input from management, employees may form an incorrect understanding of the nature or purpose of the lawsuit, and nurture unwarranted sympathies for former colleagues who are being sued. Management's focus may be questioned and the allocation of scarce company resources challenged. With input from the client, the practitioner should determine whether a memorandum or e-mail should be sent to the employees informing them of the goals to be achieved by the action and instructing them to forward all inquiries about the case to the legal department. Everyone should be requested to neither discuss the specifics of the matter internally with individuals who are likely to be witnesses nor comment about the case externally to the press or other third parties.

Other types of internal PR may also be considered, including periodic updates as the case proceeds, and an internal communications plan formulated to address morale and other concerns raised by the prospect of litigation and its potential impact on the business. This plan should consider who should be the "author" of internal reports, who are the appropriate recipients, and the manner of communications, including substance, timing, and format.

d. External Public Relations

Whether the client is a private or publicly traded company, the practitioner must determine whether any press release should be issued concerning the litigation, or other public relations efforts made to inform the public about the nature and purpose of the litigation. Where the client is a publicly traded company, special care is required regarding the content and timing of the disclosure, due to the potential impact it may have on the public markets. In this situation in particular, the best course is to mobilize an external communications team. In the absence of internal marketing personnel well versed in this aspect of public relations, the client should retain an outside consultant who has previously handled litigation-related public relations for publicly traded companies. The media plan will reflect how, and through whom, the company will respond to outside inquiries, and whether it wishes to generate media coverage or attempt to fly under the radar. Particular attention should be paid to scripting, sometimes in the form of a mock Q&A, for use by those persons who are most likely to be contacted. The client should be counseled as to how best to respond to unsolicited calls from the press or other third parties (including customers making inquiries to salespersons or to others within the organization with whom they are regularly in contact).

There are subtle differences in the public relations campaigns initiated before filing the action and during the course of the action. Before the action is filed, the client may wish to air its grievances and create the impression that it is trying to obtain cooperation from the adverse party, so the subsequent filing will appear to have been implemented only as a last resort. But whether before or after the action is filed, consideration must be given to the impact any public relations campaign will have on existing and potential customers, for both the client and the adversary. The contents of any dissemination should also be viewed with an eye toward the potential that it will give rise to a cross-claim for business interference, defamation, or trade libel. Salespersons in particular are likely to use the fact of litigation as a marketing tool in order to gain sales or market share against a competitor.

Best practices require warning the sales force of the risk such activity creates for the client, and requesting they not elaborate on the fact that the action is now pending. Fortunately, many jurisdictions have some form of privilege for communications made in the context of actual or pending litigation when made to one who is interested in the proceedings. In California, the "litigation privilege" is codified in Civil Code Section

47. In federal court, the privilege is based primarily on an extension of the Noerr-Pennington Doctrine. But there are restrictions on what can be said in order to take advantage of the privilege, as any statements must have some reasonable relationship to the dispute, both substantively and temporally.

Even if privileged, such that the adverse party is not entitled to assert a cross-claim based thereon, before any statements are released, consider the impact on the court or the jury when they learn of efforts to "market" the litigation. The public relations campaign could serve as an evidentiary basis for the defendant to argue to the jury that the true focus of the suit is not the protection of trade secrets, but rather is a ruse to generate a source of FUD (fear, uncertainty, and doubt) to sow into a competitive market. Likewise, pejorative public statements made to win the battle of public opinion may make it harder to reach a business solution, especially if the solution involves some type of combined business effort or even an acquisition of the adverse party.

In addition to managing public perceptions regarding the lawsuit, the scope of necessary external public relations must also take into consideration whether any duty exists in light of the nature of the claims to notify third parties, as when the client is handling sensitive or confidential matters for the government, or if there is a possibility that the work being handled for third parties could be adversely impacted by the trade secret theft. In addition, before any public pronouncement, an effort should be made to determine whether the litigation will impact any rights, duties, or obligations existing under contracts, warranties, disclaimers, or indemnification agreements.

CHAPTER FIVE

Identifying Additional Claims to Pursue and Preemption, Pretrial Resolution Scenarios and Mediation, Anticipating Fee Awards and Statutory Bad Faith

Pursuing a trade secret *case* requires that attention be paid to more than whether the facts support the elements of a trade secret *claim*. Other legal theories are potentially applicable as the basis to assert alternative claims. The potential also exists, throughout the process, for resolving the matter short of trial. And both sides must consider the possibility that the defendant will make a request for fees or assert a statutory bad-faith claim should the merits be adjudicated in favor of the defendant.

1. *Identifying Additional Claims to Pursue and Preemption*

When a former employee departs with confidential information, the plaintiff is not necessarily limited to assertion of a claim for misappropriation of trade secrets. There are a variety of alternative "non-trade secret" legal theories on which a claim may be based to impose liability. These include claims ex contracu, whether as expressed in a written contract (such as an employment, NDA, or vendor agreement) or implied by the conduct of the parties. The claims could be ex delicto, with the specific tort reflecting the duties that flow from the nature of the parties' relationship to both the information and each other. Or the claims could exist by reason of a violation of a statute, such as the Lanham Act or one of various unfair business practices statutes. But the inquiry as to whether other legal theories exist on which to predicate liability for the same nucleus of facts requires more than a "bar exam" approach to issue spotting. There are both legal and practical issues that must be considered.

The most critical legal issue is preemption. The majority of jurisdictions that have adopted the Uniform Trade Secrets Act apply some form of statutory preemption. As a general rule, the trade secret claims preempt the non–trade secret claims when both are based on identical facts. However, preemption is one of the areas where there is a lack of uniformity in application, even among those states that have adopted the Act. For example, courts in Minnesota and Colorado consider whether the common-law claim as pled conflicts with the trade secret claim. In these jurisdictions, a plaintiff is allowed to maintain a separate claim to the extent there is more to the factual allegations than mere misuse or misappropriation of trade secrets. Under the version of the Uniform Trade Secrets Act adopted in California, however, preemption has been applied broadly by reason of the statutory language that specifies what is *not* "affected":

> This title does not affect (1) contractual remedies, whether or not based upon misappropriation of a trade secret, (2) other civil remedies that are not based upon misappropriation of a trade secret, or (3) criminal remedies, whether or not based upon misappropriation of a trade secret. *See* Cal. Civil Code, Section 3426.7(b).

Under this version of the Uniform Trade Secrets Act, common-law claims based on the same nucleus of facts as these are preempted. However, the reach of preemption, even under this version of the Act, is not absolute. Breach of contract claims are expressly excluded from the scope of preemption. Likewise, the tort of inducing breach of contract (even one that involves the duty of confidentiality, such as a nondisclosure agreement) is not preempted. As this tort is based on interference with an identifiable contract, it does not depend on a finding of misappropriation of trade secrets.

Additional alternative theories, potentially applicable to the same general factual setting that supports a misappropriation claim, include breach of confidence, conversion, trespass to chattels, interference with prospective business advantage, unjust enrichment, unfair competition, and fraud. The first question that the practitioner must address in deciding whether to plead additional claims based on these theories is whether the operative facts pled under these alternative theories are sufficiently "additional," such that the non–trade secret claims avoid preemption. But even in a "narrow" preemption jurisdiction, the asserted legal theories only provide a basis for evaluating the legal relevance of the additional facts. Applicability of the facts to these theories does not end the inquiry. For example, a claim for breach of the duty of confidence requires additional facts that give rise to the duty. But when the heart of the claim is a breach by reason of the disclosure of trade secrets without consent by the owner, the claim will likely be preempted. For each theory, the practitioner must first consider whether an interest in "property" is identified, other than one arising under trade secrets law. If not, to proceed on a non–trade secret theory, the plaintiff must be able to identify "conduct" that does not depend for its supposed wrongfulness on the use of trade secrets.

The practitioner faced with choices between various theories must ascertain whether the jurisdiction determines the question of preemption at the pleading stage by way of a demurrer or motion to dismiss. In these jurisdictions, given the practitioner's ethical obligation to plead only those allegations that have evidentiary support, or will likely have evidentiary support after a reasonable opportunity for further investigation or discovery, the plaintiff can face a Hobson's choice.

Sometimes the practitioner will not know sufficient facts, when the complaint is filed, to affirmatively claim that the information constitutes a trade secret. This situation can occur when the information is undoubtedly "proprietary," but the available information does not yet satisfy the other elements necessary to constitute a trade secret. For example, the business could apply a method of operation unknown to the public. An employee may take this information to a competitor. But nothing about this information, at the time the complaint is filed, supports the allegation that it provides the owner a *quantifiable* benefit as a function of being unknown to others. Should the decision be made to attempt to plead the case as a trade secret claim, there is the risk that the case may be dismissed at the pleading stage on the basis that the allegations do not qualify the information as a trade secret. And, by attempting to allege that the information constitutes a trade secret, other legal theories for recovery face the likelihood of being preempted. To avoid this result, the case could be pled as a non–trade secret case. But this choice forces the plaintiff to forgo all of the benefits and protections that exist under the Uniform Trade Secrets Act.

Courts that take the different approach, holding that the defense of preemption is premature when raised by motion at the pleading stage, tend to consider the status of information (whether it constitutes a trade secret) only a matter of allegation. In these jurisdictions, as long as the legal theories pled are sufficient, it is premature to address the preemption issue until an evidentiary distinction can be made between information that constitutes a trade secret and any other type of confidential or proprietary non–trade secret information.

In deciding whether to plead a single claim for trade secret misappropriation or to include a variety of claims and attempt to avoid preemption, the practical issue facing the client is whether there is a tangible benefit in asserting multiple legal theories based on similar—but not identical—facts. A targeted complaint, focused on a single legal theory, is less likely to result in jury confusion. It also presents a case substantially less expensive to litigate than a matter where the complaint lists 10 claims, with a different legal theory supporting each claim. However, lawyers are hesitant to proceed on a single claim, wary of being second-guessed should that claim fail, and tend to include (at least at the pleading stage) everything and anything possible. In this situation, the economic benefit to the lawyer and client are also in conflict. A lawyer being paid based on the number of hours expended has little short-term incentive to narrow the case. In defense of having brought the "complex case," the suggestion is often made that this strategy preserves options, as secondary claims can be dismissed before trial (to avoid jury confusion). While the process of narrowing claims over time will ultimately reduce the overall expense of the trial, this argument fails to acknowledge the substantial cost incurred before trial (in terms of both hard dollars and the unquantifiable cost from the distraction of counsel and client) dealing with the non–trade secret claims.

2. *Pretrial Resolution Scenarios and Mediation*

From the first discussion with the client, every practitioner should ask whether there are ways in which litigation can be avoided or mitigated. For the practitioner representing the plaintiff, asking this question will help the client focus on the ultimate goals to be achieved through litigation. For those who are representing the defendant, it will force an acknowledgment of the potential downsides to the action should the jury find for the plaintiff, and a heightened assessment of the support that must be provided to defend against the claim. Following are some of the points to consider.

- Is there any possibility that the parties would be willing to engage in informal business negotiations directly between the principals before the suit is filed? Lawyers are controlling, and many feel that there should be no direct interactions between the parties once litigation is actively contemplated. Sometimes, due to the nature of the relationship between the parties, or simply because of the personalities involved on one side or the other, it may appear that direct interactions would be a complete waste of time. Do not prejudge. Do not let egos interfere with opportunity. There may be history between individuals on both sides who either have or can be delegated with sufficient authority to begin a dialogue. Sometimes this history will involve relationships that precede their current employment.
- Are the parties willing to enter into an early mediation? Some practitioners view any suggestion to engage in early mediation as a sign of weakness. Experienced counsel knows this view is incorrect. A growing school of thought, well received by many judges, views the failure to explore the potential for early

mediation as a form of malpractice. Many federal district courts require that the parties discuss ADR alternatives as part of their preparation for the initial case management conference. In any event, even a rejected offer to mediate can be beneficial. Besides advising the court that the attempt was made and rejected, the process crystallizes the choices that the client must make—either get ready to proceed or walk away. If the suggestion to mediate is declined, counsel should ask the opposing party to identify the issues that create the impediment. Some people will say that early mediation is meaningless until there is some discovery of the extent of wrongdoing claimed or the nature of the trade secrets in issue. Others will focus on the lack of information on damages. But these issues, once identified, can be addressed in a way that makes the question of early mediation one of timing rather than doing.

- Separate from mediation, would a neutral evaluation by a third party be beneficial? The use of a neutral evaluator can occur when both parties are present, or one side can engage an evaluator without any participation by the other. The latter alternative has the benefit of allowing the client to be candid with the evaluator without the risk of exposing trial strategies prematurely to the other side. In either case, the process of having to present to a neutral evaluator forces the client to crystallize the goals to be achieved in the context of the evidence that can actually be put forth in support of the claims. This process results in the client becoming more realistic and can provide negative feedback without the risk of having the client view its counsel as having lost faith in the client's position.
- There may be outcomes achievable through negotiation that cannot be achieved through litigation. The client may be interested in an acquisition of the defendant's company, with a litigation discount on the purchase price. The dispute may be resolved by the client allowing the defendant to license the trade

secrets. In contrast, a lawsuit can only result in a judgment that provides monetary and injunctive relief. An apology cannot be ordered, and one will not be forthcoming. The defendant will not provide an admission of guilt. Rather, many defendants will continue to challenge and deride the judgment, at least in the marketplace, as having been "wrongly decided." No creative business arrangement will occur.

- A critical part of the analysis must take into account whether the amount of damages will be sufficient to justify the investment of litigation dollars in bringing the matter to trial. Likewise, are the trade secrets valuable enough to justify that expense? Clients who begin litigation eager to establish a "principle" are often disillusioned by the end of the process.

3. *Anticipating Fee Awards and Statutory Bad Faith*

Filing a trade secret action is not without risk. There is always the possibility the defendant will file a claim for malicious prosecution. But these are rare events, and the threat that a malicious prosecution claim may be made in the future rarely creates consternation on the part of the plaintiff. Not only are the standards difficult to meet, they also cannot be filed as a cross-claim. Rather, they require initiation of a brand new lawsuit, as these claims are not ripe until after the underlying trade secret case has been terminated in favor of the defendant. Leverage is more often sought by a defendant through the threat of an adverse award of fees or the potential for bad-faith sanctions. Both can be sought in the misappropriation case.

Fees in a trade secret case may be awarded where an underlying agreement contains an attorneys' fees clause in favor of the prevailing party. The primary issue, if the only claim is based on the tort of misappropriation, will be whether the fee clause applies to a non-contractual claim. This inquiry turns in part on the nature of the agreement (with an NDA or employee inventions agreement being the most typical) and the breadth of the clause. In some jurisdictions the defendant can take advantage of the clause, even where the agreement is offered only as evidence of the employee's duty or knowledge rather than as a basis for relief. The laws of the jurisdiction will provide guidance on the applicability of a contractual fee provision to a tort claim, whether a request for contractual fees must appear in the prayer of the complaint or answer, and the extent of reciprocity of fee awards where the agreement only provides for an award to the employer.

Fees may also be awarded as a form of sanction under the Uniform Trade Secrets Act, which has been construed to authorize an award for the bad-faith filing *or* continued maintenance of a groundless action. Under this construction of the Act, an award of fees may be appropriate, even when the trade secrets claim was initially brought in good faith, where the defendant demonstrates that the plaintiff pursued the claim beyond a point where it was reasonable to believe the case had substantive merit. In this situation, interactions between counsel during the case are examined, as bad faith may be inferred where the specific shortcomings of the case are identified by opposing counsel, and the decision is made to proceed despite the inability to respond to the arguments raised.

A defendant seeking to place pressure on the plaintiff in order to gain leverage through the threat of a sanctions award must bear in mind that the determination of "bad faith" involves two prongs. The claim of misappropriation must be objectively specious, and there must be subjective bad faith involved on the part of the plaintiff. An attempt to create a record sufficient to create a realistic exposure to sanctions must address both prongs.

Objective speciousness exists, even where the action as alleged superficially appears to have merit, if the court determines that there is a complete lack of competent evidence to support the claim. The focus is not whether there was a lack of evidence for every element. Similar to the analysis for determining a summary judgment motion, the defendant will "prevail" on this prong if there is an absence of evidence to establish an individual element of the claim, if that element is necessary for a finding of liability. The question is whether the plaintiff is able to present, at a minimum, sufficient evidence to establish all of the elements for a prima facie case that the information (1) constitutes a trade secret, and

(2) was misappropriated by acquisition, use, or disclosure. For example, if the defendant has mental possession of the trade secrets only by reason of knowing information learned in the ordinary course of her former employment, that evidence does not support a finding of improper acquisition. Absent evidence of improper use or disclosure, there is an absence of evidence to support a finding of actual misappropriation, even when the individual is now working for a competitor. Evidence that the plaintiff had an anticompetitive motive in filing the lawsuit can also be considered in establishing this element, such as where a California-based plaintiff proceeds on a sub silentio inevitable disclosure theory and there is neither economic harm nor actual threats of misappropriation by the former employee.

Defendants often argue, in support of their fee requests, that the trade secret claim was a function of an anticompetitive strategy. As typically alleged by defendants, the plaintiff is attempting to use the fact of litigation to gain some form of market advantage or to discourage other employees from leaving to work for the competitor. Subjective bad faith rarely is shown by direct evidence, such as an admission by the plaintiff, but may be inferred from facts that demonstrate the plaintiff filed the action to harass the defendant or harbored an improper motive. This inference can be drawn, for example, from the following:

- The plaintiff fails to identify with specificity what trade secrets would be subject to an injunction. To create the evidentiary record needed to support the sanctions motion on this point, the defendant must continue to demand a detailed designation. Should the responses continue to obfuscate, the court can conclude that the refusal to provide these details is sufficient evidence to support the finding of bad faith.

- Bad faith may be inferred by the scope of relief requested, such as where the application for an injunction seeks relief that is overbroad in duration or is not supported by the type of trade secrets identified.

- The timing of the filing of the action may raise an inference of bad faith, as the mere existence of a trade secret claim can be a material event that must be disclosed to investors and can derail a business combination or exchange offer. Initiation of the lawsuit shortly before a known funding event can support an inference that it was filed in order to interfere with that event.
- A trial court may even consider a party's bad-faith settlement demands. Bad-faith settlement demands exist when a party imposes unnecessary settlement conditions, unrelated to the trade secret action, which appear to have been made for an anticompetitive purpose. For example, a condition that prohibits the defendant from working with certain third parties can be an unlawful trade restraint. The same is true, and public policy is violated, when a plaintiff seeks a covenant from a defendant corporation not to hire any of the plaintiff's employees.

The question of subjective bad faith is not limited to the state of mind of the plaintiff at the time the action was initiated. Similar inferences may be drawn where the plaintiff proceeds to trial after opposing counsel demonstrates legal or factual deficiencies in the action. In this regard, the fact that the trial court may have denied the defendant's motion for summary judgment will not create an estoppel, or bar the court from finding bad faith after trial. Bad-faith motions are distinguishable from claims for malicious prosecution, as the denial of a defense motion for summary judgment normally precludes the trial court from finding that the lawsuit was frivolous.

When faced with the threat that a motion will seek an award of fees based on a claim of bad faith, the plaintiff should ensure that it can present a record after trial that reflects its "good faith." It can engage in a dialogue with the defendant, directly or through counsel, that seeks resolution, or clarification, of facts. The defendant is free to refuse to respond substantively, referring the plaintiff to the normal methods of discovery as the appropriate channel for conducting the investigation. But this refusal has evidentiary value on the sanctions motion, as it illustrates why the plaintiff reasonably maintained the action. The plaintiff can also consider developing evidence that finds support in reliance on the opinions developed by the experts retained during the course of the proceedings. These opinions, while primarily intended as support for the scientific basis for the claim, or to address a defendant's contention that it lawfully acquired the technology from a public source or third party, can preclude a bad-faith finding only when they are both credible *and* were reasonably (and actually) relied on by the plaintiff in pursuing the action.

When the defendant believes that the matter is being improperly pursued, it should create a record beginning at the earliest possible time that it will be seeking sanctions. This process can start in its answer and be repeated throughout the case. This will prevent the plaintiff from claiming that it did not have sufficient notice of the potential for the award. Since the plaintiff's good-faith obligation continues throughout the action, the defendant should continue to create a record by placing the plaintiff on notice of the facts and events as they develop that are favorable to the defendant's position.

While there is a tendency to hold exculpatory information until trial to minimize the potential that the plaintiff can devise a way of countering the information when presented to the jury, subjective bad faith in maintaining an action cannot be based on information that was not previously known to the plaintiff. In turn, the plaintiff must consider how best to respond to these attempts to create a record. Ignoring them completely is problematic. Pointing to evidence in the existing record, in response to a motion for sanction, provides nothing more than what can already be brought to the attention of the court. The plaintiff should treat such correspondence from the defendant as an opportunity to demand (outside of formal discovery) information relative to the positions articulated by the defendant. Assurances that the defendant did not engage in the action complained of, in the form of a detailed statement under oath, can be requested. Whether or not admissible in a hearing on the merits of the misappropriation claim, the refusal to provide such assurances or similar information can be offered in support of the opposition to a motion for sanctions.

CHAPTER SIX

Choosing between Jurisdictions and Alternative Venues: Federal versus State Courts, Jury versus Bench Trials, Arbitrations, and Proceedings before the ITC

Where a trade secret case is filed can have a significant impact on the way the action is litigated and on its outcome. "Where" means in which state, when jurisdiction lies in more than one, as well as whether to file in federal versus state court. But is there a "venue risk" associated with the client's preferred choice? Could the defendant move to dismiss for lack of jurisdiction, seek a transfer of the matter to a more "convenient" forum, remove the state court filing to federal district court, or even preemptively file a declaratory relief action in a jurisdiction other than the one preferred by the plaintiff?

"Where" to file is an observation that, while governed by the legal criteria for filing, relates to the fundamental relationship between the parties and the jurisdiction in terms of their location(s), the location of the conduct that constitutes misappropriation, and the location of the harm suffered by the trade secret owner. It also involves an analysis of which potential audience—the trier of fact, whether judge or jury—will be favorable, and whether one forum will be more hospitable than another by reason of a variance in the law or the attitudes in the locale toward the protagonist and/or antagonist. If the client is from out of state, and the adverse party well known and liked locally, the prospect of that party being able to exploit a home court advantage is to be avoided if possible.

A plaintiff may thus seek to use diversity jurisdiction as the basis to file in federal district court, or a defendant may seek to remove on that basis. Alternatively, the plaintiff may want to file in state court because it is a significant employer in the city where the courthouse is located and must consider ways of preventing removal. If several jurisdictions have personal jurisdiction over the defendant, the law of one may be more favorable to the plaintiff's case than the law of another. Within a particular jurisdiction, federal court may be a better choice than state court because of the quality of the bench. Alternatively, the best approach may be to avoid the court system entirely and proceed through arbitration, or before an administrative agency such as the International Trade Commission.

1. Selecting Federal or State Court, and Between Alternative Venues

a. Personal Jurisdiction

The first question in deciding whether to file in a particular locale, regardless of the choice between federal or state court, is whether the identified court can exercise personal jurisdiction over the defendant. Where the facts lead to the conclusion that the plaintiff will be able to assert jurisdiction in only one location, the matter is simple. But sometimes the analysis leads to the conclusion that personal jurisdiction will lie in several courts in different states.

When there are multiple defendants, these choices can increase exponentially. The client may have the ability to choose among several courts or several different states. Alternatively, personal jurisdiction may exist over all of the defendants in one place, but over only some of the defendants in the client's "preferred" location. If not all of the defendants are subject to jurisdiction in the available courthouse, the client must consider whether to proceed against less than all in a particular case. This decision may result in some defendants not being sued at all, or in multiple suits being filed in several courthouses. Fortunately, the need to file in multiple locations because of issues with personal jurisdiction rarely arises when all of the defendants are U.S. citizens, or foreign business entities with a significant presence in the United States. The personal jurisdictional statutes of most states are coextensive with federal due process requirements. Under these "long-arm" statutes, a court is permitted to exercise personal jurisdiction as long as the defendant had "certain minimum contacts" with the jurisdiction, such that the maintenance of the suit does not offend "traditional notions of fair play and substantial justice."

Personal jurisdiction, of course, may be either "general" or "specific." Misappropriation claims are unlikely candidates for the court to find that it has general jurisdiction over a non-resident defendant, especially when the acts of misappropriation are considered alone. The tort of trade secret misappropriation does not usually involve "continuous and systematic" forum activity. The acts of most misappropriators involve discrete acts over a relatively short period of time. Whether the court has personal jurisdiction in these cases more often involves an analysis of specific jurisdiction.

Specific jurisdiction focuses on whether the defendant purposefully directed conduct at the forum state, and is generally determined by applying the "effects test." In a trade secret case, this analysis considers where the defendant's actions were felt, regardless of whether the actions themselves occurred within the forum or took place in a foreign jurisdiction. The right to proceed against foreign-based conduct is in sharp contrast to other forms of intellectual property. By way of example, a patent owner, faced with someone who is making, using, offering to sell, or selling any device or product that incorporates the patented invention, is limited to recourse for infringing activity that occurs within the United States. The U.S. Patent Act does not have an extraterritorial reach. A device or product manufactured and sold in China and used in that country does not infringe a U.S. patent, even when the claims of that patent read directly on that device or product.

To establish personal jurisdiction in a misappropriation case based on "purposeful direction of conduct," the defendant must have committed an intentional act, expressly aimed at the forum state, causing harm that the defendant knows is likely to be felt in the forum state. Importantly, a corporation's principal place of business determines where the corporate injury is felt as a result of misappropriation. The fact that the impacted market for a plaintiff's products or service is in a different jurisdiction, or that the actual misappropriation occurred elsewhere, does not change this result. Under this reasoning, the fact that the act of wrongful acquisition of the trade secrets took place in China, and the use of those trade secrets also occurs in China, will not negate specific personal jurisdiction in the United States over the China-based defendant where the trade secret owner is located in the United States. Of course, in this scenario there still may be difficult issues with respect to service, discovery, and enforcement of a resulting judgment. Many countries decline to routinely domesticate or enforce judgments that result from proceedings in the United States. In Germany, for example, the extent to which a judgment from a state court in the United States will be recognized and enforced is far from settled. Like other countries, Germany is eager to protect its citizens from "foreign" judgments that result from procedures considered incompatible with the fundamental standards of its domestic law, including the ability in the United States to engage in extensive and compelled pretrial discovery, and the potential for punitive damage awards.

When an issue of personal jurisdiction arises in a given case, the practitioner should also be mindful that objections to the lack of personal jurisdiction can be waived. The defendant may have previously participated in the judicial system of the jurisdiction in question. Having voluntarily accepted the benefits, the defendant will be viewed as having waived the right to subsequently ignore the concomitant burdens when they become the subject of a suit. Alternatively, when there is a preexisting relationship between client and defendant, look at the underlying agreements to see if there is a choice of venue/jurisdiction clause. This type of contract provision is routinely honored in arm's-length transactions. While not binding on third parties, at a minimum the contractual submission to jurisdiction will bind the signatories to the agreement.

b. Subject Matter Jurisdiction

Subject matter jurisdiction can be an issue when the case is filed in federal district court. In contrast to personal jurisdiction, subject matter jurisdiction cannot be waived by the parties, and an objection based on the lack thereof can be raised at any time in the proceedings. As there is no federal civil trade secret statute, federal courts will not have federal question subject matter jurisdiction. The only basis for subject matter jurisdiction, when the only claim is for misappropriation, is diversity.

Where complete diversity exists, the federal district court has subject matter jurisdiction to hear the misappropriation claim. If complete diversity does not exist in a particular jurisdiction, the matter cannot be filed in that federal district court where the only claim is trade secret misappropriation. Instead, the misappropriation claim can be heard by the federal court in that jurisdiction only under supplemental jurisdiction, as long as the supporting facts are sufficiently related to those underlying a federal question claim over which the court has original jurisdiction that they form part of the same case or controversy. An example involves a case where the plaintiff pleads a Lanham Act claim in order to pose a federal question and appends the misappropriation claim under pendant (supplemental) jurisdiction.

This jurisdictional question poses even greater complexity when the defendant seeks to assert a misappropriation cross-claim, and the court is not sitting in diversity. If the misappropriation claim is compulsory, it automatically is within the court's jurisdiction because such claims arise out of the same transaction. Permissive cross-claims, however, require independent grounds of federal jurisdiction. Which is which, in practice, is not always easy to determine. Because the cross-claim often is being asserted by the defendant primarily to create leverage, the client should be counseled on the cost-benefit involved in seeking to dismiss where an argument can be made that the cross-claim is not sufficiently related and, therefore, the court does not have subject matter jurisdiction.

Sometimes the trade secret owner will want to have the case heard in state court. To prevent an out-of-state defendant from removing and then seeking transfer to a different district or forum, consider whether complete diversity can be negated by adding a defendant (such as an individual who had sufficient involvement in the acts of misappropriation to satisfy Rule 11, perhaps as an aider and abettor or conspirator, even if he otherwise would not have been named for any number of strategic reasons). It is the citizenship of all defendants, served and unserved, that determines diversity jurisdiction.

c. Illustrative Factors When Evaluating Multiple Potential Venues

Assuming the action could be filed either in federal or state court, or in more than one state, which one is best? The following are some of the factors to evaluate when a choice exists whether to file in (or remove to) federal district court, or when selecting one state court versus another. The weight that should be attributed to any one factor can vary in application, based on the particular federal district court, state court, and even which division/branch of a court within a district (or county) of a state that has multiple divisions/branches due to its geographic reach (as few state courts are consistent in their procedures, or even their application of the same rule, within the larger districts/counties in a given state). Some of the factors to consider, in no particular order of importance, are as follows:

- Consider the local rules in the different courts, as these may impose significantly different obligations. These obligations range from the format and number of allowed motions to the content and timing of disclosure obligations. Do they favor the plaintiff or the defendant, given the particular facts of the case and the goals of the client?
- Are the time lines for each court significantly different? Some states have adopted a form of trial delay reduction legislation, designed to move matters through the system in a specified period of time. California requires, with few exceptions, that civil actions be brought to trial within five years of initiation, and has the expectation that the majority of civil matters will be resolved within 18 months of filing. Federal district courts are not subject to any outside time requirement, and, depending on the district, the average length of time the matter remains pending can vary from as little as eight months to as long as several years.
- Federal district courts assign the matter to a single judicial officer. This judge handles all aspects of the matter from initiation to

termination of the action, other than discovery matters that may be referred to a subordinate judicial officer, and any appellate matters. The parties are entitled to an Article III judge. But, upon the consent of both parties, a magistrate judge can preside over the trial. By comparison, state courts have a variety of arrangements, from the single assignment method used in federal district court to the case management method. In the case management method all pre-trial matters are handled by a case management judge. At the point where the matter is ready to be tried, the matter is referred to a trial department for all subsequent proceedings other than appeal. The trial judge typically has no prior knowledge of the action before the assignment. This lack of continuity is a benefit to a defendant in a trade secret case where a TRO and preliminary injunction was previously granted to the plaintiff. A judicial officer who has been convinced to issue such relief early in the proceedings will not have to be "re-educated," and will be inclined to act in a similar manner later at trial.

- What requirements are there for the use of local counsel? In some jurisdictions their involvement is minimal. Other courts require that local counsel be involved in all significant events, from conducting discovery meet-and-confers to being in attendance at all hearings.
- If the state court requires a formal or informal identification of trade secrets early in the proceedings, does the local federal district court adopt the same process? If not, for the given case, is one better than the other?
- Has the state adopted the Uniform Trade Secrets Act, or does it rely on the common law? Is there a disagreement between the state court and the federal district court in that state over relevant issues? For example, in California there is a difference of opinion between the state courts and certain district court judges on the question of the scope of preemption, and whether this is a

determination appropriately made at the pleading stage. The difference in legal analysis can affect the extent to which the federal district court will defer to the opinions of the appellate courts of that state.

- Are there issues regarding the manner in which the particular court addresses protective orders and confidentiality of the proceedings? Some federal district courts refuse to close the courtroom during trial. Will this affect the manner in which the evidence is to be presented?

- When venue for the underlying action is in federal district court, obtaining assistance in enforcing discovery outside of the forum is easier than when the matter is pending in a state court. There is also greater consistency in application of discovery standards among the various federal district courts than among judicial officers of different states.

- An out-of-state party, whether plaintiff or defendant, is less likely to be "home-towned" when the matter is pending in federal district court.

- Information on the assigned judicial officer—his or her background, affiliations, and prior decisions—is more readily available for judicial officers assigned to matters pending in federal district court.

- In federal district court, the defendant is obligated to specifically admit or deny each of the factual allegations asserted in the complaint. Any admissions remove the issue from being in contention, and no further proof on that matter need be presented at trial. While the standard in federal district court is "notice pleadings," detailed factual averments can force the defendant to take a position early in the process. By comparison, a defendant in California state court can respond to an unverified complaint by providing a one-line general denial to all of the allegations.

- While the Seventh Amendment right to a jury trial does not require either a 12-person jury or a unanimous verdict in federal district court, federal trials involve a six-person jury in most civil cases. Further, Federal Rule of Civil Procedure 48 mandates a unanimous verdict unless the parties stipulate otherwise. Size and unanimity requirements in civil cases vary considerably under state laws. Less than half the states require 12-person juries, and about half the states allow for non-unanimous verdicts.
- Most clients have budget requirements. Proceedings in federal district court tend to be more expensive than state court. Some of the major expense items in federal district court, not typically encountered in state courts, include the requirement that experts prepare extensive reports memorializing all of the opinions they will be offering (which is a rule originally intended to obviate the need to take their depositions, but has instead merely made the process lengthier and more expensive), and the obligations that exist in the pretrial conference process (including the major effort involved in preparing the pretrial conference statement, that lists inter alia all issues to be tried, describes and identifies all exhibits, and provides summaries of testimony to be offered).
- What differences exist in the jury pools, and manner of composition, from one jurisdiction to another? The individuals who make up the jury pool for the federal district court in Concord, New Hampshire, will have very different views from those in the jury pool for the federal district court venued in Marshall, Texas. Further, more localized jury pools exist in state court than federal district court. In Northern California, juries in San Francisco County have a record of more liberal verdicts than those 30 miles away in Santa Clara County, but do not have the same reputation of enforcing rights in intellectual property. In Southern California, Los Angeles County is more liberal than Orange County, with a reputation for higher awards, but the latter may be a better venue for an employer focusing on injunctive relief. There is a great deal of readily available

information that provides insight in this area. Yet many attorneys do not pay any attention to this issue, under the apparent misimpression that all jury pools are fungible.

- Some metropolitan areas are more likely to have jurors with technical backgrounds or who work for companies in technical markets. These jurors tend to align themselves with the side trying to protect the secrets. A plaintiff with choices can better target the prospective audience.

- Are there any substantive differences in the law that help or hinder the case? There are a number of subtle differences in trade secret law that require close attention, even between two jurisdictions that have both adopted the Uniform Trade Secret Act. Some of these differences are in the text of the statute as adopted, as compared to the model form of the Act. For example, Idaho explicitly includes a definition of "computer program" as a protectable trade secret, whereas California refers simply to a "program" in its statutory version. Other differences exist as a result of judicial interpretation, ranging from how the statute of limitations is calculated under the discovery rule to the scope of preemption. The experienced practitioner will avoid the urge to select the court in which to file based solely on the jurisdiction where she is the most comfortable. Spend the time to consider whether a less familiar location will provide greater legal leverage.

- Will there be mechanical differences, including the location of witnesses, the client's facilities, and the attorney's office, relative to the physical location of the court that makes one location more convenient than another? The practical realties of trying a case are frequently overlooked. Prudence suggests that one should try to avoid, for example, having to convince a third-party witness located in San Francisco, upon whom the case depends, to voluntarily travel to Wilmington, Delaware, in January to attend trial.

- Does the local bench have a track record in handling trade secret cases? Information on the views of trial court judges on the federal bench are easier to obtain, in part as a result of the higher publication rate of their decisions. But anecdotal information is generally available for most state court benches. At a minimum, local counsel can assist in this vetting process.

- Is the venue technologically savvy, or does it have the reputation of being technophobic? On this point, the inquiry takes into account the manner in which the local bench addresses the use of technology in the courtroom, as well as the sophistication of the jury pool toward the use of technology.

- What is the caseload of the local judges and the anticipated length of time from initial filing to trial? Jurisdictions vary tremendously, from eight months in some to five years or more in others. The maxim "justice delayed is justice denied" has great applicability to trade secret cases. Often the evidentiary basis for a TRO does not exist, and the plaintiff must use the discovery process to compile sufficient evidence to address the continued acts of misappropriation. When quick relief is not available, the defendant's potential downside is limited to the monetary award that may issue at the end of trial, coupled perhaps with a permanent injunction. But if that relief does not issue for three years or more after the action is filed, the market may have changed enough that any injunctive relief will not have real-world value. The defendant may also have used the passage of time to shield its assets in a way that eviscerates the benefit of the damages award.

- Is the connection to the forum such that, upon the adverse party's motion, there is a likelihood of transfer to a "more convenient" forum? While the mere fact of incorporation in Delaware, for example, was once a sufficient basis to preclude transfer, that absolute has diminished in recent years. The potential for a case being transferred sometimes is a reflection of the current political climate and the pressure placed on the transferor court when handling transfer motions.

2. *Jury and Bench Trials*

Whether state or federal court is the selected venue, at some point the question may arise whether to present the case to the court rather than to a jury. The question may come from opposing counsel, who is offering to stipulate to try the matter as a bench trial. The issue may present itself due to a statute or local rule that requires a decision early in the proceeding. While most courts are reluctant to find a party has forfeited the right to a jury, in federal court the jury demand must be made by including it in a pleading to the court or by providing written notice to the other party within 14 days of the last relevant pleading served. State court requirements differ from jurisdiction to jurisdiction, with some providing that any form of demand at any time prior to commencement of trial is sufficient. As the nature of the presentation of a trade secret case can vary based on the audience, the practitioner should consider this issue very carefully, and discuss it with the client, in order to timely make the decision on which way to proceed.

Juries add significant expense to any action. The proceedings become more formal, as there are many points during a trial where the jury must be excused in order for the court and counsel to address evidentiary or procedural issues out of their presence. The process of authenticating documents and laying foundations for witness testimony requires more time. The court will not be as quick to extend the luxury of taking witnesses out of turn, such as when experts have scheduling issues. Communication of complex technologies is more difficult to a lay jury than to the court. Judges are better suited to follow the presentation of technical experts, regardless of subject matter, as they have experience listening to the proffer of opinions and thus have a more refined ability to grasp the essence of an expert's presentation. Separate *Daubert/Frye* motions are not required. Without the concern over the jury hearing improper opinion testimony, the court can act as the gatekeeper while the expert is being presented on direct, through a voir dire cross-examination.

While a dry presentation to a judge runs the risk of losing his or her full interest, and anecdotes exist of judges watching ESPN on their computer screens while witnesses testify, jurors in particular need to be entertained in a manner consistent with their out-of-court experience in order to maintain their attention. Entertainment today is marked by the sheer volume of variety available, both in content and methods of delivery. Whether through movie-mega-multiplexes, cable broadcasting, or Internet streaming, the entertainment industry has recognized the need to continually adapt to an increasingly fragmented and demanding audience. Broad-based themes and genres are bypassed in favor of message pieces that target narrow, demographically identified markets. The former luxury of slow plot and character development has given way to conversation voice-overs, rapid changes in camera angles, and multilayered character interactions that are not always unified into a cohesive story line. The viewing choice of the individual has become the paramount determinant to the presentation, with the chance to grab ever-shortening attention spans made increasingly difficult. Jurors, while not having a similar wealth of choice with respect to the content of the drama they are forced to consider, are no different with respect to their expectations and desires regarding the manner in which they will be "entertained."

Unlike most other audiences, jurors do not self-select into a group that has some base level of interest in the subject matter being presented. When called to duty, their choice whether to participate diminishes swiftly. Once sworn, they have no input into what type of case they will hear and no say in the manner in which they will be entertained. There is no pause button, nor can they "hop" to something more interesting during the dull points. As a result, the modern juror is stuck in a system that bears little resemblance to how they commonly interact with the bombardment of sensory input now available. Rather, the average juror is essentially sequestered during the proceedings, unable to choose either the content or method of delivery of the information critical to the fact-finding process.

In this setting, there is a trade-off between providing testimony that focuses on the intricacies of the trade secrets, and the need to retain the thematic elements of the case presentation. The former aspect is undoubtedly important, as a proper record must be created that details the information that is the subject of the dispute. But alternative sub-examination dialogues should always be prepared, addressing the "story" side of a misappropriation case, in order to emphasize or avoid issues that correspond to the backgrounds of the jury. Too much emphasis on the intricacies of the trade secrets can often devolve into technical subtleties, lost on a jury that has mentally tuned out for the afternoon. The nuanced differences in the manner in which the story can be delivered must also be factored into the overall case theme, with a premium placed on having the flexibility to adapt to the varied expectations of those who will render the verdict. This is where careful examination during voir dire of juror preferences in the *manner* by which they obtain information, as reflected in the method of transmission as well as the choice of entertainment that reflects the style of delivery, can assist in educating the near-spontaneous directorial decisions that face all trial counsel.

Volumes have been written on jury selection, and much of the attention has focused on the need to determine the predispositions of prospective jurors with respect to particular facts or issues. But just as knowing the substantive beliefs and prejudices of your audience is a key aspect to making any presentation successful, determining what method of delivery works best in reaching and holding the attention of this form of audience is paramount. Is the audience generally older and more familiar with the pace of "Mayberry RFD"? Or do the jurors appear never to have experienced life before IM, YouTube, and Facebook, so they need a rapid-fire stream of content to remain intellectually engaged? Trying to explain the concept of cloud computing to the former, in a case involving secrets used in infrastructure convergence, will require the use of analogies that can cause the latter to roll their eyes.

The classic form of extracting information at trial, through the use of methodical examination, is surely the one that is the least effective. Learning through the oral transmission of information is difficult and requires both clear articulation and reception. This problem is intensified where the jurors are being provided new concepts to grasp along with the more traditional aspects that come up in a civil dispute. The use of a question-and-answer form of presentation is not only hard to follow, as the information from each witness is seldom placed before the jury in a self-contained and comprehensive fashion, but it also tends toward the tedious in tone and character. While an older jury who recalls "Perry Mason" may appreciate the careful organizational framework of an element-by-element examination, younger jurors will tune out long before they hear the *raison d' etre* for the line of questions. Being able and ready to tailor the manner of presentation to the audience means more today than tinkering with the case theme in light of the jurors' substantive life experiences. Likewise, although the form of oral combat that constitutes cross-examination has been described by the profession as the "crucible of truth," and traces its roots to Socrates' artful questioning of his accuser Meletus, the typical exchange between examiner and witness is far less dramatic (or interesting) than common cinematic treatment would suggest. Worse still is the bland and prepackaged direct examination, with its premium on making a record that complies with evidentiary strictures that tend to inhibit rather than engage the audience in a search for rapt attention.

Most trial counsel, recognizing these issues, more recently have relied on sophisticated demonstratives to communicate the nature of highly technical trade secrets. Recognizing the need to enliven the proceedings—at a minimum the use of poster boards and ELMOs—has become commonplace. Even at the risk of being portrayed by opposing counsel as constituting nothing more than an attempt to cozen the jury, more experienced counsel have realized that the introduction of various forms of media into the proceedings has become an essential vehicle through which they can maintain the interest of their audience through long proceedings. From "life in a day" videos that take the jury through a production facility to help them understand the process of manufacturing integrated circuits, to production-quality graphics, demonstratives are a sure way of breaking up the monotony of examination. But as the desire to inject flash has increased as more choices in technology have become available, caution is required, as the pace of judicial acceptance has not always been as rapid. Trial counsel do not have the right to choose the judge who will preside over the action, as newly filed lawsuits are assigned on a random basis to one of several trial departments. Notification of these assignments typically occurs prior to the first appearance by counsel.

At the first appearance, the newly assigned judge may ask counsel to provide an overview of the dispute and the nature of the issues that the court will be asked to address. However, while the legal issues on any given occasion may be the same regardless of the particular judge to whom the matter is assigned, no two judges are alike, and there is no guarantee that they will approach the identical issues in the same fashion. In that regard, a manner of presentation that may have been well received by one may not be allowed by another.

In federal proceedings, the court is given broad discretion in deciding evidentiary matters, including demonstratives, experiments, and reenactments. Usually addressed under the balancing test articulated in Federal Rule of Evidence 403, the issue of admissibility often comes down to whether the demonstrative is intended to illustrate general principles or to re-create an event, incident, or occurrence. Where the latter is true, the proponent typically must demonstrate a "similarity of circumstances and conditions" between the tests and the subject of the litigation. Of course, innovation by counsel is not improper simply because it may have a significant impact on the jury, as demonstrated by one enterprising defendant's use of a virtually life-sized mock-up of a scanning electron microscope as a demonstrative aid in the course of the jury trial. There is no doubt that counsel in that matter had the full attention of the jury during the portion of the examination where the expert used the mock-up to illustrate his opinions.

Consideration of the manner in which the evidence will be presented should be an action item on the drive sheet from the beginning of the case. To that end, the tendencies of the assigned judge will provide an insight into the manner in which the presentation should be made, especially given the significant appellate deference paid to trial court's decision whether to allow counsel to proceed on such evidentiary issues. To that end, local bar associations are good sources of information regarding the proclivities of sitting judges. Another source of information is the courtroom clerks, who can provide some guidance regarding the "unwritten local rules" judges apply in their courtroom. These "rules," while tending more toward the manner in which the judge runs his or her courtroom, often reflect the judge's pet peeves, and compliance can avoid an embarrassing admonition. A third source, and one that provides greater insight into the judge's substantive legal reasoning, is appellate decisions that review the decision of the trial court or are authored by the jurist before the parties will be appearing.

The manner of delivery must also take into account the time constraints imposed by the court, as well as the amount of time that can be used in developing a point before the judge's attention wanders. Trial judges have long been recognized as having the authority to set reasonable time limits on the presentation of evidence at trial. Likewise, it is hard to gain credibility and ensure the attention of the jury when the presentation takes overly long to develop. Further, for those courts that place strict time limits on counsel, careful thought must be given to the trade-off between the amount of time a given point takes to present and the likely weight the jury will place on that point in their overall deliberations. Many lawyers are so close to the case, and their own work, that they have a difficult time understanding that the incremental value provided by a particular line of questioning is not worth the time or potential distraction from other, more direct points. If you are not sure about the schedule, asking how much time is available shows a sign of respect, as well as providing an opportunity to modify the presentation to fit within the expectations of the audience.

In the theater, experienced performers know that each performance is unique, even though the lines and venue are identical. As the audience changes, the experience will be different. Audiences change, not just in their overall composition, but also in how their individual life experiences prepare them to receive the presentation. The complexities that arise out of the composition of a given audience are magnified by the significant differences in possible presentation formats that depend on whether one intends to entertain, educate, or persuade. Understanding the biases and tendencies of the audience allows one to adapt, as a presentation is only as effective as its ability to hold their attention.

3. *Whether to Proceed by Way of Arbitration*

Trade secret cases, when they proceed by way of arbitration, most often do so as a result of an arbitration clause in a preexisting agreement between the trade secret owner and the misappropriator. On rare occasions the parties stipulate to resolve the matter through arbitration after the dispute arises. Sometimes one of the parties to an agreement containing the arbitration clause will be reluctant to proceed by way of arbitration. The plaintiff may be hesitant because discovery in arbitration is limited. The defendant may be wary of the looser evidentiary requirements of arbitration. Where only the plaintiff seeks to have the matter adjudicated by an arbitrator, a typical path is to file a complaint that sets forth the essentials of the claim and make a contemporaneous demand for arbitration with an arbitration provider. When the defendant is the only party that wishes to force the matter into arbitration, the demand for arbitration is set forth in the responsive pleading. In either case, the next step is to seek an order staying the court case pending completion of the arbitration proceedings.

As the right to compel arbitration can be waived by either party, when they engage in acts inconsistent with the right to arbitration (such as proceeding with extensive judicial discovery), the decision on whether to have the matter referred to arbitration should be made early in the proceeding. However, in trade secret cases, the earliest action can involve a request for expedited relief in the form of a temporary restraining order or a preliminary injunction. The case law in the relevant jurisdiction will provide guidance on whether seeking this relief from the court will be deemed an act inconsistent with the right to compel arbitration. If so, the client will have to decide whether to seek such relief from the court and forgo arbitration or wait until the appointment of an arbitrator and seek the same relief from that source. Consider the arbitration provision in the relevant contract, as many provide that an aggrieved party may seek preliminary equitable relief from the court notwithstanding the obligation to arbitrate any disputes arising thereunder.

Because the policy in favor of resolving disputes through arbitration is very strong, a plaintiff stands little chance of avoiding arbitration if the defendant seeks to invoke a contractual arbitration provision. But, where a choice can be made between use of arbitration or standard court proceedings, some of the factors to consider are as follows:

- Will there be difficulties in gathering proof of wrongdoing or of the fact/amount of damages in a form that would be admissible under the stricter evidentiary standards applied in a court proceeding? Where the wrongdoing occurs overseas in jurisdictions that do not support efforts at compelled discovery, or when non-hearsay proof of causation requires testimony from a customer, proceeding with the arbitration is a better choice. Few businesses are eager to ask their customers to testify in these disputes, and fewer customers look forward to the process of a deposition followed by the rigors of cross-examination at trial. In arbitration, witnesses can appear by telephone, or even through declarations. Hearsay evidence is likewise admissible. The fact that hearsay evidence is often accorded lesser weight than non-hearsay evidence is preferable to a situation where no evidence on the point in dispute is admissible.
- Preliminary injunctive relief is quicker and easier to obtain in court, compared to the process of obtaining this relief through the arbitration process. An arbitrator's order has to be brought within the judicial system for purposes of enforcement. The process of moving the court to adopt the arbitrator's order provides the losing party an opportunity to challenge the order, although on fairly limited grounds. The mere pendency of a judicial action, by itself, will also have an impact on the defendant's conduct.
- In the absence of the need to seek expedited relief, such as exists in the extreme case where the trade secrets have already been published, there is little reason to hurry the process. The plaintiff can file in court initially, wait for defendant's counsel to file a responsive pleading, and then decide whether to make a motion to compel/stay (assuming the defendant does not stipulate to arbitration). When the motion to compel/stay is filed, the

plaintiff can contemporaneously file a Demand for Arbitration with the arbitration provider. As a slight variation on the foregoing strategy, the plaintiff could file the Demand for Arbitration immediately and start that process. But the sooner a Demand for Arbitration is filed, the sooner the plaintiff will have to present to the defendant whatever information may exist that pertains to the wrongful conduct and its impact on the plaintiff's business. For example, if the client believes that there is a significant amount in lost profits, such as may result from having to lower prices as a consequence of the defendant's conduct, can this loss be documented (both the fact of the loss and the causation)? Will delaying the process in order to further develop the information assist in that aspect?

- If there is a desire to seek some form of preliminary injunction, a fairly significant evidentiary presentation is required. Making this presentation in court will provide the defendant with a significant insight regarding the plaintiff's position, with respect to the nature of the secrets misappropriated and the complained-of acts of misappropriation, earlier than they would obtain if the matter is in arbitration. There is the risk that a weak presentation on the application for a preliminary injunction will embolden the defendant to fight the claim, and may condition the arbitrator to think that the claim is not very strong.

- A choice is presented to a plaintiff when the defendant engages in efforts to avoid arbitration. When the action is initiated, the plaintiff cannot tell if the defendant will want to avoid arbitration. If the defendant does not want to proceed through arbitration, the plaintiff can "accept" this waiver and head down the road of standard court proceedings. This will be a lengthier and more expensive process, but will provide an opportunity to engage in significantly more discovery.

- When the to-be-filed action involves multiple potential defendants, and only one has an arbitration agreement with the plaintiff, there are a multitude of issues. When arbitration cannot be compelled as to all defendants, the plaintiff must decide whether to pursue all contemporaneously through a court filing and ignore the right to compel arbitration altogether. The plaintiff could stagger the proceeding and first pursue the defendant, who also has the right to seek arbitration. Or the plaintiff could leave that defendant outside the pleadings as an "unindicted co-conspirator." Once the choice is made, the play is with the defendants. They may collectively waive arbitration, seek to compel arbitration solely as between the parties to the agreement (with a request to have the balance of the proceedings stayed as to the remaining defendants), or seek to have the entire matter arbitrated. Sometimes a defendant can compel arbitration when it is not a signatory to the arbitration agreement, such as where its exposure is only derivative.

- The application of res judicata and collateral estoppel can be different when a matter is resolved by arbitration, rather than through judicial proceedings. First, consistent with the concept that arbitration is merely a contractual undertaking unless and until an award is adopted by a court of competent jurisdiction and reduced to a judgment, as a general rule an arbitration award standing alone does not have preclusive effect in a subsequent proceeding involving different parties. Further, because of the different standards applicable in arbitration proceedings and the lack of similar rights to discovery and appeal, third parties are not able to defensively use a judgment based on an arbitration award in the same fashion as a final judgment that follows a court proceeding.

4. Pursuing Misappropriation Claims Before the ITC

The U.S. International Trade Commission (ITC) is an independent, quasi-judicial federal agency with broad investigative responsibilities on matters of trade. In addition to investigations into unfair trade practices that involve the effects of dumped and subsidized imports on domestic industries, the ITC also adjudicates cases involving imports that infringe intellectual property rights. These proceedings are commonly referred to as Section 337 investigations.

Section 337 investigations involve all manner of IP claims. While the matters before the ITC with the highest profile involve allegations of patent or trademark infringement by imported goods, the ITC may also handle claims of misappropriation of trade secrets. But the statutory mandate authorizes the ITC only to address unfair methods of competition/unfair acts in the importation of the articles, and to exclude articles from entry into the United States. A Section 337 investigation will not address conduct that occurs wholly within the United States.

For the ITC to exert its jurisdiction, in the context of a trade secret claim, there is no requirement that any part of the act of misappropriation occur in the United States. Rather, Section 337 is expressly directed at unfair methods of competition and unfair acts in connection with articles imported into the United States. The rationale for extending jurisdiction to a "foreign" act of misappropriation lies in the fact that importation is an inherently international transaction that touches and impacts the United States. The act of misappropriation, even where it occurs wholly outside of the United States, becomes relevant to the ITC when use of the misappropriated trade secrets results in the importation of goods into the United States. In this manner, purely foreign conduct is not being addressed. Rather, the foreign conduct is used only to establish one of the elements of a Section 337 claim—i.e., domestic injury resulting from the improper foreign conduct. By seeking a wholly domestic remedy (exclusion of the imported articles) for this domestic injury, the necessary basis for ITC jurisdiction is thus provided.

The primary remedy available in a Section 337 investigation is the exclusion order. Similar in effect to a court-issued injunction, an exclusion order is a very powerful remedy against a company attempting to import products. The exclusion order directs U.S. Customs to stop infringing imports from entering the United States. In addition, the ITC may issue a cease-and-desist order against named importers and other persons engaged in unfair acts that violate Section 337. These orders can be broad enough to prohibit the sale of infringing products already in the United

States, beginning at a point in time when the ITC's determination becomes effective. Expedited relief, in the form of temporary exclusion orders and temporary cease and desist orders, may also be available in certain exceptional circumstances.

Section 337 investigations, which are conducted pursuant to 19 U.S.C. § 1337 and the Administrative Procedure Act, include trial proceedings before administrative law judges, followed by a review of the ALJ's initial determination by the Commission. There is no right to a jury trial. The process is very quick compared to a standard court proceeding, and its fast-track procedures typically produce an initial determination by the ALJ within 12 to 16 months of initiation of an investigation.

Monetary relief is not available through a Section 337 investigation. The aggrieved party may instead file a parallel court action through which monetary relief is sought. A standard strategy is to file both proceedings contemporaneously, and then stay the court proceedings pending the outcome of the Section 337 Investigation. Once the Section 337 investigation has concluded, the stay over the court proceedings is lifted, and the plaintiff can then seek any monetary relief that may be appropriate.

The ITC, in analyzing the alleged acts of misappropriation, does not automatically apply state trade secret law in the same fashion as would a federal district court sitting in diversity. While the ALJ will typically look to the law of the state in which the complainant resides for guidance, the question of whether particular conduct constitutes "unfair methods of competition" and "unfair acts" in importation, in violation of Section 337, has been described by the Federal Circuit as an issue of federal law to be decided under a uniform federal standard rather than by reference to a particular state's tort law. As there is no federal civil trade secret statute, as a practical matter this means the ITC will look to a combination of the *Restatement of Unfair Competition*, the Uniform Trade Secrets Act, and the federal criminal statute governing theft of trade secrets, which in turn bases its definition of trade secrets on the Uniform Trade Secrets Act.

CHAPTER SEVEN

Protective Orders and Document Preservation Orders

In garden-variety civil cases, there are few occasions where information produced during discovery requires special handling due to confidentiality concerns. Due to this infrequency, the parties to such actions rarely consider adoption of a blanket protective order to govern the manner in which confidential information is handled. By contrast, in trade secret cases both sides begin the process with equally strong concerns over the ability of the adverse party to access substantive discovery responses that contain the producing party's sensitive business information. The plaintiff will not want to make its trade secrets available to people it believes already engaged in acts of misappropriation. The defendant will not want its former employer or business competitor to learn the details of its current operations. Counsel for both parties should meet early in the process of discovery to discuss adoption of protocols for handling sensitive information produced during the pendency of the case and at its termination. This effort will maximize the productive allocation of time and effort to substantive issues by both sides, instead of having counsel tied up in unnecessary procedural distractions.

However, where it appears that critical evidence may be destroyed or concealed absent prompt action, adoption of a protective order that governs how the parties are to handle confidential information is not sufficient protection. Counsel for a trade secret plaintiff must also be ready to immediately take steps, when it appears that evidence may become inaccessible, to obtain an order directing the defendants to affirmatively preserve all relevant information.

1. *Protective Orders*

After being counseled regarding the importance of effectively implementing reasonable measures to protect the secrecy of confidential business information, and having decided that it is necessary to invest substantial sums in a lawsuit over the theft of those trade secrets, the client must now be advised that it is obligated to produce in discovery all documents that refer, relate to, or contain the trade secrets at issue. When the client responds that it is reluctant to voluntarily provide a copy of its most sensitive information to the other side, it is told not to worry, as a special document—called a "protective order"—will completely insulate its trade secrets against any harm that could result from producing the information in discovery. Little wonder clients view the judicial system with skepticism.

Cognizant of the client's concerns, a standard response during the early rounds of trade secret discovery consists of an objection to the production of any substantive information until the court enters a suitable protective order. This objection is focused on the confidential nature of the responsive information, which may include the responding party's own information, or materials in their possession that belong to a third party to whom the responding party has a contractual obligation to maintain confidentiality. By asserting this objection, the responding party protects against unrestricted dissemination of information they consider confidential (as this could result in destruction of its trade secret status). Through this process the responding party creates a significant delay, as it is not obligated (absent rule or court order) to physically produce responsive materials until the terms and conditions of a stipulated protective order have been fully negotiated and entered by the court.

A number of jurisdictions have adopted local rules to short-circuit incipient disputes tied to the absence of a protective order. Where applicable, these rules provide a default form of protection from unauthorized access while a more comprehensive order is being negotiated, and thus forestalls the ability of a responding party to use that excuse to delay production. For example, under Rule 26.2 of the U.S. District Court for the District of Delaware, if any documents are deemed confidential by the producing party and the parties have not stipulated to a confidentiality agreement, until such an agreement is in effect, disclosure shall be limited to members and employees of trial counsel's firm who have entered an appearance. People falling within the scope of the foregoing rule are under an obligation to keep such documents confidential and to use them only for purposes of litigating the case. Similarly, by local rule in the Northern District of California, absent a court order, responding party cannot withhold a discovery production on the basis of a confidentiality objection. Instead, if the parties have not otherwise agreed, the generic form of protective order authorized by the Northern District of California and available on its website automatically governs discovery unless the court enters a different order. A copy of the Northern District form of protective order is included in the appendix.

Neither Delaware District Court Rule 26.2 nor the directive to the default protective order in the Northern District of California addresses all of the issues a trade secret practitioner must face in handling confidential materials. They are designed primarily to truncate disputes over the form of a stipulated protective order that can stall initial productions. There are a number of additional decisions involved in tailoring a protective order to a given case that can significantly impact the value of the protections afforded, as well as the tactical games that can be played by counsel, in the course of the action. Some of the key issues are set forth below.

How many "tiers" is a gating issue for parties to address in drafting a stipulated protective order. Each tier delineates who can review materials designated for protection within that tier. When there is a single tier, information produced during discovery can be designated as "Confidential" in order to limit the risk of public dissemination and preclude any use by the receiving party outside of the action. Under a single-tier system, the parties who can review the materials include litigation counsel and their employees, and generally anyone to whom it is reasonably necessary to disclose the information for the purposes of the litigation. As such, the parties and their employees may also review these designated materials, subject only to the requirement that they agree to be bound to the terms of the protective order (in order to ensure that the court has jurisdiction over those individuals in case of a violation of the protective order) and agree not to use any of the information for any purpose outside of the action. More complicated are multi-tier systems. These most commonly involve a second, but sometimes a third, tier.

In a two-tier system the designating party marks the production with a legend that corresponds to the sensitivity of the information and the scope of persons who can access the information in light of its sensitive content. The first tier in this system is the "Confidential" designation, typically drafted to include information (regardless of how generated, stored, or maintained) and tangible things, the disclosure of which would, in the good-faith judgment of the designating party, be detrimental to the conduct of that party's business. This category can include trade secrets, proprietary business information, or information that is competitively or personally sensitive.

The second tier is a subset of the former, usually bearing the notation "Confidential—Attorney's Eyes Only" or some variation of this phrase to reflect the more restrictive status. Under this more restrictive tier, access is limited to the trial teams and their approved consultants. Neither the adverse parties nor their employees have a right to access. To qualify for this designation, the discovery being produced generally must include extremely sensitive information, such that the disclosure to another party or non-party would create a substantial risk of serious injury to the producing party that could not be avoided by less restrictive means.

Parties do not generally include a significant amount of specificity in describing the types of information that qualify for designation under the second tier. While a discrete list of materials could be included, when a party has a particular item or items in mind when the protective order is being drafted, at the commencement of the action it is difficult to exhaustively list everything that may be requested. Further, that list can serve as a directory for the opposing party in drafting document requests. Most often some form of catch-all category is used. Whether a particular document is appropriately designated is an issue best addressed in a specific challenge to that document. At that point, the burden is on the designating party to articulate to the court a reasonable basis for its decision to restrict access.

Whether the designation is tier one or two, "Confidential" or "Confidential—Attorney's Eyes Only," the persons who can review the materials generally include retained experts (a term usually defined in the protective order, as discussed below), court reporters (who are present at depositions and trial), video operators, and related professional vendors (such as copy services and electronic database services) to whom disclosure is reasonably necessary for the litigation and who have agreed to be bound by the protective order. The parties should consider whether to include, within the concept of "professional vendors," jury consultants and mock juries. For this last group, the parties should be mindful that use of confidential materials during a mock trial exercise has a higher risk of inadvertent dissemination, even when the mock jurors have agreed to be bound by the protective order. This is a group whose individual identities will rarely become known, and there is no opportunity to object to any specific person who may be included on the adverse party's mock jury.

It is customary to expressly state that the officers, managers, and employees of the producing party have the right to review that party's own production without a waiver of confidentiality, as well as "anyone shown to be a sender or recipient of the information." But these two concepts are not coextensive. The first is stated in the present tense, and allows the producing party to police its own decision of who may see what. The latter may involve former employees, even including those who are now accused of engaging in the acts of misappropriation. To avoid arguments over what is meant by the term "shown to be a sender or recipient," as that phrase standing alone could include a "showing" by oral testimony, the phrase should include additional language that reflects a more limited approach, such as: ". . . officers, managers, and employees of the producing party have the right to review that party's own production, as well as anyone shown *on the face of the document* to be a sender or recipient of the information." To further prevent the unauthorized use or disclosure of second-tier designated materials, a further caveat should be included as follows: "Provided, however, that anyone who is entitled to review materials designated as Confidential—Attorney's Eyes Only, because they are shown on the face of the document as a sender or recipient of the information, may only review the document in the office of trial counsel of record, and may not make copies or take any notes of the contents of the document."

In contrast to the officers and employees of the producing party, when the discovery response (and/or documents being produced) bears the designation "Confidential—Attorney's Eyes Only," the officers, directors, managers, and employees of the receiving party cannot access the information, even though they can otherwise view information designated as "Confidential" and are persons to whom disclosure may be reasonably necessary to provide support and advice to counsel in the litigation.

Both sides to the dispute may want to allow their inside counsel access to second-tier information produced by the opposing party in order to provide assistance to their outside legal team. This can be a topic that creates a great deal of discord, due to the perception that in-house counsel are not as independent as outside counsel of record and are at greater risk of disclosing sensitive information to the company issuing their paychecks. But, as they are officers of the court, most courts will allow access by inside counsel to second-tier designated materials when such disclosure is reasonably necessary to the litigation, and as long as these lawyers are not involved in competitive decision-making activities for their client. At a minimum, the protective order should specify the limits on the type of activities that in-house counsel may perform for his or her employer, in order to avoid arguments over the scope of "competitive decision making." The protective order should further confirm that access to second-tier materials terminates once their responsibilities change. The parties should also consider a provision that limits the number of inside lawyers on each side who may have access, lists them by name or title, and requires that any changes or additions be identified in advance, with an opportunity to challenge their designation as an authorized individual.

A third tier of confidentiality is sometimes included where source code, specifications for the design of integrated circuits, or other extremely sensitive information is involved. This tier is focused on a small subset of the materials likely to be produced in any given case. Whether indicated by a "Highly Confidential" designation or some variation on "Confidential—Source Code" or "Confidential—ICD," the description for items falling within this third tier tends to have greater specificity than either of the other two tiers (such as "Information or Items representing computer code and associated comments and revision histories, formulas, engineering specifications, or schematics that define or otherwise describe in detail the algorithms or structure of software [or hardware] designs . . ."). Where this third tier is being considered, the client should be consulted to confirm whether there are persons otherwise entitled to access information designated "Confidential—Attorney's Eyes Only" who should be expressly denied access.

Most courts will decline to grant a receiving party's request, over the objection of the producing party, to allow access to third-tier information, such as source code, by their inside counsel. Inside counsel, in their role of providing litigation advice to the businesspeople and assisting outside counsel, do not require access to highly technical information such as source code. A party seeking access to third-tier information by its inside counsel should be prepared to explain why limiting access to retained experts will interfere with the progress of the litigation and the potential for settlement. To the extent a party insists that inside counsel have this type of access, the designating party should consider alternatively offering access through the use of a stand-alone terminal/CPU located in the office of counsel for the trade secret owner. That level of access, as it is neither connected to a printer nor accessible by a peripheral device (such as a thumb drive), will protect the information without interfering with the ability of counsel for the alleged misappropriator to prepare a defense.

The individuals accused of misappropriation may separately take the position that they should have direct access to second- and third-tier-designated information, at least to the extent it contains that which they are accused of wrongfully appropriating. The theory behind this argument is that the plaintiff has already taken the position that these individuals have had access, at least by reason of their alleged acts of misappropriation, and due process requires they have a right to review the information to prepare a defense. To the extent this argument seems to carry some weight with the court, the practitioner should focus on steps that minimize their access (such as through the use of a stand-alone terminal/CPU, as suggested above) and that limit the potential that they will be able to use, outside of the action, the information that they are now able to review inside of the action.

The default group with access to information designated at every tier is outside trial counsel, typically defined as "the attorneys of record who are not employees of a party, and the members and employees of those law firms to whom it is reasonably necessary to disclose the information for purposes of the litigation." But this definition does not address cooperating law firms (or individual lawyers at such firms), who are asked to assist counsel of record without themselves making an appearance. Can they have access as long as they agree to be bound by the protective order? The definition also does not address what should take place with respect to counsel who were initially "of record," but who were replaced during the pendency of the action by another firm. Do they have to turn over or destroy all designated materials that remain in their possession? What happens to their internal files? Are they still subject to the jurisdiction of the court?

The term "of record" is a term of art that encompasses only those people who have made an appearance. The reason for this definition is simple: once an attorney has made an appearance, the court has the ability to hold him in direct contempt for a violation of the protective order. A careful practitioner will look at this definition carefully to determine whether these issues—which will arise only once the suit is well under way—are worth addressing when the stipulated protective order is being negotiated.

A separate issue with outside counsel exists with respect to the varied duties that counsel may have for the client. In IP cases it is not unusual for a member of the litigation team to also have some involvement in the client's patent prosecution, acquisition, or portfolio development strategy. Prosecution bars prohibit members of a litigation team from also prosecuting patents for the client for a defined period of time. These are requested ostensibly to avoid a patent application being submitted on behalf of the reviewing attorney's client using information learned during the course of reviewing the adverse party's technology. The less frequently conceded purpose is to deprive the adverse litigation team of the use of a member well versed in the technology.

The proponent of a prosecution bar will argue that it is necessary because of ongoing patent prosecution and other competitive activities by the outside attorneys retained by the adversary in the areas being litigated. In particular, the concern is that, based on their nature, those activities could create a significant risk that the technical information will be used, inadvertently or otherwise. In this regard, it is very difficult for a human brain to compartmentalize and selectively suppress information once learned. Further, there are concerns flowing from the view that the separate and independent duty of candor owed by a prosecuting attorney to the USPTO may require disclosure of information learned through a review of designated materials.

Some of the issues to be considered in connection with prosecution bars include who should be within the scope of the bar and its duration. The party at "risk" (typically the trade secret owner) will argue for a broad scope of people, including all members of the firm handling the litigation, but will likely have to settle for a more limited group (members of the litigation team; only members of the litigation team who have access to second- or third-tier-designated materials; or members who also are licensed to appear and who actively are appearing before the USPTO). The bar can also extend to technical experts retained by the litigation team, who would be prohibited from prosecuting patents either on their own behalf or for others for the specified durational period.

The bar provision should specify what is meant by "prosecution." To avoid any uncertainty, it should be stated as including participation in reexaminations and reissues, in addition to the process of directly or indirectly drafting, amending, advising, or otherwise affecting the scope or maintenance of patents and patent applications in the United States, or with respect to any foreign counterparts. The prosecution bar can be subject-matter based, relating to the field of use (a bar from prosecuting patents related to the particular market segment or technology). In lieu of an absolute bar, the provision could impose a limitation on the types of materials that can be reviewed by individuals who fall within one of the classifications (such as a restriction on access to source code or technical documentation). This is more difficult to police and requires greater reliance on others engaging in proper conduct.

Durational issues include a prosecution bar that lasts only through the conclusion of trial and through exhaustion of all appeals, or that continues for a defined period (usually two years) after expiration of the case. The length should correspond to the technology, with a longer bar when the technology has a longer lifespan. With the change from a first-to-invent to a first-to-file system of acquiring patents under the America Invents Act, the client is at greater risk without a lengthy prosecution bar. While the client could always prove its prior conception and diligence in reduction to practice under the first-to-invent system, and even provoke an interference if necessary to acquire patent rights initially issued to another, under the first-to-file system the client will now have to prove that its invention was the basis for the patent application filed by another.

Once there is agreement on who may have access to what tier, the focus of the protective order turns to the manner of handling the materials during the course of the action. The protective order should address the wording and placement of the legends affixed to each document, reflecting the tier of confidentiality selected, so everyone has a clear and uniform understanding of how any particular document should be handled. The confidentiality legends should be unobtrusive, and, while most protective orders state that the legend does not constitute a finding by the court that any particular document contains confidential information, defense counsel in particular should consider the impact that particular terms may have on the jury. Anyone handed a document that conspicuously bears the legend "Highly Confidential" is likely to become conditioned to view its contents in that light. This problem can be addressed through an admonition by the trial court to the jury to the effect that the designations were for purposes of expediting discovery and are not in any way an indication how the jury should view the contents, or by a provision in the protective order to the effect that the legends must be deleted from any documents shown to the jury upon the request of any party.

The parties should address the timing on designations, requiring the notation on written materials before they are produced, and within a limited period after the testimony is given. With respect to testimony, the parties must specify whether there will be a default designation (typically level two) during the agreed period after testimony is given to allow the designating party a reasonable opportunity to review the transcript, with any party being free to use any undesignated testimony thereafter for any purpose. In addition, careful thought should go into whether to require a line-by-line designation or allow a party to simply designate an entire transcript on the basis that confidential material was discussed in the process of the deposition. Here the balance is between efficiency (cost savings) and flexibility. It is expensive to go through a transcript after a deposition to determine which pages and lines should be designated, and then to provide the other parties a written explication. On the other hand, it is cumbersome during a jury trial for the receiving party to use a transcript that contains materials both designated and not designated.

One must also consider whether to provide for the ability to "late designate." In the course of every action, documents are inadvertently produced without a legend, or appear later at a deposition unmarked. If so, the protective order should address the standards pursuant to which a party can avail itself of the right to late designate. With the proliferation of electronic means of data storage, multiple copies of the same information can appear in a variety of locations, and flexibility should be built into the protective order to accommodate this reality.

With respect to documents marked by another party, particular care is needed to address the obligations of the receiving party when they use those documents during the course of the proceedings. What is the obligation of the receiving party if they include a designated document inadvertently in a motion not filed under seal? Do they have a burden to seek an order sealing the motion, and if so, on what time frame? What are the consequences if their attempt is not successful? As far as the world is concerned, once a document is filed in a public record, it no longer retains its status as a trade secret.

Here the question is not whether the document was entitled to protection in the first place; that issue is left to provisions allowing a receiving party to challenge a designation. Absent a timely challenge, all parties must respect the designation and adhere to the requirements that apply to designated documents, regardless of the lack of confidential material contained therein. The party that included the materials in a filing must take immediate steps, upon notification by any other party, to ensure that the materials are either properly filed under seal or otherwise eliminated from the public records. As the party that included the materials in the filing is not protecting its own information, in order to ensure full compliance, adequate penalties should exist in case of a continued failure to comply. At a minimum, the protective order should provide a defined period, after receipt of notification, for the filing party to address the problem. Then, if the problem persists, the designating party can take action and seek reimbursement of any fees and costs incurred in the process.

There is one major limitation on the obligation to file designated materials under seal. Nothing the parties place in a stipulated protective order will trump a court's local rules regarding the filing of confidential information under seal. Even if the court does not strike language in a voluminous proposed protective order that changes the standard for filing under seal, it is merely a matter of time before a clerk in the filing department refuses to file something under seal or brings the issue directly to the judge, in either case teeing up the issue for the court to address directly. In the absence of extremely extenuating circumstances, the court is going to require the parties to follow its existing procedures and apply the standards articulated in the local rules when seeking permission to file materials under seal. This is a function of public policy, in the form of the public's historic right of access to civil court files and records. The unwillingness to permit filing everything under seal also reflects the practical limitation on the courts' ability to manage the volume of sealed materials. This problem is exacerbated by the propensity for counsel to overdesignate. Sealed materials must be maintained separately from other parts of the court files, which in turn creates a number of administrative headaches and staffing challenges.

Sometimes the difficulty with handling designated materials arises with respect to third-party witnesses. The receiving party may want to show a designated document to a third-party witness at a deposition, but that witness refuses to agree to be bound by the protective order (this is not a surprising situation; there is no reason why a third party should agree to be bound to an order issued in an action to which he or she is not a party). The parties can agree to include language in the protective order to the effect that a third-party witness who refuses to be bound by the protective order can be shown the document, but cannot retain a copy or take notes of its contents. The protective order should also specify that counsel for the witness, if not otherwise bound by the protective order, cannot retain a copy of any designated documents unless he or she agrees to be bound thereby. But what happens when the witness is asked, after the deposition ends, to review the transcript for accuracy? To ensure protection of the trade secrets that may be included in designated documents, the protective order can provide that the party noticing the deposition shall make any exhibits available for the witness to review in counsel's office in connection with his or her review of the deposition transcript.

The protective order must have a fair and efficient process for one party to challenge designations. Parties routinely use designations, and in particular tier-two designations, as a tactical device to make it harder for the receiving party to use the materials because of the special handling that is required, both internally at the law firm and when using the materials in court filings. Broad designations also frustrate an attorney's ability to easily consult with clients or interview third-party witnesses. Some parties will designate an entire production as "Confidential—Attorney's Eyes Only," wait for the other party to challenge the designation, and then try to excuse the overdesignation as simply a desire to rapidly make the production to the receiving party. Parties sometimes overdesignate to save the expense of having a person go through each of the documents and decide which level, if any, is appropriate. And, regardless of how frivolous a designation may appear, in the first instance the receiving party must honor the designation. Challenging the designation is a time and money sink. There typically are meet-and-confer obligations, a period to respond, followed by the burden and delay in preparing a motion, and then finally waiting for the court to rule thereon.

In negotiating the challenge provision, the parties must consider whether to provide a specific period after production in which a challenge must be made. Alternatively, they can provide language to the effect that, unless a prompt challenge to a confidentiality designation is necessary to avoid foreseeable and substantial unfairness, unnecessary economic burdens, or a significant disruption or delay of the litigation, a party may challenge a designation at any time. The former route has the benefit of clarity, but can be an unnecessary trap in fast-paced litigation. If the latter route is selected, additional language should be included to make clear that a party does not waive its right to challenge a confidentiality designation by electing not to mount a challenge promptly after the original designation is disclosed.

The burdens involved in challenging should reflect an allocation to the party who benefits most from the designation, and who is in the better position to provide a basis for the court to make its determination. A party who is making the challenge should be required to articulate the basis for the challenge by specifying the particular items and describing the attempts to meet and confer. The burden of persuasion then shifts to the party who made the designation. That party must substantiate its tier selection, as it is the party most familiar with the reason for the particular tier and the alleged harm that may occur should the protections be removed. Typically, if the parties cannot agree on the proper designation after meeting and conferring, the party seeking de-designation is the one required to make a motion to challenge the original designation.

To avoid a situation where the designating party refuses to meet and confer in good faith, but instead forces the receiving party to expend time and effort in making the motion, the designating party should be required to respond in writing in a specified period of time. Arguments in favor of the designation will be limited to those provided during the meet and confer. Time periods in which to make a challenge and in which to respond in order to maintain the designation should reflect a realistic period for the parties to operate, given the speed in which the particular jurisdiction handles the case (in a rocket docket, the time periods may be compressed). To ensure that the issue is brought to rapid conclusion, the protective order should provide that the failure of the designating party to respond to a challenge within the specified time frame constitutes a waiver of the designation. However, the party challenging the designation should also be allowed (after satisfying the obligation to meet and confer) to make a motion at any time. To avoid situations where one party routinely overdesignates in order to place additional administrative burdens on the receiving party, or the receiving party challenges every designation in the hope that an untimely response deprives the designating party of the protections of the protective order, the protective order can direct the court to assess a monetary sanction in an amount equivalent to the fees incurred by the party prevailing in the challenge (to the challenger, if the designation is revoked; to the designating party, if the challenge is denied).

In addition to challenges to the designation of materials, disclosures and challenges to experts is an area in the protective order where problems exist. Professional experts pose the problem of cross-contamination, given the breadth of their relationships with other law firms, and as they are often asked questions regarding their current work in the course of the next assignment. Industry-based experts can be a problem, as they may be working for a competitor, or move to a competitor shortly after the assignment terminates.

In addressing access by retained experts, two general alternatives exist. Most protective orders provide that a party's outside experts, once duly approved, will have access to all materials designated under the protective order. Under this "once approved, full access" approach, the focus is on the expert's background and professional relationships. The party seeking to use the expert bears the obligation to disclose and obtain approval at an initial stage of the process. Alternatively, the parties can proceed item by item, with the party seeking to disclose designated information to its retained expert required to first make a written request that identifies the categories of information to be provided to the expert. Once again, the disclosure must set forth the same "identifying criteria" described below. Under either approach, the processes for challenging disclosures and resolving such challenges are similar to the mechanism for challenging designation of materials, with the party seeking to prohibit access by the expert bearing the burden of making the motion and substantiating the challenge.

The benefit of allowing an expert full access, once disclosed to the other party, is the freedom of the retaining party and expert to fully interact without the delays inherent in having to constantly obtain approval before submitting additional information for consideration. The benefit of the alternative approach lies in the ability to control, when the information in question is extremely sensitive, exactly what is being provided to an otherwise independent third party. Most attorneys dislike the alternative (item by item) approach, as they do not want to disclose to the adverse party, prior to the submission of expert reports (or expert depositions), what the expert is being provided as part of his assignment.

Under either approach, an important part of procedure involves what the retaining party must disclose concerning the expert, the grounds for challenging the expert's access to designated materials, and the timing of the challenge. With respect to the contents of the disclosure, and the question of whether the expert's ability to see designated materials can be challenged successfully, the focus is on the identification of disqualifying criteria in the form of other consultancies, business endeavors, or relationships that can compromise the confidentiality of the information. Here the plaintiff has the advantage, as it should already have identified and retained appropriate experts in the subject matter of the trade secrets well prior to initiating suit. Then, when negotiating disqualifying criteria, the plaintiff can manage the language to exclude its expert from the scope of the criteria, but otherwise include as many other areas as possible.

There is a distinction between what constitutes disqualifying criteria for access, and whether the expert either is sufficiently qualified in the subject matter to express an opinion or has the ability to survive a *Daubert/Frye* challenge in light of the basis for the opinions to be rendered. The inquiry, when the question is the right to access, addresses the potential risk of harm to the designating party should its confidential information be placed in the hands of a person who might use that information outside of the litigation. A challenge to the ability to testify does not consider protection of the information and is not an appropriate basis for a challenge to access under the protective order. Cautious counsel can, however, include language in the protective order confirming that the failure to object to access by a retained expert shall not constitute a waiver to any challenge to admissibility of that expert's testimony.

A successful challenge does not mean that the party retaining the expert cannot continue to use her services. There are many situations where an expert may still provide value without seeing any material designated by the opposing party. For example, the trade secret owner may wish to use an industry expert to opine that the information in question constitutes a trade secret, even if a different expert may be required to opine whether the defendant is in possession of those trade secrets. The party may also want to designate one or more of its own employees as a testifying expert, knowing that it is extremely unlikely they will be able to see any items designated by the other party under the protective order.

Required disclosures for experts before they can access designated information can include:

- A complete list of matters for which the expert is currently being retained;
- An identification of all matters for which they were retained during the previous five years;
- An identification of all cases in a specified period of time (usually the prior five years) for which they provided an expert report, testified in a deposition, or participated at trial;
- A confirmation that the expert will not consult for a list of competitors for a specified period of time;
- A list of duties, obligations, or relationships to or with any business group or association, whether or not currently adverse to the client or the position being taken in the litigation;

- A statement of the extent to which the expert is involved in his own business endeavors where he could make personal use of the designated materials, along with an identification of those endeavors; or
- The extent to which the expert receives compensation or funding from any third parties, and the basis for the compensation/ funding.

Experts are very reluctant to provide information regarding their current consultancies, and their other assignments may be highly sensitive (such as where they are assisting an unidentified client who is determining whether a suit should be filed against an unsuspecting third party). However, the requirement of detailed disclosures creates additional value to the opposing party by providing insights into the work of the expert, which may lead to possible sources for impeachment. One way to resolve any concern over this aspect of a mandatory disclosure is to allow designation of that portion of the information under the protective order, so the proposed expert can be assured that this information will not be available to anyone other than counsel for the opposing party.

Even where the proposed expert does not have any disqualifying relationships, consider whether the protective order should impose a bar against the expert working in a specified or related area for a defined period after termination of the action. Alternatively, the limitation can focus on a restriction on working for, or on behalf of, a specified person or entity. These restrictions help ensure that the integrity of the designated information is not compromised and avoids the need to monitor the expert's post-litigation activities.

Counsel must also consider how to handle the designated materials at the end of the action, typically defined as a final termination of all proceedings, whether by dismissal or otherwise, along with the expiration of all rights to appeal. If the plaintiff is successful at trial, these steps can avoid the "loose end" of having a copy of the trade secrets remain in the hands of an adverse party's representative or agent. Whether the requirement is to return or destroy, with a certification of having done so, attention should be paid to the ability of the adverse counsel to retain his or her "file copy" or "working papers." This could involve a complete set of everything produced or just what was attached to pleadings and discovery. The client, however, may be under the impression that everything it produced will be returned or destroyed at the end of the action. The time to address the issue is during the drafting of the protective order, for it will be difficult to gain traction with opposing counsel after the action is over.

2. Preservation Orders

At the initiation of a trade secrets case, circumstances often suggest that any delay in securing discovery will result in the disappearance of evidence of misappropriation. Sophisticated and unsophisticated defendants alike understand the need to cover their tracks, and computers suddenly fail to operate. Files are "accidentally" deleted. Notebooks disappear. Even apart from premeditated acts designed to destroy incriminating evidence, in the normal course of IT operations computers can be reimaged or repurposed, backup tapes can be overwritten as a result of a standard tape-rotation policy, and routine document maintenance protocols may result in hard-copy items being discarded. Trying to later determine what has been "lost" is a huge distraction and a nearly impossible task.

The initial evidentiary problem facing trade secret plaintiffs exists by reason of the fact that, whether in state or federal court, they are not entitled as of right to immediately commence discovery. In many state court jurisdictions, a specified period must elapse after service of the complaint before the plaintiff can serve discovery. The defendants will then have an extended time before they will have to respond or make a physical production. In federal district court, the delay can also be substantial. Federal Rule of Civil Procedure 26(d) provides generally that a party may not seek discovery from any source before the parties have conferred on the topics outlined in Rule 26(f). Since the Rule 26(f) conference need not take place until at least 21 days before the scheduling conference, significant time will pass between service of the complaint and the first response to a request for production. A preservation order obtained at the initiation of the case, directing the defendants to take affirmative steps to secure potential evidence from loss or destruction, is the surest way to preserve the evidentiary status quo until standard discovery can commence.

Preservation orders, sometimes referred to as "turnover" orders when they also direct one party to provide immediate access to the information, are a form of injunctive relief. At the request of one party, the trial court is issuing a prohibitory injunction against the other party to prevent the potential destruction of evidence. While they are most often sought at the commencement of the action, this type of injunction is not limited to a particular point in time. Preservation orders may be granted at any juncture during the litigation when it appears that a party is doing, threatening to do, or is about to do an act "in violation of the rights of another party to the action respecting the subject of the action, and tending to render the judgment ineffectual." *See* California Code of Civil Procedure § 526, subd. (a)(3).

When sought ex parte contemporaneously with the filing of the complaint, an application for a preservation order can serve both a strategic and tactical function. In addition to the ostensible strategic purpose of the request—preservation of the evidence that is the subject of the order—rapid action places immediate and significant additional pressure on the defendants. The plaintiff is able to use the application as an opportunity to get before a judicial audience very early in the life of the lawsuit in order to begin the process of pre-conditioning the audience to the theme of the case, without having to make the more complicated factual showing necessary to obtain a temporary restraining order regarding use of the underlying trade secrets. All the concerns the plaintiff has regarding the alleged misconduct by the defendants can be laid out for the court, as well as the problems that give rise to the need for an order to preserve evidence. Even if the defendants have the time and ability to respond to the substantive charges, that rejoinder will have little impact on the relief being requested. The merits are not being litigated. Once issued, the preservation order then forces the defendants to immediately allocate their time and resources to taking proactive steps to preserve the specified evidence before they have analyzed the merits of the allegations in the complaint.

In making the request, the plaintiff should provide as much detail as possible regarding the nature of the evidence to be preserved, with respect to both its substance and the medium in which it may be contained. This will allow the drafting of an order with precision. The application should include as much substantiation as possible for the stated concern that delay will result in disappearance. Any evidence of surreptitiousness by the defendants in taking the information in the first place, or to hide those acts, should be detailed, as it will illustrate why it is reasonable to conclude that they will also take steps to destroy evidence of their actions.

Defendants may argue that the request is at best premature, that there is no evidence that they will fail to comply with the discovery vehicles available in every civil case, and that any failure to do so can be adequately addressed by the variety of sanctions available for any misuse of the discovery statutes. But preservation orders are designed to stop spoliation before it occurs, whether by inadvertence or willfully. After-the-fact issuance of monetary sanctions rarely constitutes an adequate remedy for the failure of a defendant to preserve evidence, and in many states, including California, there is no separate tort cause of action for intentional spoliation of evidence. Evidentiary sanctions precluding the introduction of evidence when spoliation has occurred generally issue only upon a showing of some form of willfulness. This level of sanction in a trade secret case can actually benefit the defendant, who does not intend to offer any of the evidence that now has become unavailable. Terminating sanctions require a significant record of noncompliance before a court can be convinced to issue that draconian level of relief. Even then, the plaintiff faces the risk that the judgment will be limited, as the full extent of wrongdoing is rarely known when the complaint is filed.

At its core, like any other type of preliminary injunction, the purpose of a preservation order is to preserve the status quo pending a determination on the merits of the claim. As with any request for injunctive relief, the plaintiff must frame its factual showing in the context traditionally considered by the courts in determining whether to issue a preliminary injunction: (1) how likely it is that the moving party will prevail on the merits, and (2) the relative harm the parties will suffer in the interim due to the issuance or non-issuance of the injunction. Here the right to conduct discovery regarding the specified evidence constitutes the "merits," and its continued availability the "status quo" that would be changed absent some form of judicial assistance.

In seeking a preservation order, it is not necessary to establish a probability of success on the question of whether misappropriation occurred, or even if the defendants are purposefully destroying potential evidence, although such evidence will suitably instruct the court in favor of granting the requested relief. The focus of any application for a preservation order is the evidence itself and its continued availability during the course of the proceedings. The plaintiff must only establish that the right to discovery will be impeded by events or conduct that will result in the destruction of potentially discoverable evidence.

Using computer-sourced media as an example, the first factor concerns whether there may be evidence in the defendant's computers and other electronic storage media, relevant to the dispute, that the plaintiff should be able to obtain through discovery:

- Were the trade secrets maintained by the plaintiff in a database to which the defendants had access?
- Can the plaintiff present a record that shows copying of the electronic documents during defendant's employment, in a volume inconsistent with normal duties, during time periods that were outside of normal work periods, or exceptionally close in time to the end of the employment relationship?
- Is there any evidence that the defendant forwarded emails containing confidential data, whether technical or customer information, price lists, or market reports, to a personal email address?

- Does the network reflect access in ways inconsistent with historical patterns, normal job responsibilities, or copying of computer files onto portable drives or other peripheral devices before separation from employment?
- Are there concrete reasons to believe that the computers now operated by the defendant contain other evidence that will bear on resolution of the trade secret causes of action, such as source code development records in a control version system where the issue is whether the defendant used the trade secrets in developing competing software?
- If a significant customer account suddenly transferred its business to the defendant, will the email servers provide evidence of the interactions that preceded the transfer?

On the second factor, the balance of harm, once the first factor is established the plaintiff has shown that it could irretrievably lose identified evidence that otherwise would have been relevant to the case if the preservation order does not issue. In this circumstance the record should also show that the harm to the defendant would be negligible. The media could be copied or a forensic image of the hard drives made, in the presence of the defendant, and after working hours so as to not interrupt the ability to conduct business. No damage to or loss of information would result from the copying. The copied material would be secured in an agreed location, but otherwise unavailable to anyone except upon agreement of the parties or upon an order of the court. Thus, concerns over privacy and privilege can be minimized to the point of nonexistence. Further, the plaintiff can offer to bear the reasonable cost to copy the materials, subject to reallocation by the trial court, and any access by the plaintiff can be deferred until the defendant has an opportunity to review the copied files for irrelevant or privileged documents. Under these circumstances, the trial court is unlikely to determine that the defendant would suffer greater harm should the injunction issue than the plaintiff would suffer if it does not.

To assist the court in producing an order that can be readily enforced in case of a later dispute over compliance with the obligation to preserve, the plaintiff should provide as much detail as possible regarding what it wants preserved, and the specific steps that the defendant should take to comply. For example, back-up tapes are routinely overwritten on a periodic basis that can be as frequent as daily or weekly. The defendant should be instructed to terminate any rotation or overwriting of back-up tapes. Document preservation protocols, a euphemism for document destruction policies that call for the periodic culling of documents, should be halted. Computers should be inventoried, secured, and made available for extraction of data. A process for inspection by a computer forensics specialist should be identified as part of the process of preservation, specifically authorizing this expert to make copies of available data off all computers and computer media in order to preserve evidence of any stolen or potentially relevant information.

In view of the ability to transfer data to highly mobile devices, including USB storage devices and external hard drives, it is highly likely defendants will be able to conceal stolen computer files unless the plaintiff specifically asks the court to extend the preservation order to a wide range of mobile devices in addition to the defendant's desktops and servers. However, the client should be advised that the cost of compliance with a preservation order when electronic forms of potential evidence are involved can be substantial, as there are personal hard drives, back-up tapes and media, and servers to consider. These expenses include the costs of hosting the recovered data as well as the fees for forensic experts, who will study the entire drive, including unallocated spaces, for the existence of documents or their destruction.

CHAPTER EIGHT

TROs, Preliminary Injunctive Relief, and Expedited Discovery

The trade secret plaintiff often seeks a temporary restraining order (TRO) contemporaneously with initiation of the action. But a TRO has limited effect. By statute, after the TRO is granted, the parties must return for a further hearing to determine whether a preliminary injunction should issue. Throughout this process, the plaintiff is focused on barring any use or further dissemination of the trade secrets pending a trial on the merits.

Why would a plaintiff seek, or refrain from seeking, a TRO/preliminary injunction? If successful, the plaintiff gains an immediate advantage. The likelihood of success on the merits at trial has been established. The resulting leverage can drive an immediate settlement. But what is the impact on the broader case if extraordinary relief is not granted? The prospect for settlement recedes. The defendant can continue to use or disclose the information during the pendency of the action without the prospect of being held in contempt. The "only" risk remaining is the potential for civil liability, months or years in the future, in the form of a monetary judgment and the potential for some form of permanent injunction. But in evaluating whether to seek this relief, the plaintiff must also consider the court's reaction. Impressions of the case may still be shaped in ways that can harden into a bias in favor of one side, subtly impacting everything from case management decisions to substantive rulings. Further, while a plaintiff is not required to seek this form of relief in order to later obtain a monetary award at trial, the failure to seek immediate injunctive relief can affect the contours of a permanent injunction.

When the strategy of seeking a TRO/preliminary injunction is implemented, a substantial amount of activity must take place before the suit is filed. In addition to the averments in the complaint, additional legal analysis is necessary to support the request. Detailed factual declarations must provide an identification of the trade secrets, address the plaintiff's ownership, and delineate the reasonable measures taken to maintain secrecy. The method of acquisition by the defendant must be described to establish improper possession. Finally, the court must be persuaded that the risk to the trade secrets/harm to the plaintiff if injunctive relief is not granted is substantial. Given the detailed showing required and the practical limits on the relief that the court may order, not every trade secret case is appropriate for this strategy.

1. The TRO

The goal of a temporary restraining order is preservation of the status quo until further consideration of the record during the hearing on an application for a preliminary injunction. The preliminary injunction, if granted, then lasts until dissolved, either on motion of the defendant or upon the conclusion of the trial on the merits. At that point, the substance of the preliminary injunction, if "continued," is encompassed by the terms of a permanent injunction. But the breadth and scope of the permanent injunction is not simply a reflection of the terms of the preliminary injunction. Rather, at that point the court takes into account factors not ripe for consideration at the preliminary injunction stage, from the factual findings that support the verdict to the potential for an alternative award of future royalties.

Defining the "status quo" for purposes of the TRO/preliminary injunction, in the context of a trade secret dispute, considers the nature of the information. This analysis, in turn, evaluates whether the value of the information, by reason of its secrecy, is transitory or has lasting duration. Thus, if the secret nature of the information has been negated because it already has been made public, then the "status quo" is not protected by an order prohibiting further use by the defendant. If the information remains secret but the record does not suggest that the defendant's manner of use creates a risk of further disclosure, such as where the information has been incorporated into the defendant's source code, the injunction may be limited to a prohibition against further dissemination. Alternatively, if the conduct of the defendant suggests continuing danger to the secrecy of the information merely by reason of the use thereof, such as where manufacturing specifications are being shared or transferred between entities, a prohibition on use as well as dissemination is appropriate.

There are pressure point differences between applications for a TRO and a preliminary injunction. An application for a TRO is presented to the court with minimal notice to the defendant. They are reserved for use in true emergencies (such as the imminent publication of materials identified as constituting the trade secrets), such that the potential damage from any significant delay will be extensive and likely irreparable. If a TRO is granted, the plaintiff has immediately obtained significant leverage over the defendant. But, while both procedures consider the likelihood of success on the merits, denial of an application for a TRO does not mean the court will refuse to issue a preliminary injunction. Rather, this declination often reflects the view of the trial court that a delay of a few weeks, to provide the defendant an opportunity to present a full response, will not cause the plaintiff significant injury but will allow a fuller and fairer consideration by the court of all sides to the dispute.

By contrast to the fairly minimal impact that flows for the denial of a request for a TRO, the plaintiff will likely feel significantly deflated should the court decline to issue a preliminary injunction. But before the defendant takes too much comfort from that result, careful attention should be paid to the reason for the declination. As noted below, the court will often deny an application for a preliminary injunction even when it believes that the plaintiff has demonstrated a likelihood of success on the merits, because the prejudice to the defendant should the injunction issue far outweighs the prejudice to the plaintiff should it not receive injunctive relief pending trial.

A key focus when seeking a TRO is the breadth of the order requested. Crafting the language of the proposed restraining order in a manner that goes only far enough to preserve the status of the information as a trade secret increases the likelihood of prevailing at this stage. A TRO that provides that the defendant "shall not publish, transfer, or disclose the [described information] to any third party" does not, by itself, interfere with the ability of the defendant to operate its business. As such, in this situation the defendant suffers little prejudice flowing from existence of the injunction. The mere fact that the defendant is now subject to an injunction is not, by itself, the type of prejudice that should adversely impact the likelihood of relief. If the plaintiff broadly markets the order to common customers for the purpose of gaining a commercial advantage unrelated to the nature of the action, there are avenues for the defendant to seek recourse. Since this conduct is arguably outside of any litigation privilege, in addition to the right to seek sanctions within the proceedings, the potential exists for an independent action based on abuse of process or unfair competition.

For the plaintiff, a limited "shall not publish" TRO minimizes the risk of harm to the secret nature of the information. Any continuing harm to the profits being generated by the owner's business that flows from the defendant's use can be compensated monetarily. Further, when "use" is not prohibited, there is little likelihood that the defendant's business will suffer an adverse impact from the fact of the injunction. As such, the amount that the plaintiff must post as an injunction bond, to secure against any harm to the defendant should the TRO have been improperly granted, is reduced.

A TRO that directs the defendant to engage in an affirmative act is more difficult to obtain. This type of order constitutes a mandatory, versus prohibitory, injunction. The court will not as readily grant an order that requires the defendant to immediately "return" or destroy various categories of information merely because the plaintiff has identified them as constituting its trade secrets. However, a narrower description that refers to materials such as Documents or other tangible things created while [Defendant] was an employee of Plaintiff" has a greater chance of being acceptable to the court. There rarely is a dispute over ownership of materials created by an individual during the course of his or her prior employment, even where the question of its status as a trade secret is hotly contested.

A TRO is returnable after a short period—typically within two weeks, unless the defendant consents to a further extension. Often granted upon an ex parte application, the TRO directs the defendant to return to the court and show cause why a preliminary injunction should not issue. The short duration of the initial period is designed to protect the defendant in case the TRO was improperly granted. But the defendant may agree to the further extension in order to conduct its own investigation. This investigation may include engaging in some preliminary discovery in order to present a comprehensive opposition to the application for a preliminary injunction. In considering how best to respond when the matter returns for the preliminary injunction hearing, the defendant should not be sanguine simply because the language of the TRO will not adversely impact its business, even if it is later converted into a preliminary injunction. It is not unusual for a court to grant a TRO that provides a scope of relief narrower than will be considered when the matter returns in the hearing whether to issue a preliminary injunction.

At the hearing on the application for the preliminary injunction, whether or not extended beyond the statutory return date, the court will proceed on the basis that the defendant now has had a sufficient opportunity to marshal its response. Compared to the time available to a court when considering a TRO presented on an ex parte basis, at this point the court also will have had sufficient time to fully consider the matter. The difference is one of urgency. Only relief that is truly urgent should issue as a TRO. If the situation does not present true urgency, either due to the passage of time since discovery of the misappropriation or because there is not a high likelihood that secrecy will be lost before the preliminary injunction application can be heard, the plaintiff should bypass the TRO process.

2. *The Preliminary Injunction*

Preliminary injunctions are psychological turning points. As an early indicator of the potential for success on the merits at trial, a great deal of effort goes into preparing these applications and oppositions. While the court is more likely to enjoin use than when it grants a TRO, a request for narrower relief further increases the plaintiff's prospect of success. This is a reflection of the plaintiff's obligation to establish, in addition to probability of success on the merits at trial, that it would suffer more prejudice if the motion is denied than the defendant would suffer if the motion is granted. When the proposed preliminary injunction will have the practical effect of shutting down all (or even a substantial portion) of the defendant's business, the court is more likely to deny the motion on grounds completely divorced from the merits. But even here the plaintiff can gain immeasurably merely from the process of seeking this form of relief.

While almost always taking place at the beginning of a case, applications for preliminary injunctions typically are heard on the same timeline as a regularly scheduled noticed motion. Briefing occurs without impact on progression of the broader case. Sometimes, due to the court's schedule, a hearing date may not be available for a substantial period after the motion is filed. When there is greater urgency to hear the matter (but not so great as to justify seeking a TRO), an application can be made to the court to shorten the notice time lines and briefing schedules, or to set a special hearing date.

At the point when the application is made, little, if any, substantive discovery has been conducted. In jurisdictions such as California, attempts by the plaintiff at early discovery can be mired down in battles over whether the trade secrets have been adequately identified. Until this has been done, the well-represented defendant will maintain that there is no obligation to provide any substantive responses to discovery. But the defendant does not have a similar right to demand a detailed description of the trade secrets before having to respond to an application for a preliminary injunction. Instead, while the lack of detail in the trade secret description can be raised by the defendant as a basis for the court to deny the application, a detailed substantive response to the merits must also be presented to maximize the chances of defeating the application. In so doing, the defendant will have to take positions, supported by affidavits or declarations, that serve to set its factual story in concrete for the rest of the case. Regardless of the outcome of the application, the defendant's presentation will provide the plaintiff a significant benefit in the form of statements that have frozen key aspects of the defendant's narrative. If the question is one involving theft of source code, the plaintiff will receive an explication by the defendant of its independent efforts to develop the code. A similarly substantive form of declarative statements would be difficult to obtain through normal discovery, as discovery responses tend to be replete with objections (if the information is sought by way of interrogatories) or obfuscation (if answers are sought by way of a deposition). Attempts by the defendant to later provide alternative explanations after engaging in substantive discovery must address the substance of these earlier statements. This process creates the risk of inconsistencies, which can be utilized by the plaintiff to later discredit the defense.

While the plaintiff is not mandated to provide a detailed description of the trade secrets in the papers filed in support of the application, this is an area where a conservative court may have difficulty. Courts are not heavily swayed by mere recitals in an agreement that describes categories of information as constituting a trade secret. The issue of whether information constitutes a trade secret is a question of fact. The language of a provision in an agreement, which describes information as constituting trade secrets or confidential information, is neither a recitation of fact nor conclusively establishes that the information fits the description. Likewise, courts are not bound by precatory language regarding the need for an injunction (such as "the parties hereto agree that any breach of the provisions of this agreement would cause Employer irreparable harm, not compensable in monetary damages").

There is a distinction between a conclusive presumption of truth that flows from facts recited in a written agreement between the parties and a recital of consideration that can be later challenged by one of the parties at trial. The prospect of future harm falls within a construction of the contract that adopts the latter. Likewise, while the trial court can enforce an agreement that contains a stipulation to the nature or amount of the monetary remedy, equitable remedies usually remain unavailable where the remedy at law is adequate, as where damages are quantifiable.

The parties should keep in mind bonding issues that arise in a trade secret case, in the context of both a TRO and a preliminary injunction. A bond, whether in federal or state court, is designed to provide protection to the party being enjoined in case the injunction should not have been issued. The obligation to post a bond achieves this result by providing the wrongfully enjoined party a ready source of funds without the need for the defendant to resort to an independent, and subsequent, collection action. The bond requirement thus discourages plaintiffs from seeking an injunction to which they are not entitled.

The first part of the bond analysis considers whether the jurisdiction follows the bonding requirements of the federal district courts. In federal district court, no party may be granted a TRO, or a preliminary injunction, without first posting security to pay both the costs and the damages sustained by any party found to have been wrongfully enjoined. While the amount of the bond is discretionary, the failure to require a bond upon the issuance of injunctive relief is considered reversible error. In some state courts, by comparison, there is no requirement of a bond upon the issuance of a TRO. Further, the bond requirement can be waived or forfeited in some jurisdictions, such as where the party to be enjoined does not address the bonding requirement at the hearing on the injunction. The defendant must always take steps, early and often, to demonstrate the impact that the injunction will have on its operations. The same evidence that will be considered by the court when balancing the hardships to the parties may be presented in support of a request for a substantial bond.

The "harm" to be secured by the bond in federal district court is limited to those damages actually and proximately resulting from the effect of the injunction, as opposed to litigation expenses independent of the injunction. Most important to the party to be enjoined, the right to recovery in federal district court is limited to the amount of the bond. The defendant, therefore, must present to the court, at the hearing on the application for injunctive relief, sufficient evidence of the harm that will likely flow from the wrongful issuance of the injunction in order to obtain adequate compensation thereafter. By comparison, in several state jurisdictions, while a bond (or cash deposit in lieu) is also required before an injunction issues to cover any damages caused by its issuance, the bond amount is not a limit on the amount the defendant can recover.

In either case, in deciding whether to pursue a TRO or preliminary injunction strategy, the plaintiff must consider whether it can obtain a bond (or provide the cash security in lieu) if the injunction issues. If the injunction will have a devastating impact on the business of the defendant, then the bond requirement can be very substantial, and bonding companies typically require a liquid or cash-equivalent security. While a court will generally provide a brief period for the party who obtained the injunction to acquire the injunction bond, a bonding source should be located if possible prior to presenting the application, as there can often be substantial delays in obtaining the bond when the amount is significant. Likewise, the defendant should pay almost as much attention to this issue as it does to the merits of whether an injunction should issue. How will the injunction, as proposed, impact the business? If the amount can be quantified and is significant, will providing that evidence in order to force a large bond also provide the plaintiff with insight into the impact of the injunction, and extra leverage in the case of settlement discussions?

Finally, there is an unfortunate tendency for the prevailing party to market the order granting injunctive relief. A press release is usually issued describing the scope of the injunction. But more personalized transmission to interested third parties also occurs. Ostensibly, the purpose of marketing is to ensure compliance by the defendant, as well as everyone else who is doing business with the defendant. On that basis, any marketing should fall within the litigation privilege. But sales teams will see the order as a means of casting doubt on the ability of the defendant to perform, even in areas unrelated to the trade secrets in issue. Here is where potential liability creeps into the picture. Should the court later be asked to determine whether the injunction was improvidently granted or that a motion to terminate the injunction was resisted in bad faith, evidence of the use of the injunction to further the goals of the sales and marketing departments can be considered. At a minimum, nothing of an editorializing nature should be physically provided to the public. By contrast, no liability attaches to dissemination of a copy of the actual order, which is a truthful public document.

3. *Expedited Discovery*

A request for expedited discovery often accompanies an application for a TRO. In similar fashion, the focus for the court on this type of request is whether a substantial question about the defendant's conduct has been raised sufficient to justify some form of extraordinary relief. Here, however, the "relief" is from the normal response time incident to discovery requests. As such, the level of proof necessary to justify this relief is substantially lower than is required to obtain a TRO.

The evidence presented in support of the application for expedited discovery is still evaluated in light of the potential that the defendant actually used plaintiff's strategies or techniques, or obtained proprietary information in a manner inconsistent with normal or permitted forms of access. Issuance of a TRO is not a predicate for an order granting expedited discovery, and it is not necessary for the plaintiff to establish a probability of success on the merits of the action. Sometimes, the concerns that will justify an order granting expedited discovery may be as tenuous as evasive responses at an exit interview that caused serious concern over the post-employment conduct of the defendant. The ultimate focus, however, is whether there is a particularized need sufficient to justify modifying existing discovery schedules.

Notwithstanding the rule in most jurisdictions that restricts propounding discovery on the defendant for a brief period of time after service of the complaint, this form of relief authorizes the plaintiff to immediately serve discovery. The application can go further and request truncation of the time for the responding party to provide substantive responses or to produce responsive documents. It can be coupled with a request, which takes the form of a "discovery preliminary injunction," to require affirmative acts that will preserve electronic evidence. In this form, the defendant can be directed to retain, or be prohibited from destroying, deleting, or secreting from discovery, any electronic storage media. The order can direct the defendant to allow copying of the electronic media by a court-appointed or -approved expert. Here the expert should be permitted access to computer and external hard drives, to recover lost or deleted files, and to perform automated searches for evidence under guidelines agreed to by the parties or established by the court.

The plaintiff will want to obtain information as quickly as possible regarding aspects of the defendant's business that pose a risk to the trade secret status of the information. Is the defendant using the information in a manner that may disclose it to third persons through external publication? Is the defendant contemplating a business transaction, whether a sale of its business or a joint venture with another business, that would result in a third party gaining access through use? In seeking this information, counsel must direct the plaintiff (or the defendant) to avoid any appearance of "self-help" discovery that violates another's ownership or privacy interests. Searching through garbage bins outside a business, for example, may provide interesting evidence but will be accompanied by a host of legal problems. An argument that self-help was necessary because the information might disappear before judicial assistance could be obtained will be seen as an unjustified intrusion on the jurisdiction of the courts to administer the orderly resolution of disputes. A party who converts, interdicts, or otherwise appropriates documents in the pursuit of litigation, outside the legal process, acts without the general protection of the litigation privilege or other protections afforded by the laws of discovery. Rather than further its case, the litigant now risks being found to have violated the protected rights of the adverse party.

As an order expediting discovery takes the matter out of the normal procedures, the court must be convinced that good cause exists. The time to propound, and the period in which to respond, reflects a considered balance between, on the one hand, the need to compile facts and to learn an adverse party's contentions, and the importance of moving matters forward in a manner that allows for an adjudication of disputes on the merits. On the other hand, the court must consider the burden that expedited discovery can have on the parties. A party that seeks broad discovery relating to all of the issues in the case will not have a sympathetic audience in the court. The subject of the request for expediting discovery in a trade secret case should focus on information needed to prepare for matters that may, or will, be brought shortly to the attention of the court for determination.

The plaintiff should focus on securing evidence that delineates the extent of the trade secrets acquired. In support of an application for expedited discovery, the plaintiff should present grounds to conclude that good cause exists because of the potential either that the information will disappear (for example, ISPs typically retain user activity logs for only a limited period of time before erasing data) or that harm that could occur in the near future if the defendant is allowed to use the information in question (for example, where the threatened use will result in loss of the secrecy of the information). Expediting the time in which one defendant must respond is also likely where the discovery is focused on obtaining identifying information that makes it possible to name and serve other defendants. Here, the intent is to include all parties in the same proceeding. In all of these situations, however, the support for expedited discovery should not just focus on the way in which the information will be relevant. The party seeking permission to propound expedited discovery should also establish the lack of other means to obtain the information through its own efforts. Using the example, above, of the desire to use expedited discovery to identify and locate all persons who may be named as a defendant, the plaintiff should delineate the steps taken to date and the specific discovery sought in order to accomplish the desired tasks.

When presenting the application for expedited discovery, the practitioner must focus on selecting the most efficient discovery tool as well as the nature of the information sought. Where the subject of the expedited discovery seeks to determine exactly what the defendant has in its possession, the process requires more than merely propounding interrogatories. Document productions, forensic examination of computer systems, and focused depositions are the tools that will provide the clearest answers. Along with ascertaining the boundaries of the information in the possession of the defendant, the initial focus can include the question of "how" the information was acquired. Given time, even where defendants cannot avoid disclosing possession of specific information, they will try to provide an innocent explanation for how the information came into their possession. When a defendant is forced to provide this explanation rapidly, before knowing exactly what information the plaintiff already has uncovered, he or she is more likely to provide an explanation that is at odds with verifiable facts. When further discovery exposes these other facts, the discrepancies will provide a valuable tool to assist the jury in its determination of whether to believe the plaintiff or the defendant.

Both plaintiffs and defendants should consider making an application to the court for expedited discovery. Defendants do not as frequently seek expedited discovery. For one reason, they do not have the same restrictions on propounding early discovery as plaintiffs. Second, they have fewer arguments to present the court in support of a request to shorten the plaintiff's time to respond. In comparison to a plaintiff, the defendant is not typically in a position where there is some event looming in which their rights would be prejudiced in the absence of being permitted to conduct expedited discovery. Exceptions include responding to a motion for preliminary injunction and an early motion for summary judgment. Yet in every trade secret case, the defendant will want to learn as much as possible about the alleged trade secrets being asserted. What exactly are the trade secrets? In what manner is the plaintiff claiming that there was improper access? In the absence of a pending application for preliminary injunction, there is little harm a defendant can identify that would substantiate altering the normal time lines for conducting discovery. The mere fact that an action alleging misappropriation has been filed, even when it is a matter of public interest in the industry in which the defendant operates, rarely will be sufficient support for an order expediting discovery. However, when faced with the potential of an injunction that could have a significant impact on the operation of the defendant's business, a strong basis is presented for demanding immediate targeted discovery.

In a case where a TRO is being sought, in its opposition the defendant should consider including a request for expedited discovery. The defendant may have received only 24 hours' notice of the hearing on the TRO application. By statute, the TRO expires automatically within the time set in the order, generally not to exceed 14 days from the date of entry. This time may be extended by the court, for "good cause shown," for an additional 14 days. The court will then consider transmuting the TRO into a preliminary injunction. Where the plaintiff seeks to jam the defendant and objects to an extension of the time, establishing good cause for expedited discovery will also generally provide sufficient grounds for the 14-day extension of time. Further, even where the TRO is denied, combining the request for expedited discovery with the opposition provides an important benefit. The court may still believe the matter to be sufficiently serious that it will set a hearing date on the preliminary injunction without regard to the briefing schedule generally applicable to noticed motions. The time presented as necessary for the defendant to conduct preliminary discovery will likewise inform the court on the appropriate schedule for that hearing.

Whether the plaintiff or defendant is making the request for expedited discovery, the application should include:

- The actual discovery that the moving party wishes to propound, provided in the physical form that will be served on the adverse party. Merely describing the discovery being sought by the party leaves too much ambiguity and increases the potential the court will deny the request "without prejudice."
- A request in the moving papers that the court deem service of the application to constitute service of the attached discovery, such that there is no further service requirements due before the time to respond begins to run.
- The factual basis for the discovery requested, tying the information sought to an issue that will be presented to the court in the near future or to an event that may soon occur in the event that judicial assistance is not forthcoming. Here relevance is the key, as a finding by the court that the information is relevant makes it more difficult for the responding party to ignore the substance of the requests in its response.
- The precise legal issue on which the anticipated discovery responses will have a bearing.

- The exact date on which the responses are due, the manner of service (U.S. mail, electronic transfer, or hand delivery), and any related details. For depositions, the location should be specified as well as the start time and date on which they should take place, and their duration, with special attention paid to the timing of production of documents sought in connection therewith. The preferable timing of production is at least 24 hours prior to the deposition so the materials can be reviewed, organized, and copied. With respect to non-deposition document productions, a response date should be identified for the formal response to the requests and a firm date set for the physical production of all materials responsive to the requests. For interrogatories or requests for admission, this will be the date on which the responses must be served and will specify the manner of service.

The fact that the court has granted an application for expedited discovery does not mean that the defendant is precluded from responding with objections. While it is not appropriate to base the objection on the timing of the discovery, other substantive objections will not have been pre-adjudicated and should not be waived by the failure to include. The nature and extent of the objections should take into account the extent to which the court considered the substantive requests in determining whether to grant the application for expedited discovery. When in doubt, the defendant should request that the court make an explicit statement in the order granting the application for expedited discovery that the order is without prejudice to the right to submit objections. However, the defendant should be cautious in asserting objections, as the court already has found a sufficient basis to permit the discovery to proceed on an expedited schedule. Should the defendant simply stonewall, the court is likely to impose even greater pain when the matter returns to the attention of the court on a motion to compel.

CHAPTER NINE

Special Masters, Court-Appointed Neutral Experts, and Technical Advisors

Intellectual property cases tend to be heavy consumers of judicial resources. Combining high stakes with sensitive and highly technical information, these cases generate significant attention within the client's executive team and are often closely watched in the relevant industry. With market share or the continued existence of a business at risk, aggressive positions are taken by each side. To marshal an effective offense, or prepare a comprehensive defense, the outside litigation teams tend to be large in number. With an increase in legal and factual complexity, the need arises to delegate responsibility in order to maximize efficiency, which in turn reduces the number of direct interactions by the lead partners. This, in turn, increases interaction by the junior lawyers on the opposing sides. Eager to demonstrate their tenacity, these members of the outside legal teams are often unwilling (or lack the authority) to compromise on the wide variety of case management or discovery issues that exist. Motions to compel, which quickly become unavoidable, tend to be numerous, lengthy, and complex. The judges and their staffs handling these matters often lack a high level of sophistication regarding technical aspects of the confidential information in dispute, and are not even fully familiar with all of the means of data creation, storage, or retrieval of that information.

Trade secret cases fit this description and are seen by many judges as having more than their fair share of pretrial disputes that require judicial assistance. While the majority of the disagreements are substantive in nature, dealing with the boundaries of relevancy and associated burden in light of the nature of the trade secrets alleged, picayune procedural disputes can also erupt at inopportune times over the handling of evidence produced during discovery. Normal discovery calendars have a difficult time dealing with the volume in a timely and thorough fashion, resulting in an incentive by at least one of the parties to try to game the system through obfuscation, objection, and delay. Special masters can be used to alleviate these concerns.

Court-appointed experts, neutral to the dispute and used for the direct benefit of the court, are a separate tool for assisting the assigned judge in handling the substantive technical areas in issue. These experts can bring to bear an unbiased understanding of the technology, unfiltered by counsel, so the court can more accurately apply its legal expertise.

1. The Use of Special Masters

Whether in state or federal district court, many assigned judges are willing to consider any approach that can divert discovery disputes to another judicial officer. The default practice in many federal district courts is to refer all discovery matters to the magistrate judges. In similar fashion, many state courts have "discovery calendars" that operate separately from the trial departments. These calendars often are handled by a court commissioner. But these subordinate judicial officers are not necessarily enamored with lengthy discovery disputes. Many also have their own "nondiscovery" calendars, full of everything from arraignments, small claims court appeals, hearings on substantive motions, and minor trials to manage, in addition to any discovery disputes the presiding judge may send their way.

In an attempt to minimize the use of judicial resources, extensive, time-consuming, and burdensome procedures are put in place before either party can bring a formal motion. The resulting delays are then compounded by an inability to find available dates on the discovery judge's calendar, in addition to the statutory notice periods applicable to all motions. Requests to shorten time are routinely denied. Orders on discovery matters are not always "final," at least initially. While discovery rulings by a magistrate judge in federal district court are considered non-dispositive matters, reviewable by an Article III judge only for clear error or abuse of discretion except where terminating sanctions are imposed, the nonprevailing party may still file written objections. These must be resolved by the Article III judge (under some local rules, merely by no action taken within a specified time) before the discovery order becomes final. Where state court commissioners are used, absent a stipulation to the contrary, their rulings are similarly challengeable by the dissatisfied party. These procedures can inure to the benefit of a party who consistently delays, obfuscates, and frustrates attempts to get to the merits of the dispute.

The appointment of a special master (or referee, synonymous for this discussion), by agreement between the parties or as a result of a formal motion, can alleviate these problems. With a dedicated individual acting as the judicial officer, the parties can expect increased access, shortened notice periods, continuity of assignments, consistency in results, and the benefit of the special master's learning curve. A dedicated judicial officer has the time to learn the intricacies of the trade secrets as alleged, and as a result will be better informed of the way in which the intricacies (whether relating to the technology involved or the market that provides the independent economic value) impact the reasonableness of the discovery being propounded and the sufficiency of the responses provided. These benefits do not come without a price. Whether a retired judge or a local practitioner is selected for the assignment, special masters charge for their time at rates generally near the top of the local market for private counsel. In large cases these fees can add tens of thousands of dollars or more to the cost of the litigation.

In deciding whether to seek appointment of a special master, one of the first considerations is the extent of the authority to be delegated when the appointment is by motion, or as authorized when the appointment is by agreement of the parties. By definition, a special master is someone assigned to aid the court in performing a specific task or function in a pending action. While most frequently used for discovery matters in trade secret cases, they can also be appointed to report to the court on specified legal or factual matters, to supervise or report on pretrial activities, or to perform particular tasks, such as an accounting. Statutory appointments as a result of a contested motion, or a sua sponte decision by the court, tend to have significant restrictions on the scope of authority, reflecting the right of litigants to have their matters heard by the assigned judicial officer. By contrast, when the parties agree to the appointment of the special master, the scope of authority can be as broad as the parties wish to specify.

The parties to a trade secret case must exercise care in specifying the grant of, and limits to, the authority of the special master. There is significant risk of "authority creep" by a special master appointed to handle only discovery matters. Although the special master may be asked to make a determination on whether a party is entitled to discovery as propounded and to apply the fairly liberal standard for conducting discovery, reaching this determination carries potential for the ruling to instead become one that touches on the merits of the dispute. For example, in those jurisdictions where a party must identify its trade secrets with reasonable particularity before commencing discovery, the defendants will consistently object to every attempt by the plaintiff to provide that identification on the basis that the description is too vague, or does not specify information that constitutes a trade secret. The discrete discovery issue, as presented to the special master, is whether a reasonable identification has been provided sufficient to guide the parties regarding the legitimate parameters of discovery. If not carefully managed, however, there is a risk that the special master will instead issue an order to the effect that the designation does not list anything that he or she can determine to constitute a trade secret. The defendant will seize upon that ruling as an adjudication on the merits in its favor, argue that it therefore did not take anything that constitutes a trade secret, and move for dismissal of the action. Likewise, if the special master holds that the information described in the identification constitutes protectable trade secrets (and not just a reasonable identification), the plaintiff will claim that this order constitutes an adjudication of the existence of the trade secrets sufficient to leave for determination only the question of whether the acts of the defendant constitute misappropriation.

Even if the assigned judge agrees that the ruling by the special master is not binding on the parties with respect to the merits of the action, a well-reasoned order carries significant weight. This bias must now be overcome by the party who lost the motion. To minimize that risk, an order appointing the special master should be reviewed with care to ensure that the scope of authority and its limits are clear. Likewise, any agreement between the parties to appoint the special master should set forth very clear boundaries on the matters that can be submitted and the scope of, and limits to, the special master's authority.

As a corollary to the importance of specifying the scope of the special master's assignment, the parties need to consider whether to stipulate to the special master having all of the authority of a sitting judge (with the ability to issue final orders, subject only to appeal in the same fashion as would an order issued by a sitting judge) or more limited in the traditional sense with the rulings advisory, and subject to confirmation by the assigned judge. Conferring the authority to act as a sitting judge has the benefit of increasing the speed and efficiency of the proceedings. The ability of a dissatisfied party to file objections to the ruling, creating additional delay and expense, disappear. For a client on a constrained budget, or who has a timetable for resolution that requires fast action, this is a positive development. As long as the right to appeal is retained, the parties are in the same procedural position that they would have had in the absence of the appointment of the special master. On the other hand, both parties are giving up the safeguard that comes with having the right to immediately challenge the ruling of the special master to the trial court, and it is very difficult to have an effective review of discovery rulings during an appeal after a trial on the merits. And, if the special master is granted the full powers of a sitting judge, even where the appointment is specifically circumscribed to designated discovery matters and disputes, there is an increased likelihood of authority creep and a lessened ability to effectively address any authority oversteps in the resulting orders.

The decision to use a retired judge or a practicing attorney as the special master weighs significantly on the question of whether to grant the full extent of authority that inures to a sitting judge. A retired judge, by experience and training, will provide greater predictability, consistent with the manner in which disputes are handled in the courthouse in which the retired judge previously sat. This lessens the need to retain the right to submit objections to the rulings of the judge as a special master.

As their former colleagues—the judges who remain on the bench—will likely afford the rulings of the retired judge significant deference, there is less value in retaining the right to submit objections to the rulings. This, in turn, will reduce the delays that come from the process of having the court review those objections.

While it is always good practice to learn as much as possible about a potential decision maker, such as the nature of his or her prior practice and the experiences others can share about professional interactions, with a retired judge the lengthy time sitting behind the bench tends to smooth any preconceived views that resulted from experiences learned earlier in a career. However, attention to judicial assignments will provide insight into any leanings that may impact how the case is handled, as a judge who sat continually on a family law assignment may not be as quick with evidentiary issues as someone who was assigned to a complex civil trial department.

A retired judge should have greater appreciation for the intellectual side of the legal issues and discovery rules, and will focus on case management issues and preparation for the trial on the merits. They should be more decisive, less inclined to "split the baby" in ruling on a matter. However, retired judges do not always appreciate the different obligations they now have that come with their change in status. As they no longer are formal members of the sitting judiciary, the obligations to the parties directly retaining their services increase. At the same time, their overall obligations to the "civil system" as a whole decrease. Without the distractions of a full calendar, and the impediments flowing from the limited time available for a given matter, they must learn to be available at odd hours and on short notice. They need to be able to distinguish when adherence to formal procedures is helpful and when it is best to act impromptu, and they need to be comfortable working with the parties to develop procedures that take into account the needs of the particular case.

Use of a practicing attorney as the special master offers a different approach, and greater caution is suggested before bestowing all the powers of a sitting judge. On the plus side, it is easier to select a practicing attorney based on his or her specialized knowledge in trade secret issues. Practicing attorneys can be even more helpful when they have experience with the technology at issue—but caution is advised, as this factor can also be a negative, depending on whether they will listen to the retained experts or rely on their own knowledge. Practicing attorneys tend to be more familiar with the realities of the practice and will more readily take client management issues into account when helping the parties shape the boundaries of appropriate responses and obligations. But if trouble is anticipated with opposing counsel, they may not be the best choice, at least not without the power to object to their rulings, as practicing attorneys are less likely to issue sanctions for bad behavior. Finally, since most practicing attorneys who accept special master assignments also have their own clients and existing practices, diligence requires inquiry into the nature of their current practice to determine whether they will have a distinct plaintiff or defendant friendly orientation.

Once a special master is selected, the practitioner should ask for a meeting of all involved to discuss the mechanics of the process. While the parties could merely adopt all of the local rules that exist in the jurisdiction where the matter is pending, given the layer of expense generated by the use of a special master, the parties should customize the process to the extent possible to suit the needs of the particular case.

As the special master will be billing his or her hourly rate to the parties, the first item to clarify is the manner in which these charges will be allocated. If there are merely two "sides" (one plaintiff and a single defendant), the cost allocation is straightforward. Each side bears an equal share of the fees of the special master. Rather than provide the special master the authority to routinely reallocate his or her fees, which can become a distraction during the process, the parties should specify that these fees will constitute an item of costs to be awarded to the prevailing party at the end of the case. Where there are multiple parties, either because several cases have been consolidated for purposes of discovery or there are multiple defendants not completely aligned in interest, the protocol can provide that the fees on a given motion can be apportioned by the number of parties to that motion. So, for example, if the plaintiff is seeking discovery responses from only a single defendant, the fees are apportioned equally between the two "sides." If several defendants are all seeking to compel answers from the plaintiff, the split is equally divided among the parties to that motion. The same is true if one party to the action joins in a position taken by another party in a motion, even though the joining party is not the direct subject of that motion. In order to be "heard" on a given motion, every "joining" party must incur its equal share of the hearing fees. Since the special master is likely to duplicate a ruling on a particular issue when it arises again in subsequent motions, as a result of an informal application of the "law of the case" doctrine, there is an incentive for the "nonparties" to join a given motion in order to have their views heard on the topic. By doing so, they can be sure that the same legal analysis will apply to any similar circumstance that may later involve them directly.

The special master, of course, retains the power to award fees to a party on any given motion as a sanction. The parties can also specify that the special master *shall* assess the fees on any given motion, unless he or she finds that the nonprevailing party acted with substantial justification. Where the latter course is selected, the parties should also consider the nature of the meet-and-confer obligation. Before the special master can hear a formal motion, the parties are to meet and confer over the dispute in order to determine whether they can resolve it without the need for outside assistance. There is a tendency, when special masters are involved, for neither party to compromise. Positions are taken for the purpose of establishing bully pulpits for the hearing. If the special master is only going to "split the baby," the parties will want to leave themselves the greatest latitude possible during the meet-and-confer. This renders the meet-and-confer requirement meaningless in high-stakes trade secret litigation, with every dispute landing in front of the special master. One way to handle this dilemma is to require the special master to choose between the last two respective positions taken by the parties during the meet-and-confer process. While some retired judges balk at this approach, feeling that it deprives them of their judicial independence, each party is forced to be more realistic, as they will have to justify their last position when trying to convince the special master to rule in their favor.

Another way to increase the efficiency of the discovery process, whether a special master is involved or not, is to insist that an exchange of written correspondence is insufficient by itself to satisfy the meet-and-confer obligation before a formal motion can be filed. Letters, when not connected to the obligation to orally meet and confer, are merely written for effect and to create a record. They are written for the enjoyment of the client. They are written from the safety of an office, behind the comfort of the keyboard, without the need to contemporaneously react and justify absurd positions. They tend to be written by the junior lawyers on the team, who are trying to be aggressive in order to impress the partner on the file. Telephone meet-and-confer sessions are better than exchanging letters, although only slightly more so when compared to face-to-face discussions. It is far easier to say "no" to a speaker phone than in person to the colleague representing the other side. Some lawyers claim that they dislike oral meet-and-confers, as the parties disagree afterward over what was said and the terms of what was agreed to during the session. That argument is the easiest to solve, as a court reporter can attend (in person or telephonically). The presence of a court reporter has the prophylactic benefit of forcing the parties to speak slowly, and one at a time, while the other side is forced to listen, as a clear record cannot be made when people are speaking over each other. A transcript of the meeting also avoids the added expense of dueling confirmatory letters that purport to lay out the terms of the parties' agreement and the areas of their continued disagreement.

Since motions before the special master are not scheduled on a calendar that includes other cases or court commitments, the parties have the benefit of the special master's undivided attention. An entire morning, or even an entire day, can be set aside to hear matters that may arise on the case. Even when the particular calendar involves only a single motion, like gas expanding to fill a vacuum, arguments on that motion will fill an entire day if the length of the hearing is not controlled. Some parties will argue that there should not be any artificial time limits and leave the matter to the special master to manage. However, when compared to the minimal time allowed to argue a discovery motion during a normal calendar in a typical courtroom, there is no due process violation by setting forth in a hearing management order a specified time limit for each side on any given motion.

A hearing management order, prepared by the parties with the input from the special master at the very beginning of the assignment, can specify the maximum number of matters to be presented during each hearing. This limit is designed to avoid the gamesmanship that can result from one side trying to jam the other with too many matters on a given day, and has the added benefit of reducing hearing fatigue. A limit on the number of matters that can be presented by each side on any given day should be coupled with an order that directs the scheduling of matters, with each side having the right to set an equal number of matters for consideration per hearing. Other hearing protocols that can be addressed at the beginning in order to smooth the process include as the following:

- Deciding who is responsible for arranging for a court reporter (i.e., who makes the arrangements in order to avoid the delays and frustrations that occur when neither party remembers to do so). Typically the obligation alternates between the parties based on which side noticed the motion(s) to be heard on a given date. An alternative approach assigns the obligation to one side to make the arrangements for all hearings throughout the duration of the case, to avoid confusion where both parties noticed motions to be heard on the same date, A related issue involves selection of the reporter, as some practitioners have strong preferences and have established relationships with particular reporters. Having the same person(s) does have the benefit of continuity, especially where technical terms predominate, which serves to maximize accuracy of the transcripts.
- Whether a reporter will be used for all hearings, including informal calls, or limited to formal motion hearings.
- Whether the moving party pays for the original transcript, and whether the special master will automatically be provided a copy of all the transcripts at a cost to be borne equally by the parties.
- The briefing schedules (whether to use the statutory schedule applicable to the jurisdiction in which the matter is pending or some other schedule; what is the time deadline for service at the "end of the business day"—whether it be 5 p.m. or midnight).

- Whether to use formal pleadings or allow letter briefs, reply briefs, and/or sur-reply briefs, and the page limits for each.
- The availability and notice requirements (whether all motions must be formally noticed; how to handle ex parte requests; what protocol should be followed for contacting the special master for handling disagreements that may arise during depositions).
- In what physical form the motions should be provided (how to handle hard copies, including filing of the original with the special master or the court; whether the special master has a preference to be provided with copies electronically; whether service via fax or PDF between the parties is an acceptable alternative).
- The form of rulings (whether "up or down" or a reasoned award, and who prepares—the special master or the prevailing party).
- The level of formality of hearings (may only one attorney argue per side, and to what extent is the agenda limited to matters formally noticed, or may any party bring up matters ad hoc for discussion?).

To increase the value derived by the investment of time and the expense in using a special master, the practitioner should consider scheduling a tutorial for the special master on the technology in issue before the first substantive matter is heard. Especially helpful where the special master is a retired judge rather than a practicing lawyer selected in part to leverage prior experience in the technical area, a nonargumentative tutorial can facilitate more efficient hearings and better-reasoned decisions. Some practitioners favor the use of the client or internal client representative as the presenter, especially if they appear to come from central casting (in that they have a well-regarded resumé in the applicable technical art and an easily understood delivery), in the belief that subtle impressions favorable to the client will result and help influence the process. But this strategy poses a not insignificant risk that the client presenter is not persuasive to the special master, and instead colors her opinion in the opposite direction. The better course is to focus on the primary goal of educating the special master in the basics of the substantive technology, and let the facts then drive the outcome. If the special master agrees to a tutorial, the parties should discuss the following:

- Should the tutorial be transcribed, and if so, are there limits to the permitted uses for the transcript?
- Does the tutorial constitute substantive evidence that can be used later in the proceedings?
- Are the presenters to be sworn?
- Can the opposing party ask questions, even if not in the form of cross-examination?
- If there are "dueling" tutorials, should the presenters be excluded during the presentation by their counterparts (so as to avoid the question of whether one gains an advantage by having the "last word") or included to allow the special master an opportunity to fully ask questions of each?

2. *Handling the Process of Court-Appointed Neutral Experts and Technical Advisors*

The ability of the court to appoint its own experts, as compared to party-retained experts, has long been established. The authority for these appointments in federal district court is codified in Federal Rule of Evidence 706. The use of court experts as a source of neutral opinions to assist the court is especially helpful in cases involving complex or arcane areas of technology. The sitting judge may desire assistance in handling complex motions, such as for partial summary judgment on the issue of whether the alleged trade secrets were already known to the defendant. A special master, appointed to handle discovery disputes, may benefit from a neutral expert's opinions in order to assist the parties in setting the reasonable boundaries of electronic discovery. In many cases these situations are adequately addressed by the party-retained testifying experts. But, notwithstanding the ubiquitous use of "non-neutral" experts in trade secret cases, a busy court does not always have the time or inclination to sort through detailed competing reports to segregate the true areas of disagreement from the many points on which the opposing experts grudgingly agree. Hours of testimony that elaborates on the technological minutia in the experts' reports rarely result in a substantial increase in the court's edification. By contrast, court-appointed experts are considered truly "neutral," assisting with opinions the court can consider without the concern that the contents of the reports have been unduly massaged by the side that retained the expert. However, use of court-appointed experts remains an infrequent occurrence due to a lack of familiarity within the court system of the value they can bring to the process, coupled with a reluctance by the parties to suggest their appointment. These neutral experts are a source of concern to many practitioners, in part due to their comfort with the adversarial system of evidence presentation that allows them to shape and control expert content, and in part reflecting the concern that the trier of fact will place disproportionate reliance on the opinions offered by the neutral experts.

When the court suggests that it intends to appoint a neutral expert to assist the court in understanding or analyzing the technology at issue, the parties will typically be asked if they have any objections to the appointment. The court may have someone specific in mind, or may request submission of nominations of persons who might be appropriate for the case. Given the efforts already undertaken by the parties to retain their own experts in the substantive areas, each side should be generally familiar with persons knowledgeable in the art who are available. This group may include some very significant names, but they may have declined to be retained to avoid the appearance of taking sides to the dispute. The group may also include some individuals who are not appropriate as party-retained witnesses due to access issues that would have disqualified them from acting on behalf of one of the parties. Where a party objects to any particular proposed expert, in addition to a claim that the proposed expert lacks the requisite skill in the art, that party should be prepared to refer the court to the criteria specified in the protective order as the basis for objecting to any expert's access to designated materials. The objection should be coupled with alternative proposed names to avoid the implication that the party is simply resisting the appointment of a court expert under any circumstances.

A final list of proposed experts will eventually be presented to the court, which will make the appointment from the list. The neutral expert will then proceed with the assignment as delineated by the court. The parties will bear the cost of the court expert equally, unless they are able to demonstrate particular hardship from having this expense imposed. The neutral expert must advise the parties of any finding that may be made, or opinions that he or she intends to offer, and can be cross-examined by either party in connection with any report being presented to the court. However, the party on the losing end of the neutral expert's report is sure to feel that justice was not served, as the opinion bore too much official imprimatur to be successfully challenged. The party who does not agree with the report must be sure to consider, and make an appropriate record concerning, any issues that may exist under *Daubert/Frye* in the same manner as if the court expert were party retained. By requiring court experts to provide sufficient information to determine whether their opinions are also grounded in reliable methodology, the practitioner is in a stronger position to ensure that this expert's opinion will assist in a fair and rational resolution of the scientific and technological issues.

There are ways to militate against undue influence by a single court expert. In cases where the budget allows (as the expense of neutral experts is borne by the parties, in addition to the expense of their own retained experts), the practitioner can suggest a parallax approach, where displacement or difference in apparent positions can be seen when viewed along two different lines of sight. This approach is accomplished by the court appointing two neutral experts, using the same selection process that it would use for a single neutral expert. The two experts are directed to prepare one report that specifies the areas where they agree and those where their opinions diverge. The court would be particularly well served by this approach, as it can focus its efforts on the area(s) where the two neutral experts do not agree, and the parties would likewise have the benefit of knowing how best to focus their further presentations.

While there is no guarantee that either party will be satisfied with this parallax approach, even with respect to the areas where the two neutral experts agree, care during the selection process and the peer-review quality of this approach should minimize that risk. In addition, neither party would be precluded from challenging those areas where the two experts agree. A challenge can be made by showing that the two neutral experts neither had nor considered all of the information necessary to establish an appropriate foundation for their joint opinion, or otherwise included an error in their combined analysis.

Where the court desires assistance in learning more about the scientific and technical issues generally applicable to the matters in dispute, as opposed to obtaining assistance in the process of fact-finding on technical matters, the parties can suggest appointment of a technical advisor as an alternative to the court appointing its own neutral expert. Technical advisors are not subject to the provisions of Rule 706, and this person's role is significantly different from that of a neutral expert. Technical advisors are limited to providing assistance in understanding the technical terms and general concepts involved in order to assist the court to better evaluate the opinions that will be offered by the testifying experts. However, to ensure that the court uses a fair and open system for appointing a neutral technical advisor, the parties should ask for the following provisions:

- An opportunity to present (or address) any allegation of bias, partiality, or lack of qualification before the technical advisor is retained;
- A clearly defined limit on the scope of the technical advisor's duties;
- Language in the order appointing the technical advisor making it explicit that any advice cannot be based on extra-record information; and
- A requirement that the technical advisor provide the parties with a copy of any reports prepared for the court, or written notification of the nature and substance of any ex parte communications between the technical advisor and the court.

CHAPTER TEN

Addressing the Elements of Reasonable Efforts to Protect Secrecy and Independent Economic Value

A trade secret plaintiff must be able to establish—as an element of the definition of a trade secret—that he or she engaged in reasonable efforts to maintain the secrecy of the information in question. In most jurisdictions, and explicitly under the Uniform Trade Secrets Act, a determination of whether the plaintiff's actions were "reasonable" is qualified by "under the circumstances." This aspect of the claim reflects more than a highly factual question that is difficult to resolve on a motion for summary judgment. The obligation to present evidence sufficient to establish that the plaintiff's efforts were reasonable will bear also on the related requirement that the information have independent economic value by reason of the fact that it was not generally known to the public or to others who could obtain economic value from its use or disclosure. Thus, the manner in which these two elements are addressed can have an impact far broader than as a gating issue that the plaintiff must satisfy in order to avoid a nonsuit. How to handle the intertwined nature of this inquiry requires consideration of the policies involved in this aspect of establishing trade secret rights, as well as the evidentiary problems that arise.

1. *Addressing the Requirement of "Reasonable Efforts" as a Means of Implementing Public Policy*

Public policy underlying the recognition of legally protectable interests in trade secrets is implemented by identifying rights that may be vindicated through judicial process, and by placing limitations on the exercise of those rights. In this regard, the requirement of "reasonable efforts" has significance with respect to both the evidentiary burdens the parties face and the potential remedies that may be awarded once liability is established. This requirement exists for both theories of trade secret protection (arising either with respect to the owner's property rights in the trade secrets or from the nature of the relationship between the parties). And, with respect to either theory, this aspect of trade secret law provides a useful balance between the ability of the innovator to profit from the development of new or useful information and the broader societal interest in preventing unreasonable monopolies on the use of that information.

This balance of societal interests expressly takes into account the characteristic of secrecy—an attribute existing independently from the substantive nature of the information—as a means of ameliorating the impact that absolute protections can have on competitive markets. The fact that the plaintiff originated the idea, standing alone, is meaningless. Protection of novel ideas independent of their secrecy is addressed by the Patent Act. Public policy is thus furthered, in that innovation is encouraged when a party has a means to "informally" acquire enforceable rights to restrict the use of information (the formal steps necessary to obtain a United States patent or to register a copyright do not exist with respect to trade secrets), and the public interest in fair competition is protected, as the right to restrict generally ends as soon as the information becomes publicly available.

Consistent with this balance of public and private interests, the right to control the use of trade secret information is not solely a question of whether the original innovator took, or failed to take, reasonable steps under the circumstances to maintain secrecy. In some circumstances, a party cannot prevent another from using information identical to that which constitutes its trade secrets, even when its efforts to maintain secrecy are not being questioned. As expressly provided for under the Uniform Trade Secrets Act, "reverse engineering or independent derivation alone shall not be considered improper. . . ." Under this "carve-out," independent efforts to create or obtain trade secret information previously developed by another are not per se unlawful, notwithstanding the fact that the trade secret owner unquestionably took "reasonable steps" to maintain secrecy. For a defendant that intends to rely on this limitation on the rights of the trade secret owner, contemporaneously created documentation of the efforts to develop the information corresponding to the trade secrets is very important. At a minimum, the defendant should look for documentation that reflects use of the information that predates the allegedly improper acquisition.

The impact of this carve-out is best understood by comparing these rights to the monopoly rights existing in favor of original inventors arising under the Patent Act, which include the absolute right to exclude subsequent inventors. Inventors under the Patent Act are granted a 20-year absolute monopoly over the use of the inventions disclosed in the patent in return for making public the details surrounding their invention. By contrast, a trade secret owner retains in perpetuity the right to protect against the improper acquisition, use, or disclosure of its trade secret information, limited only by the requirement that the information be reasonably maintained as a secret.

The definitional aspects of trade secret law thus both evaluate the owner's efforts to protect secrecy and provide a safe harbor for the independent efforts of a subsequent innovator, as a reflection of the need to balance the right of an innovator to exclude against the interest of society in facilitating full and fair competition. The desirable goal of encouraging innovation and the development of technical skills, facilitated in one aspect by providing the original innovator with a limited right to exclude, would be hampered in a broader sense if a subsequent innovator faced the risk of infringing another's trade secret rights merely as a result of achieving success in its independent development efforts. Here the key is the extent to which the efforts of the subsequent inventor were truly independent. Efforts that were contaminated by exposure to the trade secrets are insufficient. Purely contemporaneous development negates the element of "improper" acquisition, as well as the element of value derived from the information not being known to other persons who can obtain value from its use. But this issue need be considered only after the trade secret owner first establishes that its efforts constituted reasonable steps to maintain secrecy.

Practitioners representing a defendant who wishes to assert acquisition through reverse engineering as an affirmative defense (and those practitioners representing a plaintiff facing a reverse-engineering defense) should look for the same type of evidence that one would expect in a company evaluating a clean-room setting:

- Was there any overlap in development personnel with respect to those who are (or might be) accused of the wrongful conduct or, even more expansively, to anyone who may have come in contact with those who had access to the trade secrets? The greater the separation, the more likely the court will find that the subsequent efforts were not contaminated. This also avoids the implication that the development efforts were assisted through the application of negative know-how. While the use of negative know-how can be difficult to prove, as it involves the application of experience to avoid efforts previously proven to produce unsatisfactory results, cross-team interaction with individuals who had prior access to the trade secret information, coupled with accelerated development schedules, strongly suggests its existence and use.
- Were the computers used by the "clean-room team" in the course of their development efforts networked, and if so, who has access and to which databases? Stand-alone CPUs and desktops avoid this issue.
- Has the reverse-engineering process been well documented, such that an independent audit will be able to re-create each step of the development process (gaps imply continued use of the contaminated data)?

- Was the development process assisted by the manner in which the "untainted" product or process would interact with that which uses aspects of the trade secrets (such as where tainted code is excised, but the process of architecting replacement code benefits from the unique structure of the remaining untainted code)?

From a legal standpoint, the ability to lawfully acquire knowledge of the trade secrets through reverse engineering reflects both the absence of any societal interest in having a court hold that the information should be deemed as being "secret" (as long as the source of the material used for the reverse-engineering process was not, itself, improperly acquired) and the absence of any "wrongful act" that society wishes to prohibit. From a practical standpoint, the focus will be on the time and effort that were involved in the process of reverse engineering, which should be directly proportional to the value of the trade secrets and their complexity. How the trier of fact views these attributes, in turn, will be impacted by the extent to which the plaintiff can establish an evidentiary record of having engaged in reasonable efforts.

2. *The Evidentiary Significance of the Requirement of Reasonable Efforts*

What constitutes "reasonable" efforts to maintain secrecy is an intensely factual issue. By taking into account what occurred "under the circumstances," the practitioner must closely investigate the costs and benefits that vary in any given case. The inquiry considers the steps actually taken by the client, as well as a cost/benefit analysis of the steps otherwise available that the client did not implement.

- Has the client consistently advised its employees that it considers the information in question to constitute its trade secrets, and does it limit access to the information on a "need-to-know basis"?

- Are steps routinely taken by the client to educate its employees regarding the need for secrecy and the protocols in place to maintain security?

- Are appropriate documents required and maintained, such as non-disclosure agreements, employee handbooks, or proprietary rights agreements, which specify the obligation to maintain secrecy?
- When employees are hired, are they instructed regarding the importance of these provisions and required to initial or sign the agreements that contain these terms as a condition of continued employment?
- When they leave for another company, are the former employees subjected to exit interviews where they are asked to confirm (preferably in writing) their understanding of their continuing obligations to refrain from using or disclosing the secrets?
- Are there posters at the workplace reminding employees of the need to maintain secrecy?
- Do agreements with development partners or licensees have sunset limitations on the obligation to maintain information as confidential? If so, are these limitations consistent with the true lifespan of the information's inherent value that exists by reason of its secret characteristic?
- Are there marking obligations, in agreements between development partners or merger candidates, pursuant to which the party providing trade secret information must designate it as confidential (where oral, by providing a written confirmation within a specified time period, and where written, by affixing appropriate legends to the documentation)? While labeling information as "trade secret" or "confidential" before a dispute arises does not conclusively establish that the information falls within that legal definition, it is still an important fact for the trier of fact to consider when determining if the producing party placed value on the information, and believed that it could not be readily derived from publicly available sources.

- If there are means of internally tracking these marking obligations, in order to audit compliance, does the client implement these means and/or conduct compliance audits?
- Does the client provide and require the use of locked cabinets or safes?
- Does the client have a process of logging, or identifying, materials that may include information constituting a trade secret?
- Does the client restrict the availability of the materials at only a handful of its sites, attach electronic sensors to documents, or produce copies only on non-reproducible paper?
- Does the client use locked briefcases for transporting work, have alarms installed, provide photo identifications, or use experienced security personnel?

While all of the foregoing steps are not required for every client, they are examples of what can be presented as evidence of steps taken, which were reasonable under the circumstances to protect the purported trade secrets. Alternatively, where absent, they are steps the defendant may reference as constituting the minimum the trade secret owner should have implemented to satisfy its duty to maintain secrecy.

The presentation of the factual evidence of the steps taken may also turn on what is considered reasonable in the industry. Here the analysis of reasonable efforts, particularly where technical or sophisticated measures are readily available, benefits from the testimony of experts skilled or knowledgeable in the particular field involved. A case involving software programs will benefit from a person skilled in hardware and software security systems. A case involving fashion designs may benefit from a security specialist who can provide perspective on the layout of the design facility and the ease of access to common worksites. From a persuasiveness standpoint, the greater the value the owner attributes to the information (particularly where that value exists from the fact that it is secret), the greater the protections one would expect when evaluating the "reasonableness" requirement. In turn, the more effort an owner can demonstrate to having expended to protect the secrecy of the information, the more it has established that the information has real value deserving of legal protection. In turn, this evidence will help establish that there really *was* misappropriation (reflected in part by the efforts necessary to overcome the security systems), and that there was injury in fact that exists as a result of the misappropriation.

Defendants who seek to attack the efforts to maintain the information as secret will take different tacks depending on their alleged role in the misappropriation. An indirect misappropriator, who acquired the information from a direct misappropriator, may argue that the security systems were not reasonable under the circumstances, and it should not have liability arising from the fact that someone else was able to acquire the information. These defendants will take the list of efforts actually made and present opinion testimony from their own experts that the efforts were not reasonable under the circumstances as other (even potentially less expensive) systems would have prevented the theft in the first place. A practitioner representing a party alleged to be a direct misappropriator is cautioned not to take that approach. Too easily seen as an attempt to "blame the victim," this argument can backfire, instead suggesting implicitly that the underlying acts of "appropriation"—now alleged by the trade secret owner to constitute misappropriation—were willful. The direct misappropriator in possession of the trade secrets, rather than arguing that the trade secret owner should have included additional steps to prevent a breach of its existing security, will be more effective in addressing the intent element of the claim by describing the systems in place as not "reasonable" with respect to the specific information in question, as they did not provide adequate notice that the information was considered by the owner to constitute a trade secret.

The defendant in possession who is relying on reverse engineering or independent derivation has a different evidentiary focus from the defendant who argues the absence of reasonable efforts to maintain secrecy. Rather than arguing that the lack of secrecy was a result of the actions (or inaction) by the owner, such that there is no protection for the information, these defendants may claim that they have no liability, as the information allegedly constituting the trade secrets was ascertained through legitimate efforts at reverse engineering, such as by measurements and analysis made on a finished product. Using the software field as an example, the defendant should be able to establish, through contemporaneously created materials, the efforts to dissect the structure of the allegedly copied program and to isolate each level of abstraction contained within the program. This process begins with the code and ends with an articulation of the program's ultimate function. Similarly, in the field of semiconductor devices, the documented efforts may reflect "decapping" the device, followed by use of a scanning electron microscope to analyze its circuitry. The documentation should be sufficient to enable an independent expert to later retrace and map each step of the process, and the process must rely on source information (or samples) that were not themselves improperly obtained.

The potential to reverse-engineer the information can be a factor in determining the existence of a trade secret, in that the ease of compiling the information through reverse engineering may suggest that the information did not have independent value by reason of not being generally known. But the conceptual ability to reverse-engineer a product or process to identify the trade secrets will generally not provide a viable defense to a defendant who "skipped" that step and took the trade secrets directly from the plaintiff. This is particularly true where the process of reverse engineering from legitimate sources is relatively time-consuming and expensive, as compared with the utilization of the drawings or specifications actually appropriated. For the defendant who did not, in fact, reverse-engineer the trade secrets, the ability to have done so is a presentation best offered in support of an attempt to narrow the scope of the appropriate remedy.

The practitioner should be mindful that, from the client's perspective, any efforts to maintain secrecy must be "reasonable" from a business standpoint (and not measured merely by the practitioner's desire to impress the court). While the lawyer providing trade secret advice to a client who does not have litigation pending may desire the ability to enhance an evidentiary position before the dispute arises, it is difficult to sell the client on strengthening security systems merely to buttress its position should litigation ensue. Conversely, the litigator handling a pending trade secret matter, unable to change the level of security that existed at the time of the misappropriation, must include reference to these types of business realities when preparing the presentation to be made to the court.

As efforts to maintain secrecy are increased, the indirect as well as direct costs to the client also increase. Restrictions on access to technical drawings or databases, either by or between the client's engineers or development partners, create functional impediments to the free flow of ideas and interactions that can facilitate intercompany development efforts. Product introductions can be delayed and market opportunities lost. These are examples of the soft costs faced by the client. The direct costs, in the form of the expense for security guards, hardened vaults, security systems, and other efforts, are hard-dollar expenses that must be justified. What level of security is necessary becomes essentially a business-driven question, where the real world sets the value, and few clients can be convinced that any additional benefit to be gained in court from significantly increasing security exceeds the additional out-of-pocket cost. These business considerations should be included in the trial presentation. Trial judges tend to appreciate the need for balance, and understand that a requirement to take extravagant, productivity-impairing measures to maintain the secrecy of the information will reduce the incentive (or ability) to invest resources in the development of information worthy of trade secret protection.

3. *The Relationship between Reasonable Efforts, Independent Economic Value, and Available Remedies*

The manner in which the plaintiff addresses the requirement to engage in reasonable efforts to maintain secrecy can also create a remedies issue. Even where it took reasonable steps, such that the definitional requirement to establish the information as constituting a trade secret has been met, a plaintiff may be limited in its ability to obtain the relief sought. This result occurs when the efforts to maintain secrecy of the information were not ultimately effective, or even not as extensive, as they could have been.

Separate from the obligation to establish that it took reasonable efforts to maintain the information as "secret" at the time of the misappropriation, the plaintiff must also prove the existence of some form of economic value independent from the information not being generally known to the public. But these are not independent concepts in practice. What is "reasonable" in a given case, when viewed "under the circumstances," takes into account the value of the information to the owner of the trade secrets. This attribute of value has a direct bearing on the type and degree of injury that flows from the act of misappropriation. Information can be very valuable to a company without constituting a trade secret. But the absence of this attribute of value will negate the right to trade secret protection.

The requirement of independent economic value, which exists by reason of the attribute of secrecy, is one that reflects the existence of competitive value:

- Did the client gain (or increase its ability to retain) market share over competitors, at least in part, by reason of the fact that its competitors do not have the same information?
- Can the client establish a connection between the information and any head-start advantage it may have realized when it first entered an identifiable market?
- Did the information reduce development time or increase initial manufacturing efficiencies?
- Can the client identify and quantify the advantages that the information will continue to provide in an existing market? Spiritual or emotional gain to the owner of information, even if held in confidence, does not qualify the information for trade secret status.

As an alternative to the positive impact the information has on the client's business, the practitioner should consider meeting the requirement by compiling evidence to establish that a competitor could more rapidly or efficiently gain entry into the market (or enhance existing market share) as a result of obtaining knowledge of the information. Documents that contain information concerning an out-of-date technology, or that set forth information that is so specific to the owner as to be unusable by others without extensive modifications, rarely have an aspect of value that can be attributed to not being publicly known.

Information that was never secret, or where the court concludes that the efforts were not "reasonable," in turn does not provide its owner any independent economic value from the attribute of being secret, and thus, by definition, is not entitled to trade secret protection. The trier of fact will consider the nature and extent of the efforts to maintain secrecy as an indicator of the extent to which the owner considered the secret nature of the information as having a real-world value. If the evidence suggests that the owner did not think it worthwhile to undertake serious efforts to keep the information secret, the defendant will likely argue that the information in question could not have had much value from being "secret." But the determination of value in this regard is not keyed to the subjective beliefs of the trade secret owner. Even where the evidence is not contradicted, and the client truly believed that the confidential nature of the information gave it an economic advantage, if (for example) it routinely provided information to its customers regarding the basis for its pricing and other terms and conditions of the business but did not require formal agreements to maintain confidentiality, it is unlikely that a court will conclude that the defendant's use (under a trade secret theory) constituted an improper act.

Even where the information once had value by reason of its secret nature, the failure to continue to make reasonable efforts to maintain secrecy over time, or the ability to easily reconstruct the same information through lawful means, will bear on the prospective relief that may be awarded. The calculation of damages for future use will be curtailed, and the likelihood diminished that a court will award permanent injunctive relief. From a societal perspective, the rationale for providing protection against the misuse of trade secret information does not continue to apply once the plaintiff has allowed the trade secret to fall into the public domain. A plaintiff would enjoy a windfall, out of proportion to the "true" value of the information if permitted to recover ongoing damages merely because the defendant took "non-secrets" from the owner rather than from the public domain.

Proof of the ability to uncover the trade secrets through reverse engineering, while not a defense where the defendant was a direct misappropriator, can also have a significant impact on available monetary remedies. Under the Uniform Trade Secrets Act, the measure of damages is either lost profits or disgorgement, with the court having the discretion to award a reasonable royalty if either of the first two measures cannot be established. Disgorgement is an equitable remedy for unjust enrichment. Royalties take into account what a willing licensor would charge a willing licensee. Both situations take into account the availability of alternatives, the difficulty in developing the information that constitutes the trade secrets, and the value attributed to having the information in one's possession. To the extent that a defendant can establish the lack of difficulty/expense/delay associated with the ability to reverse-engineer the information, it may also be able to establish that it was not unjustly enriched, or that a willing licensee would not pay a significant royalty for the right to use the information. In addition to the amount that may be awarded, the length of time to reverse-engineer the information can also be argued as a factor to reduce the period in which the defendant would be required to pay the plaintiff an ongoing royalty for its use.

Just as evidence of the time and expense necessary to reverse-engineer the trade secrets can be offered to the court in connection with an attempt to limit the scope of injunctive relief, a significant degree of difficulty or expense can be offered as a basis for a lengthy or permanent injunction. The defendant will alternatively argue that a permanent injunction is hardly equitable when the information can be developed through reverse engineering, even when it acquired the information directly from the plaintiff. But when the information is no longer secret at the time of trial, the court will not award a permanent injunction except in those situations where the disclosure to the public at large was a result of actions by the defendant, as one party cannot profit from its own wrongdoing. Depending on the time and manner of disclosure, the court may still be willing to consider a head-start injunction, further discussed in Chapter

11, commensurate with the time savings achieved by the defendant by reason of having used the trade secrets.

The amount of potential damages can also be impacted by public disclosure. When the plaintiff has allowed the information to become public, the damages will be measured from the time of misappropriation. But the fact that the plaintiff does not continue to directly gain economic value from its secrecy (such as where the plaintiff no longer is in the same business) will not preclude an award of "future" damages as long as there is some hypothetical value of the information if offered for sale to the general market (such as may exist where third parties would be willing to pay for a license to use the information).

Where the loss of secrecy is a direct result of the actions of the defendant, the plaintiff can present an argument that considers how much the defendant owes as a result of having effectively "purchased" the trade secrets. The plaintiff, alternatively, can present an expert's testimony on the amount that would have been realized by the owner had it been able to sell the trade secret information on the open market. Finally, the plaintiff may be able to enhance the award by quantifying the economic return attributable to ownership of the trade secret during the course of its anticipated normal "life" (from misappropriation to the point where the information no longer has economic value by reason of its attribute of secrecy, such as from a change in market conditions or the existence of anticipated technological advances).

CHAPTER ELEVEN

Headstart Injunctions and Other Forms of Post-judgment Equitable Relief

Companies and individuals who invest time and valuable resources identifying opportunities and developing innovations that garner competitive advantage from the fact that they are not generally known to the public, or to others who can obtain economic value from disclosure or use, add greatly to advancements in business and technology. Too often, unfortunately, others view opportunities for misappropriation as a clever way to quickly gain market penetration. These parties seek to shortcut the time and capital investments necessary to develop similar information by the simple expedient of using trade secrets wrongfully obtained from others. When these siuations occur, the owners of the trade secrets must act with dispatch or risk losing the ability to prevent the misappropriators from unfairly capitalizing on the fruits of their efforts and industry. However, while trade secret litigation offers a ready forum through which to engage a misappropriator, litigation should rarely be initiated without first giving careful consideration to the likely nonmonetary remedies available.

Even when acts of misappropriation are discovered before the owner of the trade secrets can monetize their use, so that a significant award of monetary damages is not likely, the potential for injunctive relief provides the owner a remedy that may justify investing the significant sums necessary to prosecute these matters. And, as a result of the wide range of potential relief available to an aggrieved trade secret owner, the potential for both preliminary and permanent injunctive relief must be considered wholly apart from the monetary damages that may be awarded (which may include awards based on actual losses, unjust enrichment, or reasonable royalties in addition to exemplary damages).

Questions often arise regarding the scope of injunctive relief that the court would consider appropriate in a specific case: Will a court issue an injunction that is temporary or permanent in duration; narrow so as to restrict use of only the specific trade secrets in question;, or broad enough to encompass any competitive activities that could utilize the trade secrets? Precise guidelines are rare, as equitable relief is a means through which the courts try to implement public policy. As an inherently discretionary matter, especially in contrast to the quantitative analysis applicable to calculating monetary relief, the ultimate form of equitable relief that may be ordered lacks a high degree of predictability. This lack of visibility frustrates novice and sophisticated clients alike, as meaningful probability analysis before engaging in any type of litigation is helpful to establish reasonable expectations and is an essential predicate for developing strategic initiatives. However, while the precise extent of available injunctive relief does not lend itself to the higher level of predictability typically desired by trade secret owners in considering whether to proceed, dissecting the alternative forms of injunctive relief that a court may issue can provide important guidance.

1. "Preliminary" and "Permanent" Injunctions in Trade Secret Litigation

The standard nomenclature used to describe injunctive relief, differentiating between "temporary," "preliminary," and "permanent" (typically denoting the timing of issuance; i.e., "temporary" and "preliminary" before and "permanent" as a part of the judgment, rather than the scope or substance of the relief), is no different in trade secret litigation than in other types of general civil litigation. In the context of injunctions that may issue after a trade secret trial as a part of the judgment, a "permanent injunction" is not always permanent. It may instead expire after a specified duration or in light of changed conditions tied to the nature or use of the trade secrets.

In simplistic terms, two categories of post-trial "permanent" injunctive relief are potentially available once a trial court has concluded that a defendant has misappropriated the trade secrets in issue: The wrongdoer can be enjoined from using the identified information, or engaging in specified conduct, without durational limits. Alternatively, the trial court can enjoin the misappropriator from using identified information, or engaging in specified conduct, for a specified period of time, generally measured by calculating the length of time that would have been required to reach a similar level of knowledge or competition without having had the benefit of the fruits from the efforts of the trade secret owner—the "headstart injunction."

2. *Availability of Headstart Injunctive Relief to Address Acts of Misappropriation*

Recognizing the importance of a uniform system of trade secret protection, a majority of states have adopted the Uniform Trade Secret Act (UTSA). In jurisdictions where the UTSA has not been adopted, the common law provides similar policy articulations for protection against acts that may constitute misappropriation and similar definitions of what constitutes a trade secret. *Compare* Cal. Civ. Code § 3426.1(d); *Restatement of Torts* § 757, cmt. b; and *Restatement (Third) of Unfair Competition* §§ 39–45. By its terms, the UTSA as adopted by the majority of states explicitly authorizes injunctive relief against both actual and threatened misappropriation, provides fairly broad discretion to a trial court in fashioning appropriate injunctive relief, and sets forth avenues to modify relief should conditions change.

As a general matter, most plaintiffs initially seek, by way of the prayer in their complaint, a permanent injunction that prohibits the use or disclosure of the misappropriated trade secrets without any durational limits. In practice, appellate courts have upheld injunctions that do not have a specified time span, under the rationale that the enjoined party is permitted to seek termination of a permanent injunction at any point. Such post-trial, nondurational permanent injunctions have been held appropriate, for example, in cases where the court found some cognizable danger of recurrent violations of the rights of the trade secret owner. In such situations, a court is free to exercise its discretion to reject a defendant's representation that the means for repeating the wrong no longer exists, or its disclaimer of any intention to commit further wrongs (although these factors may be considered in determining whether to continue an injunction against discontinued acts).

Faced with the prospect of a permanent injunction, a defendant may argue the following reasons for placing durational limits on the injunction:

- The potential danger of creating an unfair monopoly in favor of the trade secret owner;
- The difficulties in modifying injunctions post-judgment due to jurisdictional issues;
- The intricacies of addressing the impact in multiple jurisdictions given the obligation to give full faith and credit to sister-state judgments;
- The greater efficiency and use of judicial resources if the duration of the injunction is set at the time it is entered, when both parties are best suited to provide evidence and argument regarding the criteria the court should consider in issuing the requested relief, and;
- An injunction of permanent duration is not justified due to the transitory secrecy of the information in question (for example, where there has been, or is likely to be, public disclosure of the information such that it no longer derives economic value from its "secret" characteristics).

Further, it is established that disclosure of a trade secret in a patent places the information comprising the secret into the public domain. Once the information is in the public domain and the element of secrecy is gone, the right to trade secret protection is extinguished, and the patentee's only recourse is afforded under the Patent Act.

In response to these arguments, trade secret owners may consider making the observation, generally well-received, that no undue prejudice inures to a permanently enjoined defendant, as the court, even upon post-judgment application, continues to have the authority and jurisdiction to terminate the injunction, such as when the trade secret has ceased to exist. The defendant, even while arguing against that form of injunction, is well advised to ask the trial court to include a specific reservation of jurisdiction in the judgment, notwithstanding the fact that a trial court's jurisdiction to modify an injunction is inherent.

Courts faced with the conundrum of whether to place duration limits when granting injunctive relief have thus reached very different conclusions. Some have held that a headstart injunction is not sufficient, and that the injunctive relief should be permanent in duration, especially where there are "persuasive reasons to doubt that the defendants ever would have successfully developed, or even endeavored to develop," a competing device but for their exposure to the trade secrets in question. Alternatively, when granted on terms that focus on the market penetration benefit gained by the misappropriator, the courts focus on the proposition that a headstart injunction best serves the purpose of injunctive relief (i.e., eliminating the commercial advantage obtained as a result of having used the trade secret to reduce the time required to develop a competing business, service, or product) without unduly stifling competition. Authorities following this argument propose that a trade secret injunction should rarely be permanent in duration, but should last only as long as is necessary to eliminate the commercial advantage that a person would obtain through misappropriation, with the period of time that would be required for independent development being the most commonly employed standard. The result is similar in jurisdictions that follow the *Restatement of Torts*, as these courts also generally apply the principle that the duration of injunctive relief in trade secret cases should be limited to the time necessary to protect the plaintiff from any harm attributable to the appropriation and to deprive the defendant from any economic advantage attributable to the appropriation.

While the Uniform Trade Secrets Act does not expressly use the term *headstart injunction*, several of its provisions directly provide support for that form of relief. For example, even when a trade secret has ceased to exist, a court is authorized to continue the injunction "for an additional period of time in order to eliminate commercial advantage that otherwise would be derived from the misappropriation." See Cal. Civ. Code § 3426.2(a). This is consistent with the proposition that a wrongdoer who has made an unlawful disclosure of another's trade secrets cannot assert that publication to escape the protection of trade secret law. This provision of the Uniform Trade Secrets Act implements the policy underlying trade secret law of eliminating any unfair advantage obtained by a wrongdoer. Consistent with the foregoing, where a misappropriator can demonstrate the ability of the public to have quickly developed the same information that a trade secret owner claims to constitute the misappropriated trade secrets, the owner will have greater difficulty convincing a court either that the economic value of the information was derived from it not being generally known or that a substantial "headstart" was improperly derived by the misappropriator from the alleged acts of misappropriation.

3. *The Impact of Reverse Engineering and Preliminary Injunctive Relief on the Duration of a Headstart Injunction*

While the act of reverse-engineering a device, or engaging in independent development, to uncover the underlying trade secrets can negate a finding of misappropriation, the potential that one could have reverse-engineered a device to uncover the incorporated trade secrets is not a defense to liability where the misappropriator in fact engaged in improper means to acquire the trade secrets. However, establishing this possibility is a relevant consideration when the court is considering the duration of an injunction, and a showing that one of reasonable skill could have developed the same information through proper means can limit the scope and duration of relief.

In determining the appropriate duration for a permanent injunction, the trade secret owner should argue to the trial court that it can take into account the effect of any pretrial preliminary injunction, including whether the preliminary injunction had the same effect or accomplished the same result as sought by the permanent injunction. In such situations a misappropriator should consider arguing that the effect of the preliminary injunction was the same as the relief being sought by the permanent injunction such that, in a fashion similar to applying credit for time served, the amount of time elapsed during the pendency of a preliminary injunction should be credited against the length of time the trial court determines otherwise appropriate for a post-trial headstart injunction. In response, the trade secret owner should consider the extent to which the pretrial preliminary injunction in fact did not serve the same purposes as a post-trial permanent injunction, or the extent to which it did not deprive the misappropriator of all of the benefits that were gained from using that which was misappropriated.

4. *Setting the Breadth of a Headstart Injunction*

There is a difference between deciding how long to enjoin a misappropriator from using the misappropriated trade secrets—either for a defined headstart period or to last forever—and the breadth of the injunction's scope, regardless of duration.

The question of an injunction's breadth takes into consideration whether to prohibit a misappropriator "only" from using the specified information found by the court to constitute a trade secret, or, more broadly, to prohibit the misappropriator—without regard for the source of the information being used—from engaging in the particular field or activity that embraced the trade secrets. While the former scope of prohibition—sometimes referred to as a "use injunction"—meets the goal of preventing the misappropriator from further using or disclosing the trade secrets without the owner's consent, the latter scope—sometimes referred to as a "production injunction"—also satisfies that goal, with the additional benefit of "doing equity" where the trade secrets are broad in nature. This is particularly the case when it would be difficult for the misappropriator to separate his or her knowledge of the trade secrets from any further work in the same area. As a result, the production injunction would operate to block access to a field or endeavor, especially where the end product in question could not be developed without some use of the trade secrets. Although production injunctions are significantly broader than use injunctions, some jurisdictions have expressly held that production injunctions are not invalid per se simply because they permanently bar a defendant from engaging in a particular business.

Use injunctions have the benefit of being facially narrow, which is a characteristic that appeals to most trial courts, even when they extend further than the specific description of the misappropriated trade secret to also prohibit use of materials "substantially derived" from the trade secret. The rationale behind extending injunctive relief to derivations and derivatives of the secret is reflected in the truism that "outright and forthright duplication is a dull and very rare type of infringement."

Production injunctions, by contrast, are more commonly considered for situations where a typical use injunction is deemed ineffective to eliminate the competitive advantage gained by the misappropriator. This is because a production injunction places broad limits on the misappropriator by describing the activities that are prohibited rather than the information that may not be used. The common rationale for a production injunction is that a use injunction would be ineffectual where the misappropriated trade secrets are inextricably connected to the manufacture of the product, and the misappropriator cannot be relied upon to "unlearn" or abandon the misappropriated technology. An inextricable connection can be established where the trade secrets form such an integral and substantial part of a comprehensive manufacturing process or technology that, absent the misappropriated trade secrets, the misappropriator would not be able to independently manufacture or design a comparable product.

5. *The Impact of Headstart and Future Damages on the Scope of Injunctive Relief and Conditional Use Injunctions*

Similar in concept to a headstart injunction, some courts have awarded "headstart damages" to compensate for the profits the plaintiff lost as a result of the competition from the defendants. "Headstart damages" are sometimes referred to as "accelerated market entry damages" or "shortcut liability." Similar to the analysis applicable to a headstart injunction, the measure of damages consists of the profits the trade secret owner can be shown to have lost as a result of the competition from the misappropriator for the period of time that the misappropriator would not otherwise have had its products in production absent the misappropriation or misuse of the trade secrets.

Both headstart damages and headstart injunctions seek to readjust the competitive landscape to that which existed before the acts of misappropriation. Public policy considerations, such as avoidance of awarding duplicative recovery for a single wrong, militate against a trade secret owner being awarded both forms of relief. A post-trial headstart injunction against a defendant's future sales would be redundant of the legal relief for headstart damages which the jury has already awarded. However, both forms of relief may be awarded where the trade secret owner can prove that the misappropriator will continue to enjoy the benefits of its headstart in the form of increased sales when it re-enters the market after the expiration of an injunction.

A trade secret owner, by seeking future damages, may also be held to have elected a legal remedy that precludes the equitable remedy of an injunction that prohibits future use. The Uniform Trade Secrets Act, reflecting the reality that situations may exist where it would be unreasonable to prohibit future use, authorizes the trial court to issue a "conditional use" injunction. This type of injunction conditions future use upon the payment of a reasonable royalty for no longer than the period of time the use could have been prohibited. The misappropriator is presented the choice of paying the royalty and being able to use the trade secrets in question or remaining subject to the injunction.

In some jurisdictions, the duration of the royalty period, referred to as the "sunset period," is calculated by determining the length of time that the defendant would not have been in production absent the misappropriation or misuse of the plaintiff's property. The appropriate length of time is a highly factual question, as it is often difficult to approximate with precision the time it would have taken the infringer to have developed a process, or to have brought to market a product, that does not infringe on the rights of the trade secret owner. Where the process or product has been designed into the operations of innocent third parties, the time period may be extended to take into account the time and effort necessary for these parties to move to a non-infringing alternative. In calculating the reasonable royalty during the sunset period, any rate normally applicable to an arm's-length transaction should be increased to reflect the fact that the activities during this period are now a result of conduct found to infringe the trade secret rights of the trade secret owner. Here the court is well placed to apply the multiplier that the jurisdiction typically applies when there is a finding of willful infringement, and the trade secret owner should request as part of the judgment an obligation on the part of the defendant to provide an accounting for these royalties to be due the fifteenth day after the close of each calendar quarter, with payment due within 30 days after the close of each calendar quarter. The trade secret owner should also request that a notice provision be included to ensure that all parties associated with the manufacture and sale of the infringed products are informed of the restrictions under which the defendant must now operate.

6. *Addressing Divergent Private and Public Interests When Considering the Potential for a Headstart Injunction*

One of the primary policy goals behind trade secret law is "the maintenance of standards of commercial ethics." Indeed, as noted in the Official Comments to the Uniform Trade Secrets Act, the Act is meant to be read expansively so as to protect and maintain standards of commercial ethics. Consistent with this policy, restrictions on the disclosure of trade secret information developed as a result of the effort and investment of the trade secret owner are necessary to the maintenance of societal standards of morality in the business community. Absent these protections, trade secret owners would be discouraged from making investments in innovation and would face greater risk of employee espionage, deceit, and fraud.

By contrast, the interests of the alleged misappropriators are rooted in the belief that overly aggressive restrictions on the use and disclosure of information reduce competition that benefits the public by impeding the free flow and use of information throughout society. These restrictions can reduce, rather than encourage, competition either by preventing a competitor from setting up a new business or by limiting an employee's access to positions at a new enterprise that can provide more meaningful opportunities to that employee as well as add to the competitive strength of a new employer. In California this policy is also articulated in statutory prohibitions against agreements that restrict post-employment competition (*see* Cal. Bus. & Prof. Code § 16600 (West 2010)), as well as in the philosophy that the burdens they impose upon the employee and society increase in proportion to the significance of the employee's accomplishments and the degree of his specialization.

In assessing whether a headstart injunction should issue in a given case, the parties should consider the need for a trial court to take into account the independent interests of the public that may be affected in balancing the competing interests of the trade secret owner and the alleged misappropriator. The primary purpose of trade secret law is to encourage innovation and development, and the public has a strong interest in the law not being used to suppress legitimate competition. Thus, while the interest of the trade secret owner is focused on retribution and compensation, the public has an interest both in the desire to prevent an alleged misappropriator from competing unfairly through the use of the trade secrets of another and in permitting fair competition through the use of publicly available information and the parties' respective talents and experiences.

One of the benefits of using a headstart injunction rather than a permanent injunction is the ability to achieve a balance between these sometimes divergent interests by allowing adjustments in duration and scope that are more responsive to the competitive advantage obtained. While broad-form injunctions are appropriate in cases where compartmentalizing the trade secrets is difficult, or because of their manner of operation or application, tying these prohibitions to a duration limitation can address the public interest by lessening the chance that a misappropriator will be improperly penalized by constraints on use of public information, general know-how, and experience.

Headstart injunctions, by focusing on the length of time appropriate to level the playing field, also have the benefit of lessening the potential for being impermissibly vague. Because an injunction prohibits conduct under threat of judicial punishment, including contempt, the parties subject to the injunction must receive explicit notice of precisely what conduct is outlawed. For this reason, trade secret injunctions that are deemed too vague will be set aside on appeal. The trade secret owner must balance the desire for a broad injunction against the potential for ambiguity sufficient to render it constitutionally unenforceable. For example, an injunction against "using or disclosing trade secrets and confidential technical information" may be too vague to give fair notice of prohibited conduct.

Sometimes the nature of the trade secrets, or the extent of derivation, makes it difficult to frame their scope in a manner that obviates the potential for impermissible vagueness. In addition to the focus on the durational aspect of the injunctive relief, a trade secret owner can address this situation by asking the trial court to implement a procedure by which the misappropriator can seek prior approval from the trial court with the aid of a special master. The master can be tasked with assisting the court and the misappropriator in distinguishing between the trade secrets and information that falls outside of the injunctive prohibitions.

CHAPTER TWELVE

The Impact of Contractual Boilerplate Provisions on Trade Secret Litigation

When the battle appears inevitable, the wise general seeks first to shape the battlefield to his advantage. Likewise, as trade secret cases arise typically out of a preexisting relationship, the practitioner can assist the trade secret owner to shape the manner in which the dispute will be handled well before a problem arises. This can be accomplished by giving careful thought to the documentation that will be used in that relationship.

Whether with respect to former employees, merger candidates, joint venturers, distributors, contractors, or consultants, the majority of these relationships all involve some form of written agreement that documents the nature and parameters of the parties' substantive and procedural rights and obligations. The documentation may take the form of an employment agreement, a memorandum of understanding and non-disclosure agreement, purchase and sale documentation, or a consulting agreement. When the documentation is being drafted, the focus is on the substantive deal—the structure of the transaction or relationship, or how to allocate the benefits that will flow to all parties from the anticipated success to be achieved. Little time or thought is typically spent on the provisions that address what will happen should the relationship falter, and even less time on the "boilerplate" that counsel for the parties insert routinely at the end of the documentation. To the extent considered at all, any discussion concerning these clauses centers on whether to include a particular type of boilerplate rather than an in-depth discussion of the specifics contained within such provisions. Yet, from the standpoint of the trial lawyer, these provisions can have a significant impact on the manner in which a case must be litigated, thus playing an important role in the evaluation of the return on investment of litigation dollars. Small changes in the language of these provisions can have a dramatic impact on the potential for leveraging a favorable return on that investment.

The following clauses are selected examples, offered to illustrate the differences that simple word choices in boilerplate clauses can have on the parties' relationship and any subsequent litigation that might ensue. These clauses are not the only ones that can create opportunities for mischief or pose traps for the unwary.

1. The Arbitration Clause

Arbitration provisions are the classic example of contract terms that can trigger the law of unintended consequences. Included often by one party to accomplish a specific goal, such as in the employment context, where the principal purpose is ensuring that wage or discrimination claims will be addressed in a nonpublic forum, these clauses can include a wider class of claims than intended originally. When the question of whether to include an arbitration provision arises, the party who may have intellectual property rights at risk should be mindful that the courts often construe these provisions broadly, in a manner that sweeps into the scope of arbitral claims those that involve intellectual property rights.

Arbitration is a creature of contract, in that the powers exercised by the arbitrator flow primarily from those created by the parties. Statutory provisions tend to fill gaps where the parties did not otherwise provide specifics. As such, the parties are free to set limits on the scope of matters that can be considered by the arbitrator.

When parties decide to arbitrate, they often select a "standard" clause along the following lines:

> "Any controversy, claim or dispute including the determination of the scope of this agreement to arbitrate, arising out of or related

> to this Agreement or the breach, termination, enforcement, interpretation or validity thereof, shall be determined by arbitration. The arbitration shall be administered by the American Arbitration Association pursuant to its Comprehensive Arbitration Rules and Procedures."

This is an example of a broad form arbitration clause. Inclusion of the "or related to" language in the clause will sweep within its ambit almost any claim that has a connection to the relationship between the parties to the underlying agreement. Trade secret claims will most certainly fall within the scope of this provision where included in an employment agreement, even when the claim is based on conduct that postdates the end of an employment relationship.

In addition to the scope of claims that may fall within the obligation to arbitrate, in deciding whether to include an arbitration provision, the parties at the drafting table should consider the breadth of persons who can invoke the obligation to arbitrate. The authority of the court to compel arbitration of a claim of trade secret misappropriation is not limited to situations involving only the signatories to the agreement. Although the general rule is that only the parties to an arbitration agreement may enforce it, there are exceptions. Decisions involving both the Federal Arbitration Act and similar statutory schemes under state law have held that a nonsignatory may claim the benefit of, as well as be bound to, an arbitration agreement pursuant to ordinary principles of contract law, including incorporation by reference, agency, alter ego, estoppel, and third-party beneficiary principles.

The estoppel exception in particular has been applied in situations where the signatory to a written agreement containing an arbitration clause is in a position where it must rely on the substantive terms of the agreement in asserting the claims against the nonsignatory. This situation may arise where the nonsignatory is alleged to have acquired the trade secret by acting in concert with a signatory. Likewise, the exception can be applicable where the signatory has raised allegations of conduct by both a signatory and a nonsignatory that is "substantially interdependent and concerted." This occurs, for example, where the claim against a competitor is essentially derivative, arising out of misappropriation by acquisition of the trade secret by a former employee. In this setting the equitable estoppel exception can be invoked by a nonsignatory to compel arbitration of the signatory's claim, based on the court concluding that the claim against the nonsignatory is founded in and inextricably bound up with the obligations imposed by the underlying employment agreement containing the arbitration clause. This result can take place even when the former employee is not named as a party defendant in the litigation.

Discovery is another issue that is not often considered when the parties decide whether to include an arbitration provision. In the arbitration provision referred to above, the Comprehensive Arbitration Rules and Procedures of the American Arbitration Association have been incorporated by reference. An arbitrator presiding over an arbitration that follows these rules has a great deal of discretion regarding the nature, type, and extent of discovery that will be allowed. For example, the parties are to engage in the voluntary exchange of documents, exhibits, and information within their control, but only to the extent the arbitrator considers such production to be consistent with the goal of achieving a just, speedy, and cost-effective resolution of the matter. Depositions and interrogatories are allowed, again at the discretion of the arbitrator and to the extent the arbitrator determines that the persons to whom the discovery is propounded may possess information necessary to the determination of the matter. This level of discretion itself causes several problems, the foremost being the lack of predictability and consistency from arbitrator to arbitrator regarding what discovery will be allowed and the manner in which objections to discovery will be handled. Also, as the arbitrator is now the gateway to the requests being propounded, the party seeking the discovery must make a preliminary showing that is unlike any process required in federal district court or most state courts.

For plaintiffs and defendants alike, the standard restrictions on discovery that typically occur in an arbitration setting simply do not work in the context of resolving disputes involving claims of trade secret misappropriation. A plaintiff will often begin with only an indication of wrongdoing and, at that point, otherwise will lack information regarding the extent of the misappropriation. Without extensive discovery, the plaintiff might not be able to learn all of the specific items of information taken, with the potential that any future claim in a subsequent proceeding is barred by principles of res judicata, collateral estoppel, or application of the statute of limitations (as an act of misappropriation arises only once in most jurisdictions upon the initial theft, even when use of an aspect of the items stolen is continuing or does not occur until some point in the future). The plaintiff also has the difficulty in discovering the extent of use or dissemination of the misappropriated information. Without the ability to determine the specifics, the plaintiff is hampered in its ability to seek appropriate injunctive relief, or to decide whether it needs to include additional parties as a defendant in order to bring before the arbitrator all who have access to the information. In addition, the plaintiff cannot prepare a damages model with the same degree of specificity and detail as when the full panoply of civil discovery is available. Compounding the problem further is the inherent reluctance of arbitrators to allow for extensive third-party discovery.

A defendant in an arbitration proceeding involving trade secrets has similar concerns over the lack of "full" discovery. First and foremost, in a court proceeding, the defendant usually has a number of different opportunities to demand that the plaintiff provide a detailed identification of all of the trade secrets at issue. This is a critical aspect of any defense to a trade secret claim, and the plaintiff will try to keep many details vague until the merits hearing. In the absence of being able to pin down the specifics of the trade secrets at issue, a number of potential defenses become problematic, including establishing that the information does not constitute a trade secret because the substance of the alleged secret is already generally known to the public.

The defendant will also want freedom to explore the development and ownership of the trade secrets in order to challenge whether the plaintiff has the proper standing to assert the claim. Damages issues, in a similar but mirror image to those that face the plaintiff, must also be considered, as the defendant will lack the tools necessary to challenge the plaintiff's damages models without the ability to engage in extensive discovery.

Both parties will want to consider the impact that the lesser evidentiary framework in arbitration may have on their case and the consequences of modifying the standard provisions to meet their specific needs. The AAA Comprehensive Arbitration Rules and Procedures state unambiguously that conformity to legal rules of evidence shall not be necessary. In practice, the issue is not one of authentication or privilege, as arbitrators are generally consistent with the courts in being less than enamored with disputes over the former and willing to be strict about the latter. The most significant issue that exists, when the evidentiary rules are relaxed, arises in the use of hearsay evidence and opinion testimony.

Even making an objection when hearsay is being offered in arbitration is frowned upon, with many arbitrators tersely responding that "it goes to the weight" of the evidence. Arbitration practitioners thus focus on deciding when to risk the arbitrator's ire by making the objection, knowing it will be overruled, for the purpose of highlighting the hearsay (lesser probative) nature of the testimony. But when one considers the problems with hearsay, coupled with the limitation on the ability to conduct full discovery, it is easy to see the mischief that can occur. Not only is the ability to cross-examine difficult when the subject of direct is an out-of-court statement being offered for the truth of the matter, but the lack of discovery will impede the ability to gain advance notice of the likelihood for that testimony.

A similar problem exists with the use of opinion testimony, whether offered through percipients or expert witnesses. In federal district court and state courts, a number of procedural protections exist to guard against the abusive use of experts in connection with identification and discovery, as well as the gatekeeper role of the court to ensure that only appropriate testimony is being offered. Arbitrators by rule do not have similar restrictions on the use of experts, and the standards that arbitrators apply are as varied as the types of arbitrators available. As trade secret litigation historically is a heavy user of experts, this is an area where the lack of predictability can result in surprise and unjust results.

Consistent with the "flexible" approach to application of evidentiary principles traditionally attributed to arbitration proceedings, arbitrators generally are not required (by the terms of the arbitration provision or the rules of the AAA) to apply strictly the law of the forum (or of any specified jurisdiction). While all parties believe that the arbitrator will apply generally understood legal and equitable principles, there is neither predictability nor consistency from arbitrator to arbitrator regarding their own views and application of governing legal or equitable standards. Without comprehensive guidelines that restrict the evidence that forms the basis for their decisions, a party considering whether to initiate arbitration or facing a potential business solution is handicapped in evaluating the potential for success in litigating the dispute or in quantifying the risk inherent in proceeding to award. A corollary to the foregoing is the almost complete absence of the ability to appeal from an arbitration award when the challenge is based on an arbitrator's error in law or the improper application of equitable principles.

When time is available at the drafting stage, many of the foregoing issues with arbitration clauses can be managed, as illustrated by the following clause:

> "*Arbitration*. Any dispute or controversy between the Company and Executive, arising out of or relating to this Agreement, the breach of this Agreement, or otherwise, shall be settled by arbitration only in New York, New York administered by the American Arbitration Association in accordance with its Employment Arbitration Rules then in effect. **The arbitrator shall be required to apply the substantive law of the State of New York, in the same manner as if the proceeding was before the Supreme Court of New York, and shall have the authority to award any remedy or relief that a court of competent jurisdiction could order or grant, including, without limitation, the issuance of an injunction.** Judgment on the award rendered by the arbitrator may be entered in any court having jurisdiction thereof. **Any such arbitration shall not extend to, or include, any disputes over the ownership or use of the intellectual property of either party, or conduct that is claimed to infringe either parties' intellectual property rights.** Except as necessary in court proceedings to enforce this arbitration provision or an

award rendered hereunder, or to obtain interim relief, neither a party nor an arbitrator may disclose the existence, content or results of any arbitration hereunder without the prior written consent of the Company and Executive. To the extent allowed by law, each party shall bear its or his costs and expenses in any arbitration hereunder and one-half of the arbitrator's fees and costs; provided, however, that the arbitrator shall have the discretion to award the prevailing party reimbursement of its or his reasonable attorney's fees and costs."

In this version of an arbitration clause, the two boldface sections reflect limitations on the authority of the arbitrator. The first is an express requirement that the arbitrator apply the law of the specified jurisdiction. This language provides both the benefit of enhancing predictability of results before the arbitration begins in order to better assess the value and risk involved, and a mechanism for protecting against a "rogue" arbitrator, as one of the few grounds for challenging an award is when the arbitrator exceeded his or her powers. Failing to apply the law of a specified jurisdiction when the arbitration provision is explicit on this point is an act in excess of the arbitrator's authority.

The second boldface section is an explicit carve-out that excludes from arbitration any dispute over the ownership or use of the intellectual property of either party. The carve-out ensures that the arbitrator cannot include an adjudication of such issues in the award. While the cases often speak in terms of the grant of arbitral authority, the job of a trial court (on either a motion to compel arbitration or when considering a petition to confirm an award) is made easier when it is considering whether the issue is within the scope of a carve-out rather than outside of a specified grant of authority. By making the clause reciprocal, the employer also lessens the chance that a court will find the carve-out to be unreasonable, with the potential of then finding the entire provision unconscionable and therefore void, as to an employee with lesser bargaining power than the employer.

This form of arbitration provision also contains an express confidentiality clause. While arbitration is inherently nonpublic, in the absence of a confidentiality provision the risk remains that one of the benefits of arbitration—the private nature of the proceedings—will be lost. The court will have nothing upon which it can base an order directing a party to maintain the information as confidential or otherwise seal the court files upon request by one or both of the parties.

2. *The Choice of Law Clause*

A choice of law clause specifies the body of law, typically by reference to a specific jurisdiction, that the trier of fact should apply when adjudicating the dispute. While a court is not bound to follow the parties' selection, especially where there is an overriding public policy issue that militates against the use of the laws of a foreign jurisdiction, by identifying beforehand the body of law the parties wish to have applied, they can create more predictability regarding how a court will handle a given dispute.

Parties generally select the body of law with which they are the most familiar rather than engaging in a comprehensive analysis of which jurisdiction's law may be the most favorable in case a dispute arises. More to the point, the choice often reflects the body of law with which *each party's lawyer* is most familiar—which corresponds usually to the law of the jurisdiction in which the lawyer has his or her office. But there are significant differences in the laws of the several states over trade secret misappropriation claims, and there is no comprehensive body of federal law that preempts inconsistent state law in this area. There are also issues regarding exclusivity of choice and concomitant scope of application that must also be considered. The following examples are presented to illustrate this point.

> "This Agreement shall be governed in accordance with the laws of the State of New York."

This is a narrow form of a choice of law clause, using the mandatory "shall" language. If applied literally, the court will apply only the laws of the state of New York. But there is an important distinction with respect to procedural versus substantive law, with most courts taking the position that a choice of law provision directs, but does not oblige, the choice of substantive law. Certainly a federal district court faced with the foregoing choice of law provision will still apply the Federal Rules of Civil Procedure and the Federal Rules of Evidence, notwithstanding the parties' agreement. Where a party wishes to incorporate a specific procedural law, the choice should be clearly specified. Thus, should a party in New York wish to require a procedural rule that exists in California, e.g., requiring a plaintiff to identify with specificity its trade secrets before being allowed to commence discovery, that party should insist on including a specific provision to that effect ("In any future dispute between the parties involving the ownership of trade secrets, the provisions of California Code of Civil Procedure Section 2019.210 will be applied in full, as follows: 'In any action alleging the misappropriation of trade secrets . . . before commencing discovery relating to the trade secrets, the party alleging the misappropriation shall identify the trade secret with reasonable particularity. . .'"). Further, with respect to this provision, there is an argument that the choice of law directive is applicable only in connection with issues of contract interpretation. While that position is somewhat of a stretch, the possibility exists that a court will limit the contractual choice of law to issues involving only the rights, obligations, or duties of the parties arising directly under the terms of the agreement.

> "This Agreement shall be construed, and the legal relations of the parties **hereto** shall be determined in accordance with, the laws of the State of New York."

In contrast to the first example, this form of a choice of law provision is extremely broad, capturing any issue of contract interpretation as well as any matter involving the signatories to the agreement—even with respect to disputes that do not touch on (that is, arise from or can be argued as related to) the agreement.

> "This Agreement shall be construed, and the legal relations of the parties **hereunder** shall be determined in accordance with, the laws of the State of New York."

The last example, substituting only the term "hereunder" for the term "hereto," arguably limits the reach of this choice of law provision to disputes that do not touch on (arise from, or can be argued as related to) the agreement. To the extent that one of the parties intended that the common law of New York be applied to a trade secret dispute, should the matter be litigated in a forum other than New York, that party may be disappointed.

3. *Venue/Jurisdiction Clauses*

Like a choice of law clause, venue and jurisdiction clauses are intended to increase leverage by ensuring that any subsequent dispute will occur in a particular (or "home") court, which the drafter perceives to be more conducive to resolving the matter in a fashion that is consistent with its expectations. It seems simple enough to specify where a matter will be resolved, but, once again, minor word choices can have significant differences in results.

While the terms "venue" and "jurisdiction" are often used interchangeably in this context, the principles underlying each remain very different in application. Venue refers to *where* a matter may be heard (i.e., in which physical location), whereas the question of jurisdiction is directed at whether the given court has the power or authority to hear the matter. Consent to a particular venue does not mean, however, that the matter will be heard in a particular locale. The court can still decide that there is no connection between the subject matter of the dispute, or the parties, and the locale. In this situation the court may conclude that it has no "interest" in hearing the matter or expending its limited judicial resources thereon, and order that the matter be dismissed or transferred to a different venue. But while a court is not required to accept the parties' choice of venue, as objections to improper venue can be waived either by agreement or acquiescence, the dispute more likely will be heard in a specified locale when the parties have so agreed. Merely choosing a particular venue, however, does not mean that the court has the power or authority to hear the matter at that location.

Jurisdiction clauses are generally focused on two areas—personal and subject matter jurisdiction. The first area addresses whether the court has the authority over *a person or entity*, given the nature or extent of their contacts within the geographic area over which the court presides.

In this sense jurisdiction and venue are similar in concept, and a party can waive by agreement any subsequent objection to the lack of personal jurisdiction, just as it can waive the objection by making a general appearance in a pending matter. Jurisdiction clauses that reflect an agreement by the parties to submit to the jurisdiction of a particular court can be very helpful to the party who subsequently wishes to initiate litigation in that court, especially against a foreign defendant, as the quagmire of attacks on personal jurisdiction can thus be eliminated.

In contrast to personal jurisdiction, however, the authority of the court over the *issues* in dispute is the focus of subject matter jurisdiction. The parties cannot waive objections to subject matter jurisdiction, nor can they confer subject matter jurisdiction on a court where it does not otherwise exist.

The following examples are illustrative of the manner in which parties have tried to address the foregoing issues.

> "Any United States District Court will have jurisdiction over any claim or controversy arising under or in relation to this Agreement."

This jurisdiction provision was used in an agreement to settle and resolve disputes over the alleged infringement of various patents relating to semiconductor manufacturing methods and devices. Neither party to the agreement was a U.S. citizen or a domestic corporation. But, as the license grant in the agreement encompassed U.S. patents, the parties agreed to jurisdiction before "any" U.S. district court both as a compromise in lieu of either party being able to select its own country for dispute resolution, and because questions involving infringement or validity of a patent under the Patent Act are within the exclusive jurisdiction of the U.S. district courts (as opposed to the courts of any individual state).

A dispute eventually arose, but the gravamen was not a question that arose under the Patent Act. Instead, state law governed, as the parties were in disagreement over the scope of the license grant, and the related arguments concerned state law issues regarding the right to use and ownership of related trade secrets that existed in connection with the implementation of the patented process. When a suit was initially filed in federal district court, the defendant immediately responded with a motion to dismiss on the basis that there was a lack of subject matter jurisdiction. Specifically, the defendant argued that there was no federal question with respect to either the license dispute or the issues arising under the Uniform Trade Secret Act. Further, as both entities were foreign corporations, there was an absence of diversity necessary for the court to exercise subject matter jurisdiction on that basis. Predictably, when the court later granted the motion to dismiss, it also noted that the jurisdiction clause in the parties' agreement was not relevant to its determination, as the parties "cannot confer subject matter jurisdiction by agreement." As the defendant had also filed a separate declaratory relief action in its own jurisdiction prior to the hearing on the motion to dismiss, once the federal district court dismissed the action based on lack of subject matter jurisdiction, the plaintiff was left to renew its claims as cross-claims in the proceeding already initiated by the defendant in its "home court."

While the foregoing result would not have occurred if the plaintiff had been able to include a secondary or tertiary claim that posed a federal question (such as a Lanham Act claim, which may have been applicable, as the defendant's advertising on its website touted the benefits of its internal development efforts giving rise to the advantages of its products), an amendment would not have cured the problem, since the court must consider subject matter jurisdiction as of the date on which the complaint is initially filed.

> "Any claim or dispute between the parties shall be brought in the state or federal courts located in the State of New York."

This hybrid venue/jurisdiction clause has the benefit of avoiding the issue of subject matter jurisdiction, as it specifies either state or federal court, with the consent to personal jurisdiction fairly implied. However, as it is not expressly stated, the risk of a lack of personal jurisdiction and a challenge thereto through a special appearance still remain. This clause also has the benefit of limiting the ability of the adverse party to choose the location, thus preempting the plaintiff's choice of forum, for example, by filing a suit for declaratory relief in a foreign location before the plaintiff can get its complaint on file (which is a tactic more frequently considered where there is a lack of a venue or jurisdiction clause). But, by including the mandatory language and thus limiting the choice of forum for disputes between the parties to a court located in New York, other problems arise. For example, how does that clause factor into a situation where the plaintiff decides to file both in a New York court and before the International Trade Commission? Given the extended reach of the ITC to cases of trade secret misappropriation, even where the act of misappropriation occurred wholly overseas (consistent with its mandate to protect domestic industry from the effect of unfair trade practices), a plaintiff may well wish to file parallel proceedings in order to maximize leverage. Likewise, what happens when the plaintiff wishes to sue a third party, such as a new employer located in a distant forum that arguably is now using trade secrets misappropriated by a former employee? Does this clause mean that, as the new employer has no ties to the area so the court does not have personal jurisdiction over the entity, the plaintiff must file two separate proceedings in two different locales? While the plaintiff can argue that the act of misappropriation, first through acquisition by the former employee and subsequently through use by the new employer, has caused harm in the jurisdiction in which the plaintiff wishes to file, the machinations this strategy entails could be better addressed through drafting the clause differently before the dispute arises.

> "The parties hereby irrevocably consent to the jurisdiction of the state and federal courts located in the State of New York in any action arising out of or relating to this Agreement."

This third provision avoids some of the issues that can arise with the prior two clauses by stipulating that an action can be filed in either state or federal court as appropriate given the subject matter analysis. There is an express consent to personal jurisdiction and venue, such that a party would not be able to challenge the right of the other parties to bring the matter in the specified court. Even if the responding party consents to the jurisdiction of the specified courts, however, it is not without means to seek to change the venue. A motion under the principles of forum non conveniens can still be considered, as some courts do not construe the foregoing language as exclusive or mandatory but merely persuasive, and thus only one factor in deciding whether another forum would be more "convenient" for resolution of the matter when all of the remaining private and public factors are considered.

4. Fee Clauses

Whether to include a fee clause is an issue that divides transactional and litigation attorneys. Those who are in favor of such provisions generally believe that a fee provision, with the potential of awarding the fees and costs of litigation to the prevailing party, has a prophylactic effect that will cause a party to pause before initiating what might otherwise be a borderline dispute (or, alternatively, to reconsider the wisdom of asserting a decidedly deficient defense in order to delay the inevitable). Proponents of fee clauses also argue that the "loser pays" system of litigation, by reallocating the full economic cost of litigation on the loser, is an appropriate means of advancing societal policy, similar to loosening foreseeability restrictions on contractual damages awards in a bad-faith breach.

Parties who do not favor the use of contractual fee provisions focus largely on the way in which these clauses disproportionately influence the economics of the underlying dispute, in that the potential for the prevailing party to recover the fees incurred becomes a significant factor in the economic assessment of any potential business resolution of the dispute.

In the specific context of agreements that may come into play in trade secret cases, additional factors must be considered. Although the complexity of the facts and the legal issues in trade secret disputes can drive the fees on each side into seven figures or more, in many cases the only realistic relief may be injunctive in nature and/or involve a de minimus royalty award when lost profits or unjust enrichment cannot be established. If all parties are required to bear their own fees, in cases where the plaintiff is not entitled to significant damages, the defendant has little economic incentive to settle early in the lawsuit. But the presence of a fee clause provides a strong economic incentive for the defendant to resolve the matter early in the proceedings. A plaintiff who may only be entitled to nonmonetary relief will be willing to forgo the right to seek fees if a resolution is reached early in the case. However, that plaintiff may refuse to accept a no-cash business solution as the case nears trial, based on the assumption that, by operation of the fee clause, the plaintiff will be able to recoup all of the fees incurred once it has "prevailed."

The absence of a contractual fee clause in trade secret cases brought under the Uniform Trade Secrets Act does not leave the prevailing party without any potential avenue to recover the monies expended on counsel. Under the Uniform Trade Secrets Act, the court has the discretion to award fees to the prevailing party, as well as a reasonable sum to cover the services of expert witnesses, if it finds that a claim of misappropriation was made in bad faith, a motion to terminate an injunction was made or resisted in bad faith, or willful and malicious misappropriation exists. However, to avail itself of these benefits, a prevailing party must prove more than required in order to obtain a contractual award of attorney's fees. In particular, a finding that the misappropriation was "willful and malicious" requires a finding of specific intent, whereas an entitlement to fees under a contractual provision may be satisfied merely by establishing that the defendant's conduct constituted a breach without the need to establish wrongful intent to acquire or use the trade secrets. In evaluating the pros and cons of a fee clause, the drafter must be mindful that the states that have not adopted the Uniform Trade Secrets Act generally will not award fees to the prevailing party who has otherwise established common-law trade secret misappropriation, whether under the Restatement or otherwise.

Parties who have the economic leverage in drafting and who are considering the use of a fee clause may be inclined to use a "one-way" clause, such as the following:

> "In any action brought to enforce the covenants set forth herein, or to recover damages for breach, the Company shall be entitled to recover reasonable attorneys' fees and other expenses of litigation, together with such other and further relief as may be proper."

The thought process behind use of a one-way clause is to gain additional economic leverage should a dispute arise. However, some states (such as California) address these clauses in two ways that render them ineffective at best, and problematic at worst, in important respects. First, they are rendered ineffective—at least as a means of creating unilateral leverage—by reason of statutes such as California Civil Code Section 1717(a), which provides:

> "In any action on a contract, where the contract specifically provides that attorney's fees and costs, which are incurred to enforce that contract, shall be awarded either to one of the parties or to the prevailing party, then the party who is determined to be the party prevailing on the contract, whether he or she is the party specified in the contract or not, shall be entitled to reasonable attorney's fees in addition to other costs."

With the fee clause now reciprocal by operation of law, the economic leverage is lost. As a result of the desire to recoup its litigation fee expenditures, the potential increases that the defendant will refuse to settle on what would otherwise be business terms acceptable to the plaintiff (such as through the use of noneconomic use restrictions).

One-way fee clauses also have the potential of rendering an employment agreement void, as this is one factor that a court may consider in determining whether the terms of the agreement are unconscionable. While the statutory scheme in some jurisdictions appears to give the trial court discretion as to whether to sever or restrict the unconscionable provision or whether to refuse to enforce the entire agreement, careful consideration should be given to the value proposition of including these provisions. In some jurisdictions where the statutory scheme and case decisions appear to contemplate the latter course, inclusion of such clauses alone can result in the court concluding that the entire agreement is void as a result of being "permeated" by unconscionability.

5. *Integration Clauses*

Trade secret cases are not just a dispute over the nature of the information in question. When a dispute arises over acquisition and/or use, the nature of the relationship between the litigants becomes a central issue to be explored, as their contractual and noncontractual interactions create and define the level and extent of the rights, duties, and obligations with respect to the information. Integration clauses, often used as a helpful guide to the court when faced with issues of contractual interpretation, can confuse the issue in the context of trade secrets due to the potential that several documents—whether or not contemporaneously created—may bear on the relationship in question.

The following provision is a fairly standard example of language used in integration clauses.

> "This Agreement expresses the full and complete understanding of the Parties with respect to the subject matter hereof and supersedes all prior and/or contemporaneous proposals, agreements, representations, and undertakings, whether written or oral. In the event of any conflict between the provisions of this Agreement and the provisions of any other agreement between the parties, the provisions of this Agreement shall control."

The difficulty with this provision in the context of a trade secret dispute arises in part from the ambiguity of the term "subject matter hereof." What the parties may think this phrase encompasses, if they were to actually give it thought at the time of execution, may be radically different from the meaning a judge might apply years later during litigation. Further, since this phrase is almost always included without any negotiation or discussion, the court is left without extrinsic evidence of the parties' mutual (or "objective manifestation of") intent to help in construction of the term. Instead, the court must rely on statutory rules on contract interpretation.

The second sentence in the above example is problematic, as it is not time-bounded (by the use of the phrase "any other agreement" without the modifiers "prior and/or contemporaneous") and creates a hierarchical approach that facially applies even with respect to after-created agreements. When multiple documents are presented by the parties as bearing upon the issue, with each side claiming that its separate document is the agreement applicable to the instant dispute, the court may instead decide to apply the rule of construction that several contracts relating to the same matters, between the same parties, and made as parts of substantially one transaction, are to be taken and construed together.

Consider the situation that may exist when a new hire is brought on board. In addition to an employment agreement that sets forth the general terms and conditions of employment, the new hire is asked to execute a proprietary inventions agreement that spells out additional employment rights and obligations—in particular, with respect to the ownership and use of company trade secrets. In this situation, it is important to ascertain whether someone with the company has considered whether any provisions between the employment and the proprietary inventions agreements are in conflict, directly or indirectly, which might bear upon the manner in which subsequent litigation is handled (such as the inclusion of an arbitration clause in the employment agreement that might result in an IP-related dispute under the proprietary inventions agreement being resolved through arbitration).

If there are multiple documents or agreements in place between the parties, such as in transactions between a company and its vendors or contractors, has someone considered whether there are prior provisions that need to be preserved or that may be impacted by application of Section 2-207 of the Uniform Commercial Code and the "battle of the forms"? In sales or licensing transactions, are appropriate safeguards in place to ensure either that there are no "side deals" being made or that they are memorialized in a fashion that will avoid conflict with the integration clause? Is there some mechanism in place (such as a modification/amendment clause in the existing agreement or a superseding clause in the after-created documents) to ensure that conflicting provisions in subsequently created documents have priority?

6. *Indemnification Clauses*

Transactional documents, such as license agreements and merger agreements, nearly always have some form of an indemnity clause tied to the ownership of and the right to use the intellectual property involved in the underlying transaction. These provisions often use language similar to the following:

> "Licensor agrees to defend, indemnify, and hold Licensee harmless against any third-party action, suit, or proceeding ('Claim') against Licensee to the extent such Claim is based upon an allegation that the Software, as of its delivery date under this Agreement, infringes a valid United States patent or copyright or misappropriates a third party's trade secret or confidential information."

While referred to as an "indemnity provision," the rights and obligations under the foregoing clause are far broader than merely whether an indemnitee is entitled to reimbursement for money it is ultimately forced to pay to a third party. As written, this clause also obligates the indemnitor to provide a defense in case a claim is made, regardless of the outcome of any suit or proceeding on the dispute, and careful thought should be given to whether to include that additional and wholly separate obligation. While the economic consequences of the duty to indemnify flows from the use of the information in question and is a generally quantifiable risk, the fees that may be involved in providing a defense to a claim of misappropriation are both difficult to estimate at the time of contracting and can well exceed the value of the information allegedly misappropriated.

From the indemnitor's standpoint, the indemnity provision should set forth in clear terms the scope and breadth of its defense and indemnity obligations, including as much specificity as possible over the circumstances in which the obligations may be triggered. According to the phrase used in the above example, defense obligations are triggered only by an "action, suit or proceeding," and do not arise merely upon receipt of a demand notice or cease-and-desist letter. However, even with this limitation, the indemnitor may also want to include a notice provision, which obligates the indemnitee to provide notice of any such demand or similar inquiry within a specified period, as a condition of its obligations and in order to allow it to promptly take action to address the situation. The indemnitor should also consider whether to place limits on the amount of the indemnification, such as tying the amount to the monies paid or earned under the agreement, or to set forth exclusions to the obligation, such as where its components are being integrated into a larger system that itself is the subject of a claim or suit.

From the indemnitees' standpoint, the right to use its own counsel, paid for by the indemnitor, should be a significant concern. The business and legal issues that face the indemnitor as the party primarily liable will be significantly different from those of the indemnitee, as are the business realities that arise in the context of any potential business solution. For example, the plaintiff alleging misappropriation by the indemnitor may be eager to enter into a business relationship with the indemnitee. But if the indemnitor has the right to require the use of its own counsel, to control whether the parties enter into any settlement negotiations, or to veto any settlement terms, a conflict is created that will interfere with the indemnitee's ability to extract itself from the litigation.

Questions that must be considered by both indemnitor and indemnitee include:

- Does the "defense" obligation refer to a lawyer selected by the indemnitor?
- Is joint representation allowed?
- What happens when there are "covered" and "uncovered" claims?
- Who has the right to control the litigation, to participate in settlement discussions, or to enter into (or veto) a settlement?
- What obligation—and to what extent—does the indemnitee have to cooperate in the litigation?
- What impact, if any, do allegations of fraud or malicious conduct have on the obligation to provide a defense or to indemnify against a loss?
- What is the ability of the indemnitor to stand behind the obligations that arise by operation of this provision, which can far exceed in dollars the amount of the transaction supported by the indemnity clause (such as the amount of license fees for software)?

- Should the indemnitee in a merger require a hold-back or escrow for a reasonable period of time to cover the anticipated expense of the duty to defend or the obligation to indemnify?
- Does the indemnitor have the right to substitute non-infringing goods in lieu of providing a defense, and what remedies does the indemnitee then have, given it will be receiving something other than the precise goods that it bargained for originally?
- Are there any limitations on the amount of the indemnity obligation or the type of damages that fall under the indemnity obligation (to include or exclude lost profits, and indirect, consequential, or incidental damages), and are those monies first or last in, or proportional, when one considers the relative contribution to settlement or satisfaction of a judgment?
- Is there any conflict between the obligations under the indemnity provision and any other provision that may extend or limit UCC warranties or remedies (such as otherwise provided for under UCC 2-312 (2) and (3))?

7. *Release Clauses*

Almost by definition, the vast majority of release clauses arise in the context of the business settlement of a dispute. The danger in trade secret cases arises in the tendency toward overbreadth in release clauses, with respect to the nature of claims being released as well as the extended list of individuals and entities who are both giving and getting the benefit of the release, as reflected in the following example:

> "Releasor, on behalf of itself and its representatives, beneficiaries, Affiliates, predecessors, successors-in-interest, agents, and assigns (collectively, the "Related Parties" and, together with the Releasor, the "Releasing Parties"), hereby remises, releases, and forever discharges each of the Companies and each of their respective past and present predecessors, successors, heirs, assigns, parent companies, subsidiaries, divisions, equity holders, owners, members, managers, partners, directors, officers, employees, contractors, agents,

representatives, consultants, accountants, counsel, insurers, associates, Affiliates, and all Persons acting by, through, under or in concert with them, or any of them (collectively "Released Parties"), of and from all debts, demands, actions, causes of action, suits, accounts, covenants, contracts, agreements, damages, and any and all claims, demands and liabilities whatsoever of every name and nature, both in law and in equity, against any or all of the Released Parties, which any or all of the Releasing Parties has, ever had or may have, whether known or unknown, for, upon, or by reason of, any matter, cause, or thing whatsoever occurring from the beginning of the world to the date hereof, including, without limiting the generality of the foregoing, those with respect to or arising out of any public policy, contract, tort, or common law obligation, including, without limitation, a breach of express or implied contract or of an implied covenant of good faith and fair dealing, and negligent or intentional infliction of emotional distress; any outstanding indebtedness owed any Released Party to Releasor or its Affiliates (collectively, the "*Claims*"). Releasor represents and warrants to each Released Party that: (a) neither Releasor nor any of the Related Parties has transferred, assigned, or encumbered all or any part of any Claims, that Releasor has full authority and capacity to execute this Release, and that no notices to, or consents, authorizations, or approvals of, any Person are required (other than those already given or obtained) in connection with the execution and delivery hereof; (b) Releasor has had the opportunity to seek, or has sought, advice regarding Releasor's legal rights from an attorney of Releasor's choice; (c) Releasor has executed this Release by the exercise of Releasing Party's informed choice and free of undue influence; and (d) Releasor has executed this Release voluntarily and without reliance on any statement, promise, representation, or other inducement of any kind or character, other than as provided for in the Stock Redemption Agreement. Without in any way limiting any of the rights and remedies otherwise available to any Released Party, Releasor covenants that neither it nor any Person acting on its behalf shall institute or cause to be instituted, or otherwise participate in or assist in any manner with, any proceeding of any kind or character against any Released Parties, which proceeding arises out of any Claim. Releasor covenants to indemnify, defend (by counsel reasonably acceptable to Companies), and hold harmless the Released Parties from any and all Claims that any Released Parties may suffer or incur or which may be alleged against any Released Parties. This is a full, final, and complete Release and settlement of all Claims and shall not be reopened in the future. If facts or circumstances concerning or relating to this Release are later found to be contrary to the facts or circumstances believed by Releasor to be true as of the date hereof, Releasor accepts and assumes the risk thereof and this Release shall remain effective. Releasor, on behalf of itself and the Related Parties, hereby represents and warrants to the Released Parties that Releasor knowingly and intentionally has waived any protection afforded to them by California Civil Code § 1542, which provides: *A general release does not extend to claims which the creditor does not know or suspect to exist in his or her favor at the time of executing the release, which if known by him or her must have materially affected his or her settlement with the debtor.* Releasor, on behalf of itself and the Related Parties, further represents and warrants that this Release is intended to cover all Claims, whether the same are known, unknown, or hereafter discovered or ascertained, and the provisions of § 1542 of the California Civil Code are hereby expressly waived."

Even where the party giving the release believes that there will not be any ongoing interactions or relationship between the parties, so that the interactions that led to the dispute can be described as "one and done," the extreme breadth of the foregoing release should be reviewed with great care. Under the language of this example, any claim for trade secret misappropriation will be barred, even if the claim that gave rise to the release had nothing whatsoever to do with an issue that might bear on misappropriation of trade secrets, such as might happen where a claim is made against a software developer for failing to complete a project on time and within budget. Because of the release of "unknown claims," if the company giving the release later learns that the developer is now marketing a product that appears to include trade secrets made available to the developer during the performance of his or her work for the company, any claim seeking to address that situation will be barred.

Care should also be exercised regarding the "and its" provisions, through which the list of persons released is expanded to a sundry list of other persons and entities who have been made intended third-party beneficiaries of the release. Similarly, a releasing party should look carefully at the "on behalf" language to ensure that it has the actual authority to provide a release on behalf of the enumerated third parties, and to conduct the necessary due diligence to ensure that it is making a properly considered decision in agreeing to a release of potentially valuable claims that belong to that third party. Finally, the nonreleasing party should buttress that language with a corresponding warranty of authority of the party giving the release to enter into the agreement.

For the same reasons as those pertaining to the care needed in considering the breadth of the claims being released, the party seeking the release should be wary about a demand from the releasing party that the releases be mutual. Absent a careful investigation into the question of whether it might have a claim that would be impacted by the release, by agreeing to mutuality of releases, the party may be unknowingly giving up an unasserted chose in action that has significant value.

8. *Marking Clauses*

In those situations where the parties anticipate an exchange of information that may constitute one or both party's trade secrets during the course of each party's performance under an agreement or during the course of their relationship, such as in joint development arrangements or in connection with the due diligence process leading to a potential merger, a specified protocol to identify the exchanged trade secrets can avoid a tangle of problems where the parties later dispute the extent to which trade secret information was exchanged, or whether the information exchanged qualifies as a trade secret. The following marking provision is an example for use in such situations.

> "*Marking requirements.* Information shall be subject to the restrictions of this Agreement if it is in writing or other tangible form only if clearly marked as confidential or proprietary when furnished to the receiving party or, if not in tangible form, only if it is identified orally and specifically as confidential or proprietary at the time of disclosure and is summarized in a writing so marked and delivered to the receiving party within thirty (30) days after such disclosure, in which case the Information contained in such summary (not information contained solely in the non-tangible disclosure) shall be subject to the restrictions herein. For purposes of this Agreement, "writing" includes without limitation paper documents, electronic mail, slide presentations, and other communications involving visually readable characters; and "delivery" includes without limitation transfer of a paper document, electronic mail, slide presentations, facsimile, and all other forms of transmitting recorded information. Each party hereto shall endeavor to keep to a minimum the amount of Information that is furnished to the other upon which restrictions are imposed. Information other than Information which is marked or otherwise identified and delivered as provided above, shall not be subject to any restriction by the transmitting party as to the receiving party's disclosure or use thereof."

The difficulties that exist with use of these types of provisions do not arise so much by reason of the particular language used, but rather in ensuring compliance with the obligations created thereby. In the absence of compliance by the delivering party the certainty exists, should a dispute arise, that the receiving party will claim that the information so provided is not entitled to any protection. If the receiving party does not compare what it received to what the other party claims to have been delivered, or to what it may have had access to by reason of its own efforts, the possibility exists that it might also face difficulties in the event of a later dispute, such as the loss of the ability to later argue that the designation by the delivering party was improper or overbroad.

When this type of provision is used, the party providing the information should make sure to have in place protocols for tracking delivery and, in particular, for adhering to the notification deadlines for information provided orally, as there otherwise may not be a consistent record of what was provided. Likewise, the receiving party should have in place protocols for keeping track of notifications and for reviewing their contents to ensure that what was received is consistent with what was described. When this provision is in place, both sides must take affirmative steps to ensure that the rank-and-file employees have been trained in its application and the consequences of failure to comply, and their supervisors tasked with ensuring adherence to its requirements. Before agreeing to a marking provision, it is important to determine whether in practice the individuals affected will be able and willing to adhere to its requirements.

CHAPTER THIRTEEN

The Trade Secret Fitness Audit

As markets climb out of recession, there is a corresponding uptick in intellectual property (IP) litigation of all types, and in particular trade secret litigation, as venture money becomes available to fund new businesses. Current employees see opportunities to monetize their ideas without the need to share with their employers. Former employees who were let go during restructuring periods now have opportunities to make use of information acquired during their prior employment. Unfortunately, few companies realize that they should be concerned, during a reduction in force, that soon-to-be-former employees may take IP with them. With the focus on overcoming challenging economic times, how to increase quarterly earnings draws more attention than protecting abstract rights. In many situations the company does not even have a clear ability to identify what it really needs to protect. When a dispute does occur, the unprepared company must spend significant funds to first determine what may have been taken and whether anything can be done in response. In essence, attempts to close the barn doors finally occur, but after the horses are already gone.

Developing and thereafter auditing the health of an intellectual property rights program is an essential part of protecting a company's key intangible assets. The nature of a fitness audit is designed to ensure that the company is employing best practices for the information that must be protected. This process involves more than reviewing relevant agreements, policies, and procedures for the treatment of confidential and proprietary information. A business must first understand what it owns in order to effectively protect its interests.

Forward-thinking companies avoid spending huge sums in litigation by recognizing they can achieve much more, while spending less, by dealing with problems before they arise. These companies consider what steps they can take to implement best IP rights practices with respect to their trade secrets. As a result, they are also well positioned once the economy improves to take advantage of the competitive edge that a strong IP portfolio can offer.

1. Key Objectives of the Fitness Audit

Intellectual property is considered to be one of the more important assets a company can own, whether in the form of patents, copyrights, trademarks, or trade secrets. An IP fitness audit is intended to identify key information to be protected, whether under common law, the Patent Act, the Copyright Act, or the Uniform Trade Secrets Act.

The nature of trade secrets poses a particular problem during an IP fitness audit. They are less likely to be catalogued by the client and are not subject to any registration requirement either to establish ownership or to assert a claim based thereon. There are, however, steps that the client can implement to assist in the process of identifying key areas where trade secrets reside. Within these areas, the client can be requested to highlight discrete blocks of information that provide the company a competitive edge. Following the process of cataloguing the trade secrets, risk factors posed by business relationships—employees, customers, joint ventures, OEMs, etc.—can be identified. Areas of weakness in the ability to protect the trade secrets can then be addressed, and best practices implemented, by examining existing and available procedures, policies, and enforcement protocols for protection of these intellectual assets.

2. *Identifying the Trade Secrets Existing within the Universe of Business Information*

A business cannot easily protect a trade secret when it has not been identified. Trade secrets are rarely recognized as such upon the epiphany that leads to a solution. Once the idea is implemented, trade secrets that exist within that concept are not generally memorialized for purposes of populating a repository the business can use for future reference purposes. Rather, trade secrets that exist within the larger universe of business information are most frequently recognized as such only upon the occurrence of an event that places the secret nature of the information in question.

For clients who have not already taken steps to identify areas where they have trade secret information, rather than waiting for an event that places the trade secrets at risk, a number of relevant questions can be asked that focus on what transforms routine business information into trade secret information. These might include the following:

- The client should be asked to provide a list of all information considered to constitute its trade secrets, a description of how they are documented and maintained, and measures routinely implemented to protect them from disclosure.
- What information does the company consider confidential, and what does it consider proprietary? This is somewhat of a "trick" question, as the term "proprietary" is not the same as "confidential." Labeling information as "proprietary," by itself, does not mean that the information constitutes a trade secret. The term "proprietary," as defined by dictionaries such as the *American Heritage College Dictionary*, 4th Edition, refers specifically to *ownership*. Yet many individuals, including most lawyers, equate the terms proprietary, confidential, and trade secret, and use them interchangeably, as if intent on implementing the maxim of jurisprudence that "superfluity does not vitiate." However, asking for an identification of company proprietary

information is a helpful way to begin a dialogue. This discussion will assist in the process of identifying the subset of proprietary information that has the additional attributes necessary to constitute a trade secret. To this end, the client should be asked to provide a list that identifies all confidential and proprietary "know-how" and a description of how the information is maintained, who has access, and under what circumstances.

- How does the company make its money? Trade secrets, under the Uniform Trade Secrets Act, consist of information that has independent economic value from not being generally known to the public or to others who can obtain economic value from its disclosure or use. Similarly, under the *Restatement of Torts*, the information must give the owner an opportunity to obtain an advantage over competitors who do not know or use it. Learning where a company makes its money is a key to identifying what information provides the economic advantage and whether that information is worthy of efforts to maintain its secrecy.
- Where is the company now, and where is it going? Some of the most valuable trade secrets are not always related to what a company is currently doing in the market, whether its revenue generation is service- or product-based. Rather, the future plans in the process of development are a fertile source of trade secret information, even if only in the nascent stage. This is a likely area for secrets to be misappropriated, as the return on monetization for this information has a greater potential yield than secrets that have long been implemented.
- What information would adversely impact the company if taken to a competitor? Some information, such as market intelligence, does not readily appear to provide independent economic value by not being known to others. However, a client may be able to more readily conceptualize the value if the question is considered in the context of the harm to its operations should the information become available to a competitor.

- What information would significantly benefit a competitor? The best way to identify a trade secret is not always by consideration of the economic benefit to the client. Sometimes the information is part of a larger whole, such that it is impossible to discern its discrete contribution, and sometimes the information is not currently being used in the operations of the business. An alternative method of identifying trade secrets looks at the value to a competitor if it was able to acquire, and then use, the information to further its business.
- Has the company developed any software or technology that is used internally in the operation of its business? If so, the client should identify and provide a list of all such items considered material to its business. The client should provide a brief description of the function of each aspect of the software or technology and identify the principal developers. This process should also include an identification of any open-source software that has been incorporated into the client's software.
- Are there techniques or concepts under development that are not ripe for seeking patent protection? Many technology companies have established patent development programs in which inventors are encouraged to submit an IDF (invention disclosure form) and are specially compensated upon issuance of a patent that encompasses the inventions disclosed therein. But not every invention in an IDF becomes a patent, or even finds its way into a patent application. The invention may have been conceived but not yet reduced to practice. There may be on-sale bar issues or prior art that make patentability problematic due to anticipation or obviousness. For these reasons and a host of others, particular attention should be paid to areas where patents are being considered.
- Are there aspects of patented technology that remain secret? Even when a patent issues, not all aspects of the invention will be disclosed, whether it involves a process for manufacturing or a

device being manufactured. Further enhancements may have been developed since the filing of the application that are not being claimed in a continuation or progeny patent, or have yet to be claimed. This is another, although related, area in which trade secrets will reside.

To facilitate the investigation and identification of trade secrets, the practitioner must identify and speak with a variety of people, including individuals in engineering, marketing, and sales, who will be well suited to identify key data. In addition, managers in IT, engineering, marketing, and sales can assist in identifying who has access to what information, and whether access is consistent with the requirement of engaging in reasonable efforts to maintain secrecy.

3. Identifying/Addressing Risk Factors to the Protection of Trade Secrets

Specification of the information that provides an economic benefit to the business from not being generally known is only the start in the process of auditing IP fitness for trade secrets. To qualify as a trade secret under the Uniform Trade Secrets Act, the information must also be subject to reasonable measures under the circumstances to maintain its secrecy. The following are some of the risk factors to consider.

a. Employer/Employee Relationships

The greatest risk of trade secret misappropriation involves employees of the business, and particularly those who will soon be former employees, as they are most likely to have means, opportunity, and motive. Protection of the trade secrets of a business begins when an employee is first hired, by ensuring that the risk of IP contamination at the point of hire has been ameliorated and continues through the employee's tenure. In addition to nondisclosure agreements, proprietary invention agreements, and post-employment noncompetes, a number of steps can be implemented that will assist with new employees. These steps will also provide additional safeguards with respect to the existing workforce during and after the term of their employment.

- Ensure that appropriate written policies exist and are provided to all new employees at the time of hiring. In unmistakable terms, the policies must make explicit the prohibition over use of IP belonging to others. The policies must include a prohibition against bringing into the workplace any materials from prior places of employment, whether in electronic or hard-copy form. Employees routinely keep copies of their "own" notes and workpapers, especially when they held a position that had an inventive component, often without any thought that these materials may contain or constitute trade secrets belonging to their former employer. As a part of the new employee orientation process, the new employee and his or her supervisor should review these policies together, to ensure that no questions remain regarding their implementation or importance. The broader workforce should be reminded, on an ongoing basis, that any violation of these policies will result in immediate adverse employment consequences, leading up to and potentially including termination.

- Require invention disclosures by all new employees before they begin work. This will avoid later disputes over conception and ownership. Any substantive disclosures should be reviewed for overlap with new assignments to minimize potential for comingling of IP.

- Generally, examine the delineation of workforce responsibilities for products or projects, especially when there are multiple teams assigned. Be clear regarding the areas to which the employee will now be assigned, to reduce unnecessary access overlap with areas where the employee has no responsibilities. The more overlap, the greater the risk of a claim of misappropriation through inevitable disclosure in those states that recognize the doctrine. Suggest the client consider "walling off" affected employees for a period of time or modifying their responsibilities to reduce the extent of overlap.

- On larger projects, consider formal compartmentalization of information. A source code development project may lend itself to discrete development teams, each of which has access only to their portion under development. Should an act of misappropriation occur, the potential for theft of the entire code is reduced and the potential for injury minimized.
- Restrict the introduction and use of any data that may be questionable as to ownership or the right to exploit (such as open-source materials). Require clearance by a supervisory-level employee before agreeing to any click-through licenses, as they may have provisions addressing derivative works that will call ownership rights into question.
- Implement restrictions to internal data and confidential materials, limiting access to those with a demonstrated need to use, and periodically review the access list to ensure the need is still extant. These restrictions are both physical (locked file cabinets and password-protected computer systems) and policy-based (position-based restrictions limiting who has the right within the organization to access materials, and separating access by function as well as by geographic location).
- Periodic monitoring of electronic databases should be implemented to look for unusual access patterns.
- Internal methods for identification, handling, and marking of confidential and proprietary information should be reviewed, and any inconsistencies within the organization resulting from legacy procedures or individual customer requirements should be noted and eliminated.
- External requirements for identification and handling of information received by the organization, or that is being shared outside of the organization, should be reviewed and monitored to ensure compliance. All relevant employees should be trained on both internal and external methods, with supervisory employees explicitly responsible for compliance.

- Document-retention programs should be reviewed periodically for compliance with litigation-based obligations of preservation. The process should be modified to review materials for sensitive and valuable information before they are destroyed to confirm that the program is being implemented consistent with the current requirements of the business, and to ensure destruction of those materials containing sensitive information the company no longer wants to maintain.
- Protocols for exit interviews should be reviewed, and established if nonexistant, so the process of separation after termination is conducted in a uniform and systematic manner. Decisions should be made whether to escort employees off the premises immediately upon notice of termination and whether their access to computer systems should be terminated before, during, or after their exit interview (and for how long, if the latter). There should be a standard process for recovering any portable electronic devices issued for use in the course of their employment. Hard drives should be imaged for technical contributors. Too often, regardless of the policy to conduct exit interviews, they are either not conducted at all or are done in a haphazard fashion. These interviews are a perfect opportunity to confirm with exiting employees their continuing obligations to maintain the confidentiality of the business's trade secrets, to affirm that they have not taken anything that belongs to the business and that might contain trade secret information, and to ask about their future plans, including whether they are going to work for a competitor. This last point touches upon issues that exist in jurisdictions where the doctrine of inevitable disclosure is recognized. An employee who is not forthright regarding future plans bears further attention. The protocol must also reflect the type of memorialization of the interview that is appropriate for the business and how (and by whom) that documentation will be created to ensure that it is prepared in a timely and consistent fashion.

- There should be a protocol to confirm compliance with proprietary rights agreements. This can involve a spectrum of efforts, from the use of "physical" tools to police compliance (such as taking and storing a forensic image of the employee's hard drives) to documentation of the status of his or her work at the time of termination.
- Where a new employer is identified as a competitor, an evaluation of risk will involve whether the business should contact the new employer to advise that the employee is under ongoing obligations of confidentiality and to request that the new employer take appropriate steps to ensure that the IP rights of the business are being respected.

b. Special Consultants and Contractors

In addition to employee issues, special attention is warranted with respect to individuals who are assisting the business on a project basis. Whether referred to as special consultants or contractors, these individuals may have access to some of the client's most sensitive information. Yet the same protections routinely used by a business for its own employees will not be as carefully implemented. The issues involved with consultants and contractors are not just the duty to maintain secrecy, which can be handled primarily through the use of non-disclosure provisions. If not addressed in the consulting agreement, potential issues can lead to competing claims over ownership of IP that may be developed during the course of the relationship. Access issues will arise and, as a practical matter, restrictions on physical access to buildings and work sites will weaken the longer the consultant is involved with the company, as his face becomes more familiar to the workforce. These issues are particularly overlooked when the consultant is working across several departments or in and out of multiple buildings. There are risks involved in open-ended arrangements, with the increased likelihood of end-point creep and the lack of termination oversight. Closure issues (along the lines discussed in connection with exit interviews, above) must be addressed once the project is over. End points should be specified, as they can always be extended, providing a trigger for reviewing the status of the arrangement and an opportunity for taking any steps necessary to secure any IP that may be implicated.

Particular attention is necessary when the consultant being retained is an expert in his area, as opposed to an individual contributor who may have a level of knowledge generally held by those in his trade or profession. Points to consider include:

- Does the "expert consultant" have conflicting obligations with contemporaneous consultancies?
- Is he teaching or publishing in his area of expertise? The desire to contribute to the larger body of technical knowledge is directly inconsistent with the obligation to maintain secrecy.
- Is it likely that she will have conflicting obligations as a result of prior consultancies, such that another business may make a claim that its IP has percolated into the client's knowledge warehouse?
- Is he likely to have conflicts with future consultancies, which can be addressed in his engagement agreements?

c. Multicompany Collaborative Relationships and Joint Ventures

Original equipment manufacturers, vendors, and joint ventures all share trade secrets as part of the process of collaborative business operations. For example, for an original equipment manufacturer (OEM) to design-in an input-output IC into a motherboard that will be sold to an end-user, detailed information is required regarding the pin-outs and registry sets. This information, however, is highly confidential to the IC manufacturer. All of the access issues previously discussed apply, but the foremost issue relates to ownership in addition to the always present question over permissive scope of use.

In the course of collaborative transactions, existing trade secrets will be used and new trade secrets created. There will be contributed IP, blended IP, developed IP, and derivative IP. There are special issues that exist regarding the extent of access and use by subsidiaries, related companies, successors, and assignees. The controlling documentation that governs the relationship must address all of these issues, as well as the protocols for ensuring complete and thorough identification of the IP as it is created and used. This documentation should be explicit regarding the rights to patents that are based on information that constituted, in whole or in part, the trade secrets of one, the other, or both, and the rights to monetize, license, or assert those resulting patents against third parties.

Protection of confidential information, with respect to both the manner of protection and the obligation, should be clear. This includes the duration and scope of the obligations and the manner by which they are policed during and after the relationship. Access and scope-of-use issues should be clarified, publication and publicity rights addressed, and claw-back and change-of-control issues delineated. Indemnity obligations, representations and warranties, and business disruption contingencies (e.g., IP escrows) also are issues that bear analysis.

d. Customer Relationships

Although customers are rarely provided with trade secret information, there are situations, including design-in projects, where it will be necessary to communicate sensitive information. Many sophisticated companies, when they have buying power and leverage, draft agreements to negate their obligation to maintain the trade secrets of their vendors, or to minimize the obligation by placing a durational limit on the period during which they are bound to protect the trade secrets of another. Marking obligations are included, with onerous obligations to mark materials as confidential and to provide confirming writings whenever any trade secrets are orally communicated. Some companies demand trade secret escrows, particularly in the context of software in the form of source-code escrows, with triggers that allow access under surprisingly innocuous conditions. In this area, the fitness audit consists (at least initially) of a review of these relationships and their governing agreements as a form of risk assessment. The next step is to determine the extent to which there is (non)compliance by either side. Once that analysis is completed, the business is better informed and can determine whether it is in its best interest, when the protection of the secrets is balanced against business realities, to take some further action.

4. After the Audit

The majority of business initiatives die out for lack of attention and follow-through within six months after initiation. To derive the highest value from an IP fitness audit, the overriding requirement going forward involves policing the obligations, policies, and procedures established as a result of the audit; ensuring and maintaining a chain of command responsible for enforcing and policing; and periodically reviewing (and, where appropriate, updating) "standard" contractual terms and agreements to preserve their desired legal effect. Relationships change over time, and rules may differ based upon the location of employees, the nature of the deal, and the goals of the business.

Appendix: Stipulated Protective Order for Litigation Involving Patents, Highly Sensitive Confidential Information and/or Trade Secrets

UNITED STATES DISTRICT COURT

NORTHERN DISTRICT OF CALIFORNIA

Plaintiff, v. Defendant.	Case No. C STIPULATED PROTECTIVE ORDER FOR LITIGATION INVOLVING PATENTS, HIGHLY SENSITIVE CONFIDENTIAL INFORMATION AND/OR TRADE SECRETS

1. PURPOSES AND LIMITATIONS

Disclosure and discovery activity in this action are likely to involve production of confidential, proprietary, or private information for which special protection from public disclosure and from use for any purpose other than prosecuting this litigation may be warranted. Accordingly, the parties hereby stipulate to and petition the court to enter the following Stipulated Protective Order. The parties acknowledge that this Order does not confer blanket protections on all disclosures or responses to discovery and that the protection it affords from public disclosure and use extends only to the limited information or items that are entitled to confidential treatment under the applicable legal principles. The parties further acknowledge, as set forth in Section 14.4, below, that this Stipulated Protective Order does not entitle them to file confidential information under seal; Civil Local Rule 79-5 and General Order 62 set forth the procedures that must be followed and the standards that will be applied when a party seeks permission from the court to file material under seal.

2. DEFINITIONS

2.1 Challenging Party: a Party or Non-Party that challenges the designation of information or items under this Order.

2.2 "CONFIDENTIAL" Information or Items: information (regardless of how it is generated, stored or maintained) or tangible things that qualify for protection under Federal Rule of Civil Procedure 26(c).

2.3 Counsel (without qualifier): Outside Counsel of Record and House Counsel (as well as their support staff).

[2.4 *Optional*: Designated House Counsel: House Counsel who seek access to "HIGHLY CONFIDENTIAL – ATTORNEYS' EYES ONLY" information in this matter.]

2.5 Designating Party: a Party or Non-Party that designates information or items that it produces in disclosures or in responses to discovery as "CONFIDENTIAL" or "HIGHLY CONFIDENTIAL – ATTORNEYS' EYES ONLY" [*Optional*: or "HIGHLY CONFIDENTIAL – SOURCE CODE"].

2.6 Disclosure or Discovery Material: all items or information, regardless of the medium or manner in which it is generated, stored, or maintained (including, among other things, testimony, transcripts, and tangible things), that are produced or generated in disclosures or responses to discovery in this matter.

2.7 Expert: a person with specialized knowledge or experience in a matter pertinent to the litigation who (1) has been retained by a Party or its counsel to serve as an expert witness or as a consultant in this action, (2) is not a past or current employee of a Party or of a Party's competitor, and (3) at the time of retention, is not anticipated to become an employee of a Party or of a Party's competitor.

2.8 "HIGHLY CONFIDENTIAL – ATTORNEYS' EYES ONLY" Information or Items: extremely sensitive "Confidential Information or Items," disclosure of which to another Party or Non-Party would create a substantial risk of serious harm that could not be avoided by less restrictive means.

[2.9 *Optional*: "HIGHLY CONFIDENTIAL – SOURCE CODE" Information or Items: extremely sensitive "Confidential Information or Items" representing computer code and associated comments and revision histories, formulas, engineering specifications, or schematics that define or otherwise describe in detail the algorithms or structure of software or hardware designs, disclosure of which to another Party or Non-Party would create a substantial risk of serious harm that could not be avoided by less restrictive means.]

2.10 House Counsel: attorneys who are employees of a party to this action. House Counsel does not include Outside Counsel of Record or any other outside counsel.

2.11 Non-Party: any natural person, partnership, corporation, association, or other legal entity not named as a Party to this action.

2.12 Outside Counsel of Record: attorneys who are not employees of a party to this action but are retained to represent or advise a party to this action and have appeared in this action on behalf of that party or are affiliated with a law firm which has appeared on behalf of that party.

2.13 Party: any party to this action, including all of its officers, directors, employees, consultants, retained experts, and Outside Counsel of Record (and their support staffs).

2.14 Producing Party: a Party or Non-Party that produces Disclosure or Discovery Material in this action.

2.15 Professional Vendors: persons or entities that provide litigation support services (e.g., photocopying, videotaping, translating, preparing exhibits or demonstrations, and organizing, storing, or retrieving data in any form or medium) and their employees and subcontractors.

2.16 Protected Material: any Disclosure or Discovery Material that is designated as "CONFIDENTIAL," or as "HIGHLY CONFIDENTIAL – ATTORNEYS' EYES ONLY." [*Optional*: or as "HIGHLY CONFIDENTIAL – SOURCE CODE."]

2.17 Receiving Party: a Party that receives Disclosure or Discovery Material from a Producing Party.

3. SCOPE

The protections conferred by this Stipulation and Order cover not only Protected Material (as defined above), but also (1) any information copied or extracted from Protected Material; (2) all copies, excerpts, summaries, or compilations of Protected Material; and (3) any testimony, conversations, or presentations by Parties or their Counsel that might reveal Protected Material. However, the protections conferred by this Stipulation and Order do not cover the following information: (a) any information that is in the public domain at the time of disclosure to a Receiving Party or becomes part of the public domain after its disclosure to a Receiving Party as a result of publication not involving a violation of this Order, including becoming part of the public record through trial or otherwise; and (b) any information known to the Receiving Party prior to the disclosure or obtained by the Receiving Party after the disclosure from a source who obtained the information lawfully and under no obligation of confidentiality to the Designating Party. Any use of Protected Material at trial shall be governed by a separate agreement or order.

4. DURATION

Even after final disposition of this litigation, the confidentiality obligations imposed by this Order shall remain in effect until a Designating Party agrees otherwise in writing or a court order otherwise directs. Final disposition shall be deemed to be the later of (1) dismissal of all claims and defenses in this action, with or without prejudice; and (2) final judgment herein after the completion and exhaustion of all appeals, rehearings, remands, trials, or reviews of this action, including the time limits for filing any motions or applications for extension of time pursuant to applicable law.

5. DESIGNATING PROTECTED MATERIAL

5.1 Exercise of Restraint and Care in Designating Material for Protection. Each Party or Non-Party that designates information or items for protection under this Order must take care to limit any such designation to specific material that qualifies under the appropriate standards. To the extent it is practical to do so, the Designating Party must designate for protection only those parts of material, documents, items, or oral or written communications that qualify – so that other portions of the material, documents, items, or communications for which protection is not warranted are not swept unjustifiably within the ambit of this Order.

Mass, indiscriminate, or routinized designations are prohibited. Designations that are shown to be clearly unjustified or that have been made for an improper purpose (e.g., to unnecessarily encumber or retard the case development process or to impose unnecessary expenses and burdens on other parties) expose the Designating Party to sanctions.

If it comes to a Designating Party's attention that information or items that it designated for protection do not qualify for protection at all or do not qualify for the level of protection initially asserted, that Designating Party must promptly notify all other parties that it is withdrawing the mistaken designation.

5.2 Manner and Timing of Designations. Except as otherwise provided in this Order (see, e.g., second paragraph of section 5.2(a) below), or as otherwise stipulated or ordered, Disclosure or Discovery

Material that qualifies for protection under this Order must be clearly so designated before the material is disclosed or produced.

Designation in conformity with this Order requires:

(a) <u>for information in documentary form</u> (e.g., paper or electronic documents, but excluding transcripts of depositions or other pretrial or trial proceedings), that the Producing Party affix the legend "CONFIDENTIAL" or "HIGHLY CONFIDENTIAL – ATTORNEYS' EYES ONLY" [*Optional*: or "HIGHLY CONFIDENTIAL – SOURCE CODE"] to each page that contains protected material. If only a portion or portions of the material on a page qualifies for protection, the Producing Party also must clearly identify the protected portion(s) (e.g., by making appropriate markings in the margins) and must specify, for each portion, the level of protection being asserted.

A Party or Non-Party that makes original documents or materials available for inspection need not designate them for protection until after the inspecting Party has indicated which material it would like copied and produced. During the inspection and before the designation, all of the material made available for inspection shall be deemed "HIGHLY CONFIDENTIAL – ATTORNEYS' EYES ONLY." After the inspecting Party has identified the documents it wants copied and produced, the Producing Party must determine which documents, or portions thereof, qualify for protection under this Order. Then, before producing the specified documents, the Producing Party must affix the appropriate legend ("CONFIDENTIAL" or "HIGHLY CONFIDENTIAL – ATTORNEYS' EYES ONLY" [*Optional:* or "HIGHLY CONFIDENTIAL – SOURCE CODE]) to each page that contains Protected Material. If only a portion or portions of the material on a page qualifies for protection, the Producing Party also must clearly identify the protected portion(s) (e.g., by making appropriate markings in the margins) and must specify, for each portion, the level of protection being asserted.

(b) for testimony given in deposition or in other pretrial or trial proceedings, that the Designating Party identify on the record, before the close of the deposition, hearing, or other proceeding, all protected testimony and specify the level of protection being asserted. When it is impractical to identify separately each portion of testimony that is entitled to protection and it appears that substantial portions of the testimony may qualify for protection, the Designating Party may invoke on the record (before the deposition, hearing, or other proceeding is concluded) a right to have up to 21 days to identify the specific portions of the testimony as to which protection is sought and to specify the level of protection being asserted. Only those portions of the testimony that are appropriately designated for protection within the 21 days shall be covered by the provisions of this Stipulated Protective Order. Alternatively, a Designating Party may specify, at the deposition or up to 21 days afterwards if that period is properly invoked, that the entire transcript shall be treated as "CONFIDENTIAL" or "HIGHLY CONFIDENTIAL – ATTORNEYS' EYES ONLY."

Parties shall give the other parties notice if they reasonably expect a deposition, hearing or other proceeding to include Protected Material so that the other parties can ensure that only authorized individuals who have signed the "Acknowledgment and Agreement to Be Bound" (Exhibit A) are present at those proceedings. The use of a document as an exhibit at a deposition shall not in any way affect its designation as "CONFIDENTIAL" or "HIGHLY CONFIDENTIAL – ATTORNEYS' EYES ONLY."

Transcripts containing Protected Material shall have an obvious legend on the title page that the transcript contains Protected Material, and the title page shall be followed by a list of all pages (including line numbers as appropriate) that have been designated as Protected Material and the level of protection being asserted by the Designating Party. The Designating Party shall inform the court reporter of these requirements. Any transcript that is prepared before the expiration of a 21-day period for designation shall be treated during that period as if it had been designated "HIGHLY CONFIDENTIAL – ATTORNEYS' EYES ONLY" in its entirety unless otherwise agreed. After the expiration of that period, the transcript shall be treated only as actually designated.

(c) for information produced in some form other than documentary and for any other tangible items, that the Producing Party affix in a prominent place on the exterior of the container or containers in which the information or item is stored the legend "CONFIDENTIAL" or "HIGHLY CONFIDENTIAL – ATTORNEYS' EYES ONLY" [*Optional*: or "HIGHLY CONFIDENTIAL – SOURCE CODE"]. If only a portion or portions of the information or item warrant protection, the Producing Party, to the extent practicable, shall identify the protected portion(s) and specify the level of protection being asserted.

5.3 Inadvertent Failures to Designate. If timely corrected, an inadvertent failure to designate qualified information or items does not, standing alone, waive the Designating Party's right to secure protection under this Order for such material. Upon timely correction of a designation, the Receiving Party must make reasonable efforts to assure that the material is treated in accordance with the provisions of this Order.

6. CHALLENGING CONFIDENTIALITY DESIGNATIONS

6.1 Timing of Challenges. Any Party or Non-Party may challenge a designation of confidentiality at any time. Unless a prompt challenge to a Designating Party's confidentiality designation is necessary to avoid foreseeable, substantial unfairness, unnecessary economic burdens, or a significant disruption or delay of the litigation, a Party does not waive its right to challenge a confidentiality designation by electing not to mount a challenge promptly after the original designation is disclosed.

6.2 Meet and Confer. The Challenging Party shall initiate the dispute resolution process by providing written notice of each designation it is challenging and describing the basis for each challenge. To avoid ambiguity as to whether a challenge has been made, the written notice must recite that the challenge to confidentiality is being made in accordance with this specific paragraph of the Protective Order. The parties shall attempt to resolve each challenge in good faith and must begin the process by conferring directly (in voice to voice dialogue; other forms of communication are not sufficient) within 14 days of the date of service of notice. In conferring, the Challenging Party must explain the basis for its belief that the confidentiality designation was not proper and must give the Designating Party an opportunity to review the designated material, to reconsider the circumstances, and, if no change in designation is offered, to explain the basis for the chosen designation. A Challenging Party may proceed to the next stage of the challenge process only if it has engaged in this meet and confer process first or establishes that the Designating Party is unwilling to participate in the meet and confer process in a timely manner.

6.3 Judicial Intervention. If the Parties cannot resolve a challenge without court intervention, the Designating Party shall file and serve a motion to retain confidentiality under Civil Local Rule 7 (and in compliance with Civil Local Rule 79-5 and General Order 62, if applicable) within 21 days of the initial notice of challenge or within 14 days of the parties agreeing that the meet and confer process will not resolve their dispute, whichever is earlier.[1] Each such motion must be accompanied by a competent

[1] *Alternative*: It may be appropriate in certain circumstances for the parties to agree to shift the

declaration affirming that the movant has complied with the meet and confer requirements imposed in the preceding paragraph. Failure by the Designating Party to make such a motion including the required declaration within 21 days (or 14 days, if applicable) shall automatically waive the confidentiality designation for each challenged designation. In addition, the Challenging Party may file a motion challenging a confidentiality designation at any time if there is good cause for doing so, including a challenge to the designation of a deposition transcript or any portions thereof. Any motion brought pursuant to this provision must be accompanied by a competent declaration affirming that the movant has complied with the meet and confer requirements imposed by the preceding paragraph.

The burden of persuasion in any such challenge proceeding shall be on the Designating Party. Frivolous challenges and those made for an improper purpose (e.g., to harass or impose unnecessary expenses and burdens on other parties) may expose the Challenging Party to sanctions. Unless the Designating Party has waived the confidentiality designation by failing to file a motion to retain confidentiality as described above, all parties shall continue to afford the material in question the level of protection to which it is entitled under the Producing Party's designation until the court rules on the challenge.

7. ACCESS TO AND USE OF PROTECTED MATERIAL

7.1 Basic Principles. A Receiving Party may use Protected Material that is disclosed or produced by another Party or by a Non-Party in connection with this case only for prosecuting, defending, or attempting to settle this litigation. Such Protected Material may be disclosed only to the categories of persons and under the conditions described in this Order. When the litigation has been terminated, a Receiving Party must comply with the provisions of section 15 below (FINAL DISPOSITION).

Protected Material must be stored and maintained by a Receiving Party at a location and in a secure manner[2] that ensures that access is limited to the persons authorized under this Order.

7.2 Disclosure of "CONFIDENTIAL" Information or Items. Unless otherwise ordered by the

---

burden to move on the Challenging Party after a certain number of challenges are made to avoid an abuse of the process. The burden of persuasion would remain on the Designating Party.

[2] It may be appropriate under certain circumstances to require the Receiving Party to store any electronic Protected Material in password-protected form.

court or permitted in writing by the Designating Party, a Receiving Party may disclose any information or item designated "CONFIDENTIAL" only to:

(a) the Receiving Party's Outside Counsel of Record in this action, as well as employees of said Outside Counsel of Record to whom it is reasonably necessary to disclose the information for this litigation and who have signed the "Acknowledgment and Agreement to Be Bound" that is attached hereto as Exhibit A;

(b) the officers, directors, and employees (including House Counsel) of the Receiving Party to whom disclosure is reasonably necessary for this litigation and who have signed the "Acknowledgment and Agreement to Be Bound" (Exhibit A);

(c) Experts (as defined in this Order) of the Receiving Party to whom disclosure is reasonably necessary for this litigation and who have signed the "Acknowledgment and Agreement to Be Bound" (Exhibit A);

(d) the court and its personnel;

(e) court reporters and their staff, professional jury or trial consultants, and Professional Vendors to whom disclosure is reasonably necessary for this litigation and who have signed the "Acknowledgment and Agreement to Be Bound" (Exhibit A);

(f) during their depositions, witnesses in the action to whom disclosure is reasonably necessary and who have signed the "Acknowledgment and Agreement to Be Bound" (Exhibit A), unless otherwise agreed by the Designating Party or ordered by the court. Pages of transcribed deposition testimony or exhibits to depositions that reveal Protected Material must be separately bound by the court reporter and may not be disclosed to anyone except as permitted under this Stipulated Protective Order.

(g) the author or recipient of a document containing the information or a custodian or other person who otherwise possessed or knew the information.

7.3 Disclosure of "HIGHLY CONFIDENTIAL – ATTORNEYS' EYES ONLY" [*Optional*: and "HIGHLY CONFIDENTIAL – SOURCE CODE"] Information or Items. Unless otherwise ordered by the court or permitted in writing by the Designating Party, a Receiving Party may disclose any information or item designated "HIGHLY CONFIDENTIAL – ATTORNEYS' EYES ONLY" [*Optional*: or "HIGHLY CONFIDENTIAL – SOURCE CODE"] only to:

(a) the Receiving Party's Outside Counsel of Record in this action, as well as employees of said Outside Counsel of Record to whom it is reasonably necessary to disclose the information for this litigation and who have signed the "Acknowledgment and Agreement to Be Bound" that is attached hereto as Exhibit A;

[(b) *Optional as deemed appropriate in case-specific circumstances:* Designated House Counsel of the Receiving Party[3] (1) who has no involvement in competitive decision-making, (2) to whom disclosure is reasonably necessary for this litigation, (3) who has signed the "Acknowledgment and Agreement to Be Bound" (Exhibit A), and (4) as to whom the procedures set forth in paragraph 7.4(a)(1), below, have been followed];[4]

(c) Experts of the Receiving Party (1) to whom disclosure is reasonably necessary for this litigation, (2) who have signed the "Acknowledgment and Agreement to Be Bound" (Exhibit A), and (3) as to whom the procedures set forth in paragraph 7.4(a)(2), below, have been followed];

(d) the court and its personnel;

(e) court reporters and their staff, professional jury or trial consultants,[5] and Professional Vendors to whom disclosure is reasonably necessary for this litigation and who have signed the "Acknowledgment and Agreement to Be Bound" (Exhibit A); and

(f) the author or recipient of a document containing the information or a custodian or other person who otherwise possessed or knew the information.

7.4 <u>Procedures for Approving or Objecting to Disclosure of "HIGHLY CONFIDENTIAL –</u>

---

[3] It may be appropriate under certain circumstances to limit the number of Designated House Counsel who may access "HIGHLY CONFIDENTIAL – ATTORNEYS' EYES ONLY" information under this provision.

[4] This Order contemplates that Designated House Counsel shall not have access to any information or items designated "HIGHLY CONFIDENTIAL – SOURCE CODE." It may also be appropriate under certain circumstances to limit how Designated House Counsel may access "HIGHLY CONFIDENTIAL – ATTORNEYS' EYES ONLY" information. For example, Designated House Counsel may be limited to viewing "HIGHLY CONFIDENTIAL – ATTORNEYS' EYES ONLY" information only if it is filed with the court under seal, or in the presence of Outside Counsel of Record at their offices.

[5] *Alternative:* The parties may wish to allow disclosure of information not only to professional jury or trial consultants, but also to mock jurors, to further trial preparation. In that situation, the parties may wish to draft a simplified, precisely tailored Undertaking for mock jurors to sign.

ATTORNEYS' EYES ONLY" [*Optional*: or "HIGHLY CONFIDENTIAL – SOURCE CODE"] Information or Items to Designated House Counsel[6] or Experts.[7]

(a)(1) Unless otherwise ordered by the court or agreed to in writing by the Designating Party, a Party that seeks to disclose to Designated House Counsel any information or item that has been designated "HIGHLY CONFIDENTIAL – ATTORNEYS' EYES ONLY" pursuant to paragraph 7.3(b) first must make a written request to the Designating Party that (1) sets forth the full name of the Designated House Counsel and the city and state of his or her residence, and (2) describes the Designated House Counsel's current and reasonably foreseeable future primary job duties and responsibilities in sufficient detail to determine if House Counsel is involved, or may become involved, in any competitive decision-making.[8]

(a)(2) Unless otherwise ordered by the court or agreed to in writing by the Designating Party, a Party that seeks to disclose to an Expert (as defined in this Order) any information or item that has been designated "HIGHLY CONFIDENTIAL – ATTORNEYS' EYES ONLY" [*Optional*: or "HIGHLY CONFIDENTIAL – SOURCE CODE"] pursuant to paragraph 7.3(c) first must make a written request to the Designating Party that (1) identifies the general categories of "HIGHLY CONFIDENTIAL – ATTORNEYS' EYES ONLY" [*Optional*: or "HIGHLY CONFIDENTIAL – SOURCE CODE"] information that the Receiving Party seeks permission to disclose to the Expert, (2) sets forth the full name of the Expert and the city and state of his or her primary residence, (3) attaches a copy of the Expert's current resume, (4) identifies the Expert's current employer(s), (5) identifies each person or entity from whom the Expert has received compensation or funding for work in his or her areas of expertise or to whom

---

[6] *Alternative*: The parties may exchange names of a certain number of Designated House Counsel instead of following this procedure.

[7] *Alternative:* "CONFIDENTIAL" or "HIGHLY CONFIDENTIAL – ATTORNEYS' EYES ONLY" information or items may be disclosed to an Expert without disclosure of the identity of the Expert as long as the Expert is not a current officer, director, or employee of a competitor of a Party or anticipated to become one.

[8] It may be appropriate in certain circumstances to require any Designated House Counsel who receives "HIGHLY CONFIDENTIAL – ATTORNEYS' EYES ONLY" information pursuant to this Order to disclose any relevant changes in job duties or responsibilities prior to final disposition of the litigation to allow the Designating Party to evaluate any later-arising competitive decision-making responsibilities.

the expert has provided professional services, including in connection with a litigation, at any time during the preceding five years,[9] and (6) identifies (by name and number of the case, filing date, and location of court) any litigation in connection with which the Expert has offered expert testimony, including through a declaration, report, or testimony at a deposition or trial, during the preceding five years.[10]

(b) A Party that makes a request and provides the information specified in the preceding respective paragraphs may disclose the subject Protected Material to the identified Designated House Counsel or Expert unless, within 14 days of delivering the request, the Party receives a written objection from the Designating Party. Any such objection must set forth in detail the grounds on which it is based.

(c) A Party that receives a timely written objection must meet and confer with the Designating Party (through direct voice to voice dialogue) to try to resolve the matter by agreement within seven days of the written objection. If no agreement is reached, the Party seeking to make the disclosure to Designated House Counsel or the Expert may file a motion as provided in Civil Local Rule 7 (and in compliance with Civil Local Rule 79-5 and General Order 62, if applicable) seeking permission from the court to do so. Any such motion must describe the circumstances with specificity, set forth in detail the reasons why the disclosure to Designated House Counsel or the Expert is reasonably necessary, assess the risk of harm that the disclosure would entail, and suggest any additional means that could be used to reduce that risk. In addition, any such motion must be accompanied by a competent declaration describing the parties' efforts to resolve the matter by agreement (i.e., the extent and the content of the meet and confer discussions) and setting forth the reasons advanced by the Designating Party for its refusal to approve the disclosure.

In any such proceeding, the Party opposing disclosure to Designated House Counsel or the Expert shall bear the burden of proving that the risk of harm that the disclosure would entail (under the safeguards

---

[9] If the Expert believes any of this information is subject to a confidentiality obligation to a third-party, then the Expert should provide whatever information the Expert believes can be disclosed without violating any confidentiality agreements, and the Party seeking to disclose to the Expert shall be available to meet and confer with the Designating Party regarding any such engagement.

[10] It may be appropriate in certain circumstances to restrict the Expert from undertaking certain limited work prior to the termination of the litigation that could foreseeably result in an improper use of the Designating Party's "HIGHLY CONFIDENTIAL – ATTORNEYS' EYES ONLY" information.

proposed) outweighs the Receiving Party's need to disclose the Protected Material to its Designated House Counsel or Expert.

8. PROSECUTION BAR [*Optional*]

Absent written consent from the Producing Party, any individual who receives access to "HIGHLY CONFIDENTIAL – ATTORNEYS' EYES ONLY" [*Optional*: or "HIGHLY CONFIDENTIAL – SOURCE CODE"] information shall not be involved in the prosecution of patents or patent applications relating to [insert subject matter of the invention and of highly confidential technical information to be produced], including without limitation the patents asserted in this action and any patent or application claiming priority to or otherwise related to the patents asserted in this action, before any foreign or domestic agency, including the United States Patent and Trademark Office ("the Patent Office").[11] For purposes of this paragraph, "prosecution" includes directly or indirectly drafting, amending, advising, or otherwise affecting the scope or maintenance of patent claims.[12] To avoid any doubt, "prosecution" as used in this paragraph does not include representing a party challenging a patent before a domestic or foreign agency (including, but not limited to, a reissue protest, *ex parte* reexamination or *inter partes* reexamination). This Prosecution Bar shall begin when access to "HIGHLY CONFIDENTIAL – ATTORNEYS' EYES ONLY" [*Optional*: or "HIGHLY CONFIDENTIAL – SOURCE CODE"] information is first received by the affected individual and shall end two (2) years after final termination of this action.[13]

9. SOURCE CODE [*Optional*]

(a) To the extent production of source code becomes necessary in this case, a Producing Party may designate source code as "HIGHLY CONFIDENTIAL - SOURCE CODE" if it comprises or includes confidential, proprietary or trade secret source code.

---

[11] It may be appropriate under certain circumstances to require Outside and House Counsel who receive access to "HIGHLY CONFIDENTIAL – ATTORNEYS' EYES ONLY" information to implement an "Ethical Wall."

[12] Prosecution includes, for example, original prosecution, reissue and reexamination proceedings.

[13] *Alternative:* It may be appropriate for the Prosecution Bar to apply only to individuals who receive access to another party's "HIGHLY CONFIDENTIAL – ATTORNEYS' EYES ONLY" technical or source code information pursuant to this Order, such as under circumstances where one or more parties is not expected to produce "HIGHLY CONFIDENTIAL – ATTORNEYS' EYES ONLY" information that is technical in nature or "HIGHLY CONFIDENTIAL – SOURCE CODE" information,

(b) Protected Material designated as "HIGHLY CONFIDENTIAL – SOURCE CODE" shall be subject to all of the protections afforded to "HIGHLY CONFIDENTIAL – ATTORNEYS' EYES ONLY" information [*Optional*: including the Prosecution Bar set forth in Paragraph 8], and may be disclosed only to the individuals to whom "HIGHLY CONFIDENTIAL – ATTORNEYS' EYES ONLY" information may be disclosed, as set forth in Paragraphs 7.3 and 7.4, with the exception of Designated House Counsel.[14]

(c) Any source code produced in discovery shall be made available for inspection, in a format allowing it to be reasonably reviewed and searched, during normal business hours or at other mutually agreeable times, at an office of the Producing Party's counsel or another mutually agreed upon location.[15] The source code shall be made available for inspection on a secured computer in a secured room without Internet access or network access to other computers, and the Receiving Party shall not copy, remove, or otherwise transfer any portion of the source code onto any recordable media or recordable device. The Producing Party may visually monitor the activities of the Receiving Party's representatives during any source code review, but only to ensure that there is no unauthorized recording, copying, or transmission of the source code.[16]

(d) The Receiving Party may request paper copies of limited portions of source code that are reasonably necessary for the preparation of court filings, pleadings, expert reports, or other papers, or for deposition or trial, but shall not request paper copies for the purposes of reviewing the source code other than electronically as set forth in paragraph (c) in the first instance. The Producing Party shall provide

---

[14] It may be appropriate under certain circumstances to allow House Counsel access to derivative materials including "HIGHLY CONFIDENTIAL - SOURCE CODE" information, such as exhibits to motions or expert reports,

[15] *Alternative*: Any source code produced in discovery shall be made available for inspection in a format through which it could be reasonably reviewed and searched during normal business hours or other mutually agreeable times at a location that is reasonably convenient for the Receiving Party and any experts to whom the source code may be disclosed. This alternative may be appropriate if the Producing Party and/or its counsel are located in a different jurisdiction than counsel and/or experts for the Receiving Party.

[16] It may be appropriate under certain circumstances to require the Receiving Party to keep a paper log indicating the names of any individuals inspecting the source code and dates and times of inspection, and the names of any individuals to whom paper copies of portions of source code are provided.

all such source code in paper form including bates numbers and the label "HIGHLY CONFIDENTIAL - SOURCE CODE." The Producing Party may challenge the amount of source code requested in hard copy form pursuant to the dispute resolution procedure and timeframes set forth in Paragraph 6 whereby the Producing Party is the "Challenging Party" and the Receiving Party is the "Designating Party" for purposes of dispute resolution.

(e) The Receiving Party shall maintain a record of any individual who has inspected any portion of the source code in electronic or paper form. The Receiving Party shall maintain all paper copies of any printed portions of the source code in a secured, locked area. The Receiving Party shall not create any electronic or other images of the paper copies and shall not convert any of the information contained in the paper copies into any electronic format. The Receiving Party shall only make additional paper copies if such additional copies are (1) necessary to prepare court filings, pleadings, or other papers (including a testifying expert's expert report), (2) necessary for deposition, or (3) otherwise necessary for the preparation of its case. Any paper copies used during a deposition shall be retrieved by the Producing Party at the end of each day and must not be given to or left with a court reporter or any other individual.[17]

10. PROTECTED MATERIAL SUBPOENAED OR ORDERED PRODUCED IN OTHER LITIGATION

If a Party is served with a subpoena or a court order issued in other litigation that compels disclosure of any information or items designated in this action as "CONFIDENTIAL" or "HIGHLY CONFIDENTIAL – ATTORNEYS' EYES ONLY" [*Optional*: or "HIGHLY CONFIDENTIAL – SOURCE CODE"] that Party must:

(a) promptly notify in writing the Designating Party. Such notification shall include a copy of the subpoena or court order;

(b) promptly notify in writing the party who caused the subpoena or order to issue in the other litigation that some or all of the material covered by the subpoena or order is subject to this Protective Order. Such notification shall include a copy of this Stipulated Protective Order; and

[17] The nature of the source code at issue in a particular case may warrant additional protections or restrictions, For example, it may be appropriate under certain circumstances to require the Receiving Party to provide notice to the Producing Party before including "HIGHLY CONFIDENTIAL – SOURCE CODE" information in a court filing, pleading, or expert report.

(c) cooperate with respect to all reasonable procedures sought to be pursued by the Designating Party whose Protected Material may be affected.[18]

If the Designating Party timely seeks a protective order, the Party served with the subpoena or court order shall not produce any information designated in this action as "CONFIDENTIAL" or "HIGHLY CONFIDENTIAL – ATTORNEYS' EYES ONLY" [*Optional*: or "HIGHLY CONFIDENTIAL – SOURCE CODE"] before a determination by the court from which the subpoena or order issued, unless the Party has obtained the Designating Party's permission. The Designating Party shall bear the burden and expense of seeking protection in that court of its confidential material – and nothing in these provisions should be construed as authorizing or encouraging a Receiving Party in this action to disobey a lawful directive from another court.

11. A NON-PARTY'S PROTECTED MATERIAL SOUGHT TO BE PRODUCED IN THIS LITIGATION

(a) The terms of this Order are applicable to information produced by a Non-Party in this action and designated as "CONFIDENTIAL" or "HIGHLY CONFIDENTIAL – ATTORNEYS' EYES ONLY" [*Optional:* or "HIGHLY CONFIDENTIAL – SOURCE CODE"]. Such information produced by Non-Parties in connection with this litigation is protected by the remedies and relief provided by this Order. Nothing in these provisions should be construed as prohibiting a Non-Party from seeking additional protections.

(b) In the event that a Party is required, by a valid discovery request, to produce a Non-Party's confidential information in its possession, and the Party is subject to an agreement with the Non-Party not to produce the Non-Party's confidential information, then the Party shall:

1. promptly notify in writing the Requesting Party and the Non-Party that some or all of the information requested is subject to a confidentiality agreement with a Non-Party;

2. promptly provide the Non-Party with a copy of the Stipulated Protective Order in this litigation, the relevant discovery request(s), and a reasonably specific description of the

[18] The purpose of imposing these duties is to alert the interested parties to the existence of this Protective Order and to afford the Designating Party in this case an opportunity to try to protect its confidentiality interests in the court from which the subpoena or order issued.

information requested; and

3. make the information requested available for inspection by the Non-Party.

(c) If the Non-Party fails to object or seek a protective order from this court within 14 days of receiving the notice and accompanying information, the Receiving Party may produce the Non-Party's confidential information responsive to the discovery request. If the Non-Party timely seeks a protective order, the Receiving Party shall not produce any information in its possession or control that is subject to the confidentiality agreement with the Non-Party before a determination by the court.[19] Absent a court order to the contrary, the Non-Party shall bear the burden and expense of seeking protection in this court of its Protected Material.

12. UNAUTHORIZED DISCLOSURE OF PROTECTED MATERIAL

If a Receiving Party learns that, by inadvertence or otherwise, it has disclosed Protected Material to any person or in any circumstance not authorized under this Stipulated Protective Order, the Receiving Party must immediately (a) notify in writing the Designating Party of the unauthorized disclosures, (b) use its best efforts to retrieve all unauthorized copies of the Protected Material, (c) inform the person or persons to whom unauthorized disclosures were made of all the terms of this Order, and (d) request such person or persons to execute the "Acknowledgment and Agreement to Be Bound" that is attached hereto as Exhibit A.

13. INADVERTENT PRODUCTION OF PRIVILEGED OR OTHERWISE PROTECTED MATERIAL

When a Producing Party gives notice to Receiving Parties that certain inadvertently produced material is subject to a claim of privilege or other protection, the obligations of the Receiving Parties are those set forth in Federal Rule of Civil Procedure 26(b)(5)(B).[20] This provision is not intended to

[19] The purpose of this provision is to alert the interested parties to the existence of confidentiality rights of a Non-Party and to afford the Non-Party an opportunity to protect its confidentiality interests in this court.

[20] *Alternative*: The parties may agree that the recipient of an inadvertent production may not "sequester" or in any way use the document(s) pending resolution of a challenge to the claim of privilege or other protection to the extent it would be otherwise allowed by Federal Rule of Civil Procedure 26(b)(5)(B) as amended in 2006. This could include a restriction against "presenting" the document(s) to the court to challenge the privilege claim as may otherwise be allowed under Rule 26(b)(5)(B) subject to ethical obligations.

modify whatever procedure may be established in an e-discovery order that provides for production without prior privilege review. Pursuant to Federal Rule of Evidence 502(d) and (e), insofar as the parties reach an agreement on the effect of disclosure of a communication or information covered by the attorney-client privilege or work product protection, the parties may incorporate their agreement in the stipulated protective order submitted to the court.

14. MISCELLANEOUS

14.1 Right to Further Relief. Nothing in this Order abridges the right of any person to seek its modification by the court in the future.

14.2 Right to Assert Other Objections. By stipulating to the entry of this Protective Order no Party waives any right it otherwise would have to object to disclosing or producing any information or item on any ground not addressed in this Stipulated Protective Order. Similarly, no Party waives any right to object on any ground to use in evidence of any of the material covered by this Protective Order.

[14.3 *Optional:* Export Control. Disclosure of Protected Material shall be subject to all applicable laws and regulations relating to the export of technical data contained in such Protected Material, including the release of such technical data to foreign persons or nationals in the United States or elsewhere. The Producing Party shall be responsible for identifying any such controlled technical data, and the Receiving Party shall take measures necessary to ensure compliance.]

14.4 Filing Protected Material. Without written permission from the Designating Party or a court order secured after appropriate notice to all interested persons, a Party may not file in the public record in this action any Protected Material. A Party that seeks to file under seal any Protected Material must comply with Civil Local Rule 79-5 and General Order 62. Protected Material may only be filed under seal pursuant to a court order authorizing the sealing of the specific Protected Material at issue. Pursuant to Civil Local Rule 79-5 and General Order 62, a sealing order will issue only upon a request establishing that the

---

An alternate provision could state: "If information is produced in discovery that is subject to a claim of privilege or of protection as trial-preparation material, the party making the claim may notify any party that received the information of the claim and the basis for it. After being notified, a party must promptly return or destroy the specified information and any copies it has and may not sequester, use or disclose the information until the claim is resolved. This includes a restriction against presenting the information to the court for a determination of the claim."

Protected Material at issue is privileged, protectable as a trade secret, or otherwise entitled to protection under the law. If a Receiving Party's request to file Protected Material under seal pursuant to Civil Local Rule 79-5(d) and General Order 62 is denied by the court, then the Receiving Party may file the Protected Material in the public record pursuant to Civil Local Rule 79-5(e) unless otherwise instructed by the court.

15. FINAL DISPOSITION

Within 60 days after the final disposition of this action, as defined in paragraph 4, each Receiving Party must return all Protected Material to the Producing Party or destroy such material. As used in this subdivision, "all Protected Material" includes all copies, abstracts, compilations, summaries, and any other format reproducing or capturing any of the Protected Material. Whether the Protected Material is returned or destroyed, the Receiving Party must submit a written certification to the Producing Party (and, if not the same person or entity, to the Designating Party) by the 60-day deadline that (1) identifies (by category, where appropriate) all the Protected Material that was returned or destroyed and (2) affirms that the Receiving Party has not retained any copies, abstracts, compilations, summaries or any other format reproducing or capturing any of the Protected Material. Notwithstanding this provision, Counsel are entitled to retain an archival copy of all pleadings, motion papers, trial, deposition, and hearing transcripts, legal memoranda, correspondence, deposition and trial exhibits, expert reports, attorney work product, and consultant and expert work product, even if such materials contain Protected Material. Any such archival copies that contain or constitute Protected Material remain subject to this Protective Order as set forth in Section 4 (DURATION).

IT IS SO STIPULATED, THROUGH COUNSEL OF RECORD.

DATED: ______________________ ________________________________
Attorneys for Plaintiff

DATED: ______________________ ________________________________
Attorneys for Defendant

PURSUANT TO STIPULATION, IT IS SO ORDERED.

DATED: ______________________ ________________________________
[Name of Judge]
United States District/Magistrate Judge

EXHIBIT A

ACKNOWLEDGMENT AND AGREEMENT TO BE BOUND

I, ______________________________ [print or type full name], of _________________ [print or type full address], declare under penalty of perjury that I have read in its entirety and understand the Stipulated Protective Order that was issued by the United States District Court for the Northern District of California on [date] in the case of ___________ **[insert formal name of the case and the number and initials assigned to it by the court]**. I agree to comply with and to be bound by all the terms of this Stipulated Protective Order and I understand and acknowledge that failure to so comply could expose me to sanctions and punishment in the nature of contempt. I solemnly promise that I will not disclose in any manner any information or item that is subject to this Stipulated Protective Order to any person or entity except in strict compliance with the provisions of this Order.

I further agree to submit to the jurisdiction of the United States District Court for the Northern District of California for the purpose of enforcing the terms of this Stipulated Protective Order, even if such enforcement proceedings occur after termination of this action.

I hereby appoint __________________________ [print or type full name] of ____ [print or type full address and telephone number] as my California agent for service of process in connection with this action or any proceedings related to enforcement of this Stipulated Protective Order.

Date: ______________________________

City and State where sworn and signed: ______________________________

Printed name: ______________________________
[printed name]

Signature: ______________________________
[signature]

Index

A

actual misappropriation, form of, 86–92, *Also see* inevitable disclosure doctrine; pre-litigation checklist; statute of limitations, impact of
  actual use or disclosure, inability to prove, 87
  categories of conduct, 86
  claim investigations, beginning, 86
  disclosure, defined, 90
  fair licensing price, calculation of, 88
  intent to secure control of trade secrets, 87
  knowledge of trade secret acquisition by accident or mistake, 89
    knowledge, determining, 89–90
    requirement for, 89
  misappropriated information as basis for investment, 90
  negative know-how, 91
    defined, 91
    injunctive relief regarding, 92
    issues regarding, 91
    value of, 91
  original misappropriator, questions regarding, 86
  royalty-based awards, 88
    determination of, 88
    purpose of, 88
  sale price of secrets, 90–91
    determining, 90
    role in setting damages, 90
  target defendants, focus, 86
  Uniform Trade Secrets Act
    damages, provisions for, 87
    misappropriation defined, 86
  unknowing possession of secrets, 87
  use, defining, 88–89
    disclosure, differentiated from, 90
    requisite mental state, requirement for, 89
    Uniform Trade Secrets Act provisions for, 89
  willful and malicious misappropriation, 87
    award of attorney's fees for, 87
    injunctive relief for, 87
  wrongful acquisition, 87
    as actionable act, 87
    mere possession, insufficiency of, 87
    monetary relief for, 87
    proof of, 87
additional claims, pursuit of, 113–17
  breach of confidence, 115
  claims ex contracu, 113
  claims ex delicto, 113
  conversion, 115
  fraud, 115
  interference with prospective business advantage, 115
  jurisdictional issues, 115
  Lanham Act violations, 113
  non–trade secret case, pleading of, 116
  operative facts regarding, evaluation of, 115
  sufficient facts, lack of knowledge of, 115–16
  trespass to chattels, 115

unfair competition, 115
unjust enrichment, 115
variety of claims, inclusion of, 116
aider and abettor, 53–54
burden of proof requirements for, 53
defined, 53
naming as defendant, 53
arbitration clause, 232–39
arbitrator authority, limitations on, 238
broad form of, 233
class of claims encompassed, 232
confidentiality issues, 238–39
court instruction to arbitrate, 233
damages, issues regarding, 235
discovery provisions of, 234–35
inappropriateness of for misappropriation cases, 234
estoppel exception, impact of, 233
evidentiary framework issues, 236
hearsay issues, 236
issues, addressing at the drafting stage, 237–38
law of the forum, application of, 237
obligation to arbitrate, invocation of, 233
opinion testimony issues, 236
ownership issues, exclusion of, 238
unintended consequences of, 232
arbitration option, consideration of, 142–45
arbitration clauses, impact of, 142
avoidance of, difficulties in, 142
collateral estoppel, application of, 145
demand for
filing of, 144
presentation of, 142
key determination factors, 143–44
multiple potential defendants, impact of, 144–45
preliminary injunction
request for, 144
preliminary injunctive relief issues, 143
proof of wrongdoing, issues regarding, 143
request for expedited relief, impact of, 142
res judicata, application of, 145
right to compel arbitration, 142
waiver of, 142

B

bad faith, determination of, 119–23
evidence in support of, 121
exculpatory information, issues regarding, 123
factual deficiencies in action, demonstration of, 122
harassment, claims of, 121
improper pursuit, issues regarding, 123
malicious prosecution, distinguished from, 122
plaintiff options regarding, 122
prongs for, 120
objectively specious claims, 120
subjective bad faith, demonstration of, 120
bench trials, considerations regarding, 136–41
evidentiary matters, decisions regarding, 140
experience of judges, benefits of, 136
information on judges sources for, 140–41
judge tendencies, determining, 140
multimedia presentations, hazards of, 139
random selection of judges, 139–40
tailoring presentations for, 136
time constraints, impact of, 141

boilerplate clauses in trade secret negotiations. *See* arbitration clause; choice of law clause; fee clauses; indemnification clauses; integration clauses; marking clauses; release clauses; venue/jurisdiction clauses
business impact of naming defendants, 43–52
  acquisitions, potential impact on, 49
  client goals, analysis of, 44–45
  client's business, impact on, 44–45
  client's competitors, impact on, 46–47
  Corporations Code, requirements of, 50
  current employees, impact on, 45
  direct competitors, suits against, 48
  economic support, companies providing, 49
  former employees, issues regarding, 46–47
    staggering joinder, consideration of, 46
  funding source considerations, 50
  indemnification issues, 50
  insurance as source for defense funds, 51–52
  joint representation options, 51
  jury views, consideration of, 49–50
  marketing professionals, advice of, 45
  separate counsel, options regarding, 50
  third parties, impact on, 48–49

C

choice of law clauses, 239–41
  broad form of, 240
  familiarity factor in selection, 239
  narrow form of, 239
  procedural versus substantive law issues, 239–40
  purpose of, 239
  reach, limits on, 240
Civil Discovery Act
  discovery and trade secret provisions, 65
client goals in trade secret litigation, 19–23
  adverse judgments, potential for, 23
  cost of investment analysis, 22
  market goals, 21–22
  message, client desire to send, 21
  monetary goals, consideration of, 21
  return on the investment, 20
    calculation of, 20
    consideration of, 20
  risk calculation, 22–23
Code of Civil Procedure
  discovery and trade secret provisions, 65
conditional use injunction, 227
  options available from, 227
  purpose of, 227
  royalty payment issues, 227
    reasonable royalty, calculation of, 227
    sunset period, impact on, 227
conspiracy allegations
  attacks against claims of, 54
  complexities involved with, 55
  requirements for establishing, 54
  third parties, filing against, 54
  vicarious responsibility, imposition of, 54

D

destruction of a trade secret, 4
development of trade secrets, 5–9
  acquisition of secrets, impact of, 7–8

chain of evidence, review of, 6
corporate entities, issues regarding, 7
history of, compilation of, 6
joint development efforts, issues regarding, 8
misappropriation suits, role in defending, 6
ownership, impact on, 5–9
passage of time, problems caused by, 7
secrecy, maintaining, 6–7
true creator, determination of, 5
warranties, impact of, 8

discovery and trade secret designation, 64–77. *Also see* discovery, defendant actions in; trade secret designations, objections to; Trade Secret List
boundaries of the trade secrets, determining, 66
Civil Discovery Act provisions, 65
Code of Civil Procedure provisions, 65
comprehensive identification, requirement for, 64
entity notices, 74–76
precision of, 74
purpose of, 74
evidence of misappropriation, importance of, 67
expert testimony of defendant, impact of, 70
generalized descriptions in complaints, 64
inadequate details, providing, 65
initial trade secret interrogatories, 72–74
interrogatories, weakness of, 74
jurisdictional considerations, 64
meeting and conferring with defendants, values of, 71
partial identification, problems of, 67
particularizing of secrets, need for, 66
productions requests, 75–76
reasonable particularity, application of, 64
requests for admission, 72
requests for production of document, 72
risks, consideration of, 70–71
separate testifying expert, retaining, 70
specificity of information, defendant desire for, 75
Uniform Trade Secret Act provisions, 65

discovery, defendant actions in. *Also see* Trade Secret List
boundaries of secrets, determining, 65
delaying tactics, 68
deposition notices, serving of, 74
expert witnessed, retaining of, 70
interrogatories
limitations of, 74
list of, 72
lack of evidence of misappropriation, identifying, 67
motion for protective order, request for, 69
narrowing of plaintiff list, advantages of, 67–68
objection options, 66
details, inadequacy of, 66
form of, 68
generalized list, insufficiency of, 66
particularized information, desire for, 66
protective order, request for, 76
specificity of information, solicitation of, 75

document retention/collection issues, 106–09

damages, documents relating to, 106
deleted documents, search for, 109
document audit, construction of, 106
document management tools, evaluation of, 106
document retention policies, review of, 106
document sources, identifying, 107
employee knowledge, review of, 107
employee notification memorandum, 107
gathering process, employee notification of, 108
hard-copy documents, handling of, 108
information management activities tools for, evaluation of, 106
insurance coverage considerations, 107
searches, conduct of, 108
support documents, identifying, 106–07
documentation in trade secret litigation. *See* boilerplate clauses in trade secret negotiations

E

E.I. du Pont de Nemours Powder Co. v. Masland, 3
expedited discovery, 182–87
application for, content of, 186–87
burden created by, 183
defendant requests for, 185
efficient discovery tool, selection of, 184
evidence supporting, 182
extraordinary relief, provision of, 182
good cause, establishing, 183–84
impact of, 182
level of proof for, 182
objections to, 187
purpose of, 182
requests for, 182
court questions regarding, 182
in conjunction with TROs, 182
TRO applications, impact on, 185
experts witnesses, court appointment of. *See* neutral experts, court-appointed

F

fee awards, anticipation of, 119–23. *Also see* bad faith, determination of
anticompetitive strategy, claims of, 121
appropriateness of, 120
sanctions, form of, 120
underlying agreements, impact of, 119
Uniform Trade Secrets Act, provisions for, 120
fee clauses, 245–47
absence, impact of, 246
benefits of, 245
criticism of, 245
factors relative to trade secret cases, 245–46
inclusion of, determination regarding, 245
one-way clauses, 246–47
defined, 246
employment agreements, impact on, 247
purpose of, 246
Uniform Trade Secrets Act provisions, 246
foreign defendants, 52–54
difficulties in suing, 52
Hague Convention, provisions of, 53

procedural hurdles regarding, 52
resulting judgment against, enforcement of, 53
future damages, 226–28. *Also see* conditional use injunction
seeking, consequences of, 227

H

headstart damages, 226–28
accelerated market entry damages, 226
measure of damages, determining, 226
purpose of, 226
shortcut liability, 226
headstart injunctions, 225. *Also see* headstart damages; production injunction; use injunction
breadth of, establishing, 225–26
considerations regarding, 225
competitive landscape, readjustment of, 227
divergent interests, consideration of, 228–30
duration of, 224–25
insufficiency of, 223
interests, balance between, achieving, 229
post-trial against future sales, 227
preliminary injunction duration, impact of, 225
public interests, consideration of, 229
purpose of, 223
reverse engineering impact on, 224–25
time issues, focus of, 229
unfair advantage, attempts to eliminate, 224
Uniform Trade Secrets Act support for, 223

I

identification of trade secrets. *See* trade secret identification for internal use; trade secrets, identification for trial
indemnification clauses, 249–52
economic consequences of, 250
indemnification amount, limits on, 250
key questions regarding, 251–52
provisions of, 249
right to counsel issues, 251
rights and obligations under, 250
inevitable disclosure doctrine, 92–96. *Also see* threatened misappropriation
application of, inconsistencies regarding, 93
appropriate equitable relief under, 95
bad facts
defined, 95–96
impact of, 95–96
defined, 93
employee obligations, disregard for, 96
inevitable disclosure, determination of, 94
jurisdiction selection considerations, 96
non-competition agreements as substitutes for, 96
purpose of, 93
shelf life of trade secrets, determining, 95
state recognition of, 93
initial complaint, issues impacting, 38–43
consolidation of actions, seeking, 43
coordination of proceedings, seeking, 43

defendants in multiple jurisdictions, 38
delayed-discovery rule, application of, 38
Doe defendants, requirements for naming, 38–39
jurisdictional issues, 40–41
personal jurisdiction, 41
subject matter, 40
multiple actions, 42
multiple defendants
naming of, 39
options regarding, 41
proof of liability, issues regarding, 41
separate actions, 42
special master, appointment of, 43
statute of limitations, issues regarding, 38–40
subsequent actions, 42–43
injunctive relief. *Also see* conditional use injunction; future damages; headstart damages; headstart injunctions; production injunctions; use injunctions
as remedy for misappropriation, 219
continuing after secret existence ends, 223
durational considerations, court, 223
modification of relief, 221
permanent injunctions, 220–21
categories of, 221
duration of, determining, 224
durational limits on, reasons for, 222
prohibitions of, 221
specific reservation of jurisdiction, inclusion in, 223
termination of, requests for, 221
potential for, consideration of, 220
preliminary injunctions, 220-25
effect of, 224
impact on headstart injunctions, 225
preliminary injunctions, 220
production injunction, defined, 225
scope of, questions regarding, 220
temporary injunctions, 220
types of, 220–21
Uniform Trade Secret Act, provisions for, 221
use injunction, defined, 225
integration clauses, 247–49
court guidance provided by, 248
difficulties regarding, 248
multiple documents, issues regarding, 248–49
potential for confusion regarding, 248
intellectual property rights program, health of. *See* trade secret fitness audits
International Trade Commission (ITC), pursuing misappropriation claims before, 145–47
function of ITC, 145
jurisdictional requirements, 146
monetary relief, filing for, 147
relevancy of claims, 146
Restatement of Unfair Competition, impact of, 147
Section 337 investigations, 146–47
conduct of, 147
focus of, 146
remedies available through, 146
state trade secret law, application of, 147
Uniform Trade Secrets Act, impact of, 147

J

jurisdiction clauses, 241–45
  personal jurisdiction, 241–42
    defined, 241
    objections regarding, 242
  purpose of, 241
  state or federal court, option regarding, 244–45
  subject matter analysis, impact of, 244
  subject matter jurisdiction, 242–45
    objection issues regarding, 242
    purpose of, 242
  venue/jurisdiction hybrid clause, 243–44
    benefits of, 243
jurisdictional considerations, 125–26. *Also see* multiple potential venues, evaluation of; personal jurisdiction; subject matter jurisdiction
  diversity jurisdiction issues, 126
  International Trade Commission option, 126
  key factors regarding, 125
  law variance factors, 125
  local attitude factors, 125
  potential audience, analysis of, 125
jury trials, considerations regarding, 136–41
  communication of complex technologies, difficulties, 136
  expenses connected with, 136
  interest level issues, 137
  juror background, awareness of, 138
  jurors, discomfort of, 137
  jury demand, presentation of, 136
    state court requirements, 136
  jury selection issues, 138
  methodical examination, ineffectiveness of, 138
  multimedia presentations, use of, 139
  need to entertain, 137
  removal of jury from courtroom, 136

L

Lanham Act
  subject matter jurisdiction provisions, 129
  trade secret claims, provisions for, 113
legally correct defendants, identifying, 26–30. *Also see* aider and abettor; business impact of naming defendants; conspiracy allegations; foreign defendants; initial complaint, issues impacting; pre-dispute demand letter
  actions to be filed, considerations regarding, 38
  legal prerequisites for, 43
  multiple defendants, naming of, 39
  pre-litigation activities, focus of, 30
  unknown defendants, issues regarding, 38–39
litigation history, 11–16
  client's litigation philosophy, understanding of, 13
  importance of, 11
  information acquired through, 11
  insight acquired through, 11
  key questions regarding, 12
  lawsuit costs, 12
    accurate depiction of, 12
    potential impact of, 12
  litigation-oriented clients, 14
    dangers of, 14
    goals of, 14

prior litigation
claims other than trade secrets, 15
facts relating to, importance of, 14
releases executed in connection with, 15–16
significance of, 13
trade secret misuse, date of, 15

M

malicious prosecution claims, filing of, 119
marking clauses, 255–57
difficulties regarding, 256
exchanged trade secrets, identification of, 255–56
provisions of, 256
recommended protocols regarding, 257
mediation, 117–19
discussion of, court requirements for, 118
early mediation, issues regarding, 118
failure to explore, hazards of, 117–18
rejected offers, benefits of, 118
willingness for, determining, 117
misappropriation claims before the ITC. *See* International Trade Commission, pursuing misappropriation claims before
misappropriation, identifying. *See* actual misappropriation, form of
misappropriation of trade secrets, 3–4. *Also see* additional claims, pursuit of; mediation; preemption, application of; pretrial resolution scenarios
development of trade secrets, issues regarding, 6
litigation pending at time of sale, 5
multiple suits, issues regarding, 4
ownership at time, importance of, 4
right to sue for, determination of, 4
subsequent owners, rights of, 4
Uniform Trade Secrets Act, definition of, 26
misappropriation, protection against, 33–34. *Also see* pre-dispute demand letter
IP protection, seeking of, 33
relevant documents, securing of, 33
repository of information, creation of, 33
misappropriation, threat of. *See* threatened misappropriation
multiple potential venues, evaluation of, 130–35
budget considerations, 133
caseload consideration, 135
confidentiality issues, 132
court time lines, analysis of, 130
discovery issues, 132
factors to consider, 130–35
federal district court, advantages of, 132
judicial officer, selection of, 130–31
jury considerations, 133, 134
local counsel, use of, 131
local rules, consideration of, 130
location considerations, 134
protective order issues, 132
substantive law, differences, consideration of, 134
technical knowledge considerations, 135
trade secret identification issues, 131
Uniform Trade Secrets Act, adoption of, 131

N

neutral experts, court-appointed. *Also see* technical advisors, appointment of
- authority for, 200
- concerns regarding, 201
- *Daubert/Frye* issues, 202
- expense of, 202
- findings of, advising parties regarding, 202
- function of, 200–02
- list of experts, presentation of, 202
- objections to, 201
- parallax approach, 202
  - benefits of, 202–03
  - implementation of, 202
  - purpose of, 202
- special master, benefit to, 200
- value of, unawareness of, 201

O

ownership of trade secrets, 2–5. *Also see* development of trade secrets; plaintiff group; property rights, trade secrets as; protected relationship, trade secrets as
- acquirer of a trade secret
  - rights of, 4
  - status of, 4
- appellate decisions, impact on, 2
- demonstrating, 2
- factors affecting, 2
- former owners, rights of, 4
- litigation is pending at the time of sale, 5
- property, trade secrets as, 2
- standing, differentiation from, 3
- subsequent owner, 5
  - rights of, 4

P

permanent injunction. *See* injunctive relief

personal jurisdiction, 126–28
- certain minimum contacts requirement, 127
- court ability to exercise, determining, 126
- federal due process requirements, 127
- foreign enforcement of U.S. judgments, 128
- general jurisdiction
  - unlikeness of finding, 127
- multiple defendants, impact of, 126
- objections to, waiver of, 128
- purposeful direction of conduct, 127–28
  - determination of, 127
- specific jurisdiction
  - analysis regarding, 127
  - effects test for, 127
  - focus of, 127
  - United States, recourse limits to, 127
- states statutes and due process, 126–27

plaintiff group, 9–11
- defined, 9
- informal structures, impact of, 10
- interactions with client, issues regarding, 9–10
- interest individuals, identification of, 9
- stakeholders, defined, 9
- structure of group, evaluating, 9

pre-dispute demand letter, 31–38
- choice of addressees and signatories, 32
- circulating of, issues regarding, 36
- content of, 31

detail, benefit of, 31
drafting of, keys to, 36
failure to respond, consequences of, 34
immediate cessation of use, demand for, 31
improper publication of, 36
legitimate purpose of, 36
purpose of, 31
recipient response to, 34
additional information, request for, 34
choice of addressees and signatories in response l, 35
course of action, determining, 32
insufficiency of, 31–32
internal investigation, undertaking, 34–35
options for, 32
preliminary report, filing of, 34–35
risks of sending, 37
pre-litigation checklist, 102. *Also see* document retention/collection issues; witness investigation, pre-litigation
external public relations, 109–11
external communications team, creation of, 110
marketing the litigation, impact of, 111
Noerr-Pennington Doctrine, impact of, 111
outside consultant, retaining, 110
press release, issuance of, 109–10
sales force, warnings to, 110
timing issues, 110
information management activities, 106–09
internal public relations, 109
case updates, providing, 109
employees, informing of activities, 109
internal reports, issues regarding, 109
morale concerns, addressing, 109
providing, importance of, 102
purpose of, 102
preemption, application of, 113–17
breach of contract, exclusion of, 114
common-law claims, impact of, 114
jurisdictional issues, 115
multiple claims, issues regarding, 116
non–trade secret cases, pleading of, 116
prematurity, rulings of, 116
Uniform Trade Secrets Act provisions for, 114
uniformity in application, lack of, 114
preliminary injunction. *See* injunctive relief
preliminary injunctions, 177–81
applications for, 178
defendant benefit from, 179
hearings on, 178
response to, 178
bonding issues, 180
analysis of, 180
harm, potential for, 180
obtaining bonds, 181
requirements of, 180
conclusive presumption of truth, consideration of, 179
impact of, 177–78
marketing orders granted, 181
potential consequences of, 178
prospect of future harm, consideration of, 179
remedy issues, 179

preliminary technical check, 16. *Also see* trade secret, defined
absolute secrecy, maintenance of, 19
confidentiality considerations, 18–19
information compilation issues, 17
information presentation issues, 17
technical information, issues regarding, 17
trade secret disclosure, history of, 18
trade secret information, identification of, 16
preservation orders, 167–72
applications for, 168
benefits of, 168
detail required in, 169
focus of, 170
arguments against issuance, 169
balance of harm, consideration of, 171
copied material, issues regarding, 171
disappearance of evidence, addressing, 167
discovery commencement, delays in, 167
electronic forms, issues regarding, 172
enforcement of, 172
evidence sought, identification of, 170–71
granting of, 168
impact on defendants, 168–69
injunctive relief, form of, 168
purpose of, 169
turnover orders, defined, 168
pretrial resolution scenarios, 117–19. *Also see* mediation
business negotiations, engaging in, 117
creative business arrangements, potential for, 119
expense considerations, 119
neutral evaluation by third party, 118
outcomes achievable through, 118–19
production injunctions
advantages of, 226
common rationale for, 226
field of endeavor, access to, 225
function of, 225
scope of, 225
validity of, issues regarding, 225
property rights, trade secrets as, 2–3
appellate decisions, impact on, 2
protected relationships, distinguished from, 3
statute of limitations, impact of, 3
protected relationship, trade secrets as, 2–3
appellate decisions, impact on, 2–3
statute of limitations, impact of, 3
protective orders, 150–67
absence of, disputes relating to, 150
accused individuals, access rights of, 155–56
challenges to, 161–63
burdens involved in, 162
costliness of, 161
negotiation of, 162
response to, failure of, 163
Confidential designation, 153
Confidential—Attorney's Eyes Only designation, 153–54
default forms of, 150
default group, access rights of, 156
designation issues, 159
designated materials under seal, 160
late designate, 159
receiving party obligations, 159
requirements, adherence to, 160
testimony, 159
timing, 159

disclosure, preventive measures, 153–54
document review allowances, 153
end of the action considerations, 166–67
experts, issues regarding, 163–64
access rights, determining, 163–64
challenges to, 163
disqualifying criteria for, 164–65
required disclosures for, 165–66
restrictions on, imposition of, 166
successful challenges to, 165
handling of materials, manner of, 158
Highly Confidential designation, 155
highly technical information, access to, 155
inside counsel review privileges, 154
of record, defined, 156
producing party review provisions, 153
prosecution bars, 156–57
defined, 156
duration of, 158
issues regarding, 157
necessity of, 157
purpose of, 157
specifications of, 157
purpose of, 150
review of materials, eligibility for, 153
reviewing tiers, 151
rules restricting access to confidential documents, 151
sender or recipient requirements, 153
tailoring of, decisions regarding, 151
terms and conditions, negotiation of, 150
third-party witness issues, 161
tiers, system of
function of, 151
implementation of, 151
single-tier system, function of, 151
third tier, 154–55
two-tier system, function of, 152
varied duties of counsel, issues regarding, 156–57

R

reasonable efforts, evidence for, 209–14
advisable actions regarding, 209–11
attribute of value, importance of, 215
business considerations regarding, 213
competitive value, establishing existence of, 215
cost considerations, 214
disgorgement, damages for, 217
efforts made, court consideration of, 216
inadequacy, claims of, 212
independent derivation claims, 212
ineffectiveness of, 214–15
key issues regarding, 209–11
level of security, determining, 214
loss of secrecy caused by defendant, 218
lost profits, damages for, 217
maintaining efforts over time, 216
public disclosure impact on damages, 218
reasonableness, determining, 211
remedies, potential, 217
reverse engineering claims, 212

permanent injunction request, impact on, 217
potential impact of, 213
remedies, impact on, 217
steps taken, identification of, 211
release clauses, 252–55
breadth of, issues regarding, 254
business settlements, application to, 252
dangers of, 252
mutual releases, issues regarding, 255
persons released, issues regarding, 255
remedies for misappropriation, nonmonetary. *See* injunctive relief
Restatement of Torts
trade secrets, defined, 98

S

secrecy, reasonable efforts to protect, 206–09. *Also see* reasonable efforts, evidence for
efforts to create or obtain trade secrets, lawfulness, 207
independent development efforts, issues regarding, 207
public and private interests, need to balance, 206
requirement for
significance of, 206
theories of trade secret protection, application to, 206
reverse engineering, issues regarding, 208–09
secrecy, characteristic of, 206
U.S. Patent Act, provisions for, 206
Uniform Trade Secrets Act, application to, 207
special masters, use of, 190–200
appointment of, 191
authority of, issues regarding, 191–92
background information, need for, 194
benefits of, 191
charges by, allocation of, 195
compromises, hindrance to, 196
costliness of, 191
discovery disputes, diversion of, 190
fees as sanctions, 196
functions of, 191
hearing fees, issues regarding, 196
hearing management order, provisions of, 197–98
hearing protocols, addressing, 198–99
judicial resources, conservation of, 190
meet-and-confer obligation, issues regarding, 196–97
meeting with, focus of, 195
motions, handling of, 197
neutral experts, benefits of, 200
orders appointing, review of, 193
practicing attorneys as, 193–94
advantages of, 194
concerns regarding, 195
retired judges as, 193–94
concerns regarding, 194
rulings, extent of, 192
seeking appointment of, considerations regarding, 191
sitting judge, authority to act as, 193
tutorials, use of, 199–200
stakeholders in plaintiff groups. *See* plaintiff group
standing in trade secret litigation, 3–5
establishment of, 3
former owner, status of, 3
issues regarding, 3

misappropriation, issues regarding, 3–4
ownership, differentiation from, 3
statute of limitations, impact of, 98–102
accrual date, determining, 99
accrual of the period of limitations, determination of, 98
continuing misappropriation as single claim, 99
drop-dead date, notification of, 101
filing of suits, timing for, 101
improper disclosure, issues regarding, 99
misappropriation discovery date, 99
state laws, application of, 98
third party involvement, consideration of, 100
time period extensions, 98
time-barred claims, 101
Uniform Trade Secrets Act, provisions for, 99
subject matter jurisdiction, 128–29
citizenship and diversity determination, 129
complete diversity, negation of, 129
diversity, not complete, impact of, 129
federal district court
complete diversity, impact of, 129
issues regarding, 128
Lanham Act, claims under, 129
misappropriation cross-claim, impact of, 129
state court options, 129
supplemental jurisdiction, application of, 129
waiver of, prohibition against, 128

T

technical advisors, appointment of, 203
function of, 203
limitations on assistance provided, 203
neutrality of, ensuring, 203
provisions governing, 203
temporary injunction. *See* injunctive relief
temporary restraining orders, 174–77
affirmative act, requirements for, 176–77
breadth of order, significance of, 176
denial of
impact of, 175
reasons for, 175
duration of, 177
emergencies, use in, 175
goal of, 174
leverage provided by, 175
notice provided to defendant, 175
returnability of, 177
shall not publish designation, 176
status quo, defining, 174–75
urgency, impact of, 177
threatened misappropriation, 96–98
attorneys' fees, award of, 98
improper purposes, potential for, 98
injunctions, issuance of, 97
proof of, requirements for, 97
relief, basis for, 97
substantial nature of, 97
Uniform Trade Secrets Act provisions regarding, 96
trade secret, defined, 16
classifying information as, requirements for, 17
economic issues regarding, 16
essence of, 16

general knowledge of, 16
idea limitations, inapplicability of, 16
information compilation issues, 17
information identification, importance of, 16
information presentation issues, 17
jurisdictions, variance among, 16
technical information, issues regarding, 17

trade secret designation for discovery. *See* discovery and trade secret designation

trade secret designations, objections to, 67–71
as delaying tactic, 68
motion for protective order
purpose of, 69
request for, 69
rulings regarding, 69
purpose of, 67
reasonably distinguished information, need for, 69
reasons for, 67
response to, 68
sufficiency of the disclosure, challenges to, 68

trade secret fitness audits. *Also see* trade secrets, identification of
as a precautionary measure, 260
cataloguing of trade secrets, 260
consultant concerns, 268–69
experts, issues regarding, 269
contractor concerns, 268–69
customer relationship issues, 270
employer/employee relationship issues, 264–68
new employees, consideration of, 264
recommended safeguards, 264–68
implementation of policies, importance of, 271
joint ventures, issues regarding, 269–70
key objectives of, 260
multicompany collaborative relationships, 269–70
process of, 260
protection measures, identifying weaknesses in, 260
risk factors, identifying, 260, 264

trade secret identification for internal use, 57, 57–63. *Also see* Trade Secret List; trade secrets, defined
comprehensive internal analysis, need for, 58
disclosure due to patent acquisition, 62–63
grouping of secrets, 61
internal client champion, 58
function of, 58
identification of, 58
requirements for, 58
key questions regarding, 63
licensure issues, 61–62
list length, considerations regarding, 60
list of trade secrets, compilation of, 59
misappropriated information, identification of, 60
negative pregnant concept, application of, 61
ownership issues, 61–62
chain-of-custody approach, 61
hidden questions regarding, 61
secrets creation/development issues, 60
technical viewpoints, divergence of, 58
tertiary items, hazards of including, 61
trade secret, understanding uniqueness of, 59
unprotected information, identification of, 59

Trade Secret List
ability to challenge, 70
amending before trial, 77–80
court questions regarding, 78–79
new secrets, admissibility of, 78
objections to, 77
reasonable notice for, 77
reasons for, 77
request for, denial of, 79
case management tool, use as, 78
challenges to, 68
defendant review of, 66
expert testimony regarding, 70
failure of, demonstrating, 70
function of, 65
incorporation in judgments, 83
lack of requirement for, 71–72
objections to, 68
response to, 66
revision of, 68
submittal of list, 77–78
sufficiency of, challenges to, 69
trade secret litigation goals. *See* client goals in trade secret litigation
trade secrets, defined, 60
conceptual datum, 60
empirical datum, 60
expressions of ideas, 60
facts as, 60
Restatement of Torts provision for, 98
trade secrets, identification of, 261–64
confidential information, identifying, 261
economic factors, review of, 262
future plans, review of, 262
information beneficial to competitor, identifying, 263
patent development programs, implementation of, 263
patented technology, 263
secrets regarding, 263
potential harm from competitors, review of, 262
proprietary information, identifying, 261
relevant questions regarding, 261–64
software development, review of, 263
technological developments, review of, 263
trade secret information, compilation of, 261
trade secrets, identification for trial, 80–82
amalgamation of elements, secrets as, 81
exacting details, need for, 81–82
independent economic value test, 81–82
post-trial permanent injunctions, issues regarding, 82–83
sufficient particularity, need for, 80
uniform standard for, lack of, 80
trade secrets, nature of. *See* property rights, trade secrets as; protected relationship, trade secrets as
turnover orders. *See* preservation orders

U

U.S. Patent Act
IP protection under, 33
secrecy provisions of, 206
Uniform Trade Secrets Act, 14, 116
actionable use, varieties of, 89
actual misappropriation defined, 86
commercial ethics, protection of, 228
continuing misappropriation as single claim, 14

discovery and trade secret provisions, 65
fee award provisions of, 120, 246
headstart injunctions, support for, 223
injunctive relief, provisions for, 221
misappropriation, damages for, 87
misappropriation, defined, 26
multiple potential venues, impact on, 131
preemption, application of, provisions for, 114
preemption, provisions for, 114
secrecy protection provisions, 207
state adoption of, 221
statute of limitations, provisions for, 99
threatened misappropriation, provisions regarding, 96
use, defined, 89
use injunctions, 225–26
benefits of, 226
function of, 225
ineffectiveness of, 226
narrow scope of, 226

V

venue clauses, 241–45
court dismissal rulings, 241
court transference rulings, 241
improper venue, objections to, 241
purpose of, 241
state or federal court, options regarding, 244–45
subject matter analysis, impact of, 244
venue choices, court options regarding, 241
venue, defined, 241
venue/jurisdiction hybrid clause, 243–44
benefits of, 243

W

witness investigation, pre-litigation, 102–11
expert consultants, use of, 104
expert witnesses, issues regarding, 104–05
neutral third-party, 103–04
considerations regarding, 103–04
plan for contacting, 103
subpoenas, need for, 103
sets of witnesses, 102
under control of client, 102–03
appropriateness of, determining, 103
contact information for, 102
interviewing, 103